SPIDER-MAN FAMILY

BACK IN BLACK

SPIDER-MAN FAMILY

BACK IN BLACK

Writers: Sean McKeever, Fred Van Lente,
Paul Benjamin & Paul Tobin
Artists: Terrell Bobbett & Gary Martin, Federica Manfredi &
Terry Pallot, Kano with David LaFuente, Vasilis Lolos, Pierre Alary
and Leonard Kirk & Terry Pallot

Colorists: Bruna Brito, SotoColor's A. Crossley,
Jean Paul Fernandez & Michelle Madsen
Letterers: Blambot's Nate Piekos

Covers Artists: Marcelo DiChiaro, Kano, Pierre Alary & Chris Sotomayor

Editors: Nathan Cosby & Mark Paniccia

Collection Editor: Jennifer Grünwald
Assistant Editors: Cory Levine & Michael Short
Associate Editor: Mark D. Beazley
Senior Editor, Special Projects: Jeff Youngquist
Senior Vice President of Sales: David Gabriel
Production: Jerry Kalinowski
Book Design: Dayle Chesler
Vice President of Creative: Tom Marvelli

Editor in Chief: Joe Quesada
Publisher: Dan Buckley

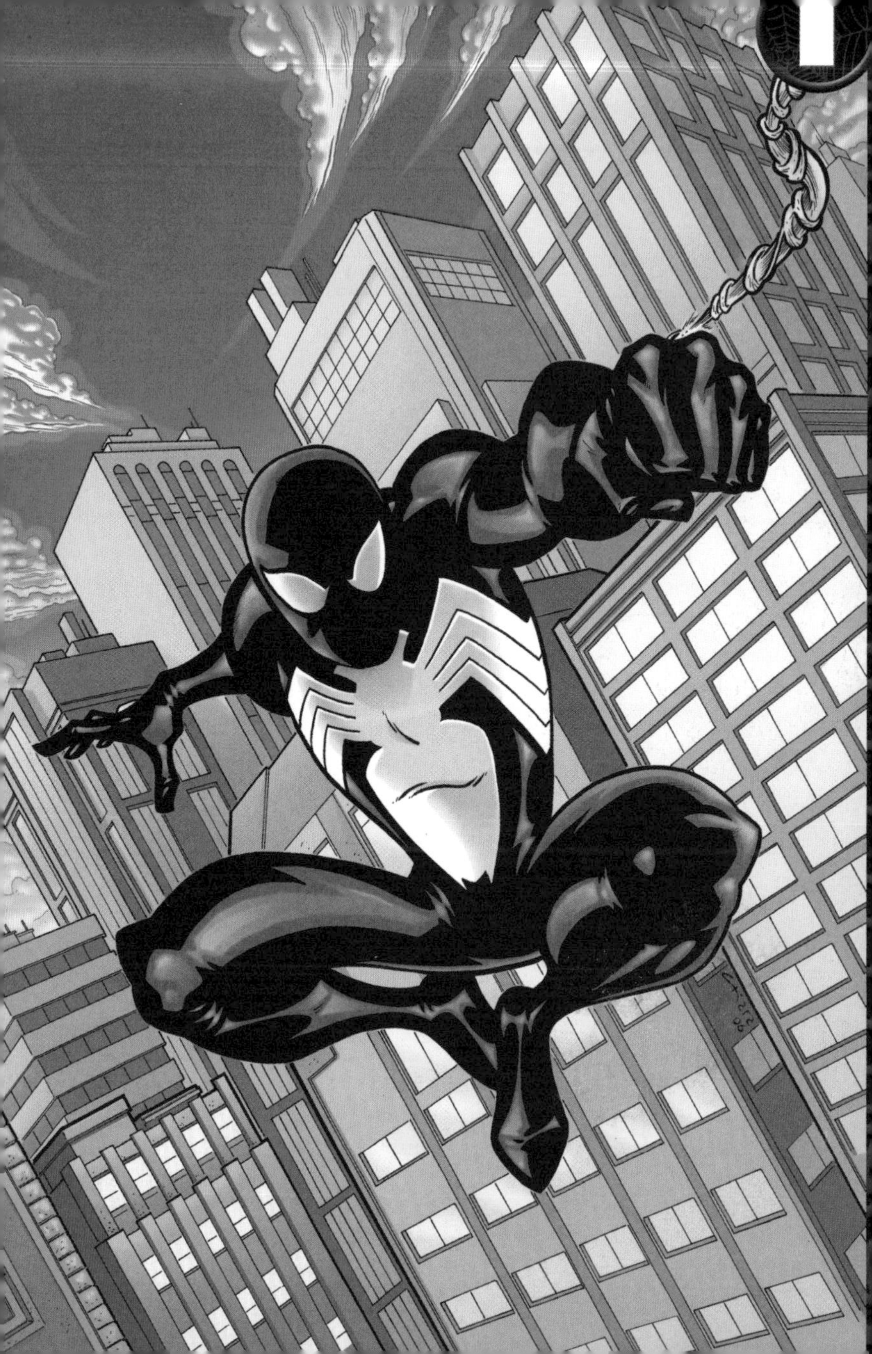

This is Peter.

He's got spider powers.
He uses them to help people.

One time, Peter ripped up [h]
costume and needed a new

He found a machine that gave
him a new outfit...

...but later found out the "costume" w[as]
alien that was sucking the life out of [h]

But before Peter discovered his clothes were becoming a little *too* attached...

HOMESICK

SEAN McKEEVER
Writer

TERRELL BOBBETT
Penciler

GARY MARTIN
Inker

BRUNA BRITO
Colorist

NATE PIEKOS
Letterer

MA[RK] DiC[ ]
Cove[r]

KATE LEVIN
Production

MARK PANICCIA
Consulting Editor

NATHAN COSBY
Editor

JOE QUESADA
Editor in Chief

[ ] BU[ ]
Pu[ ]

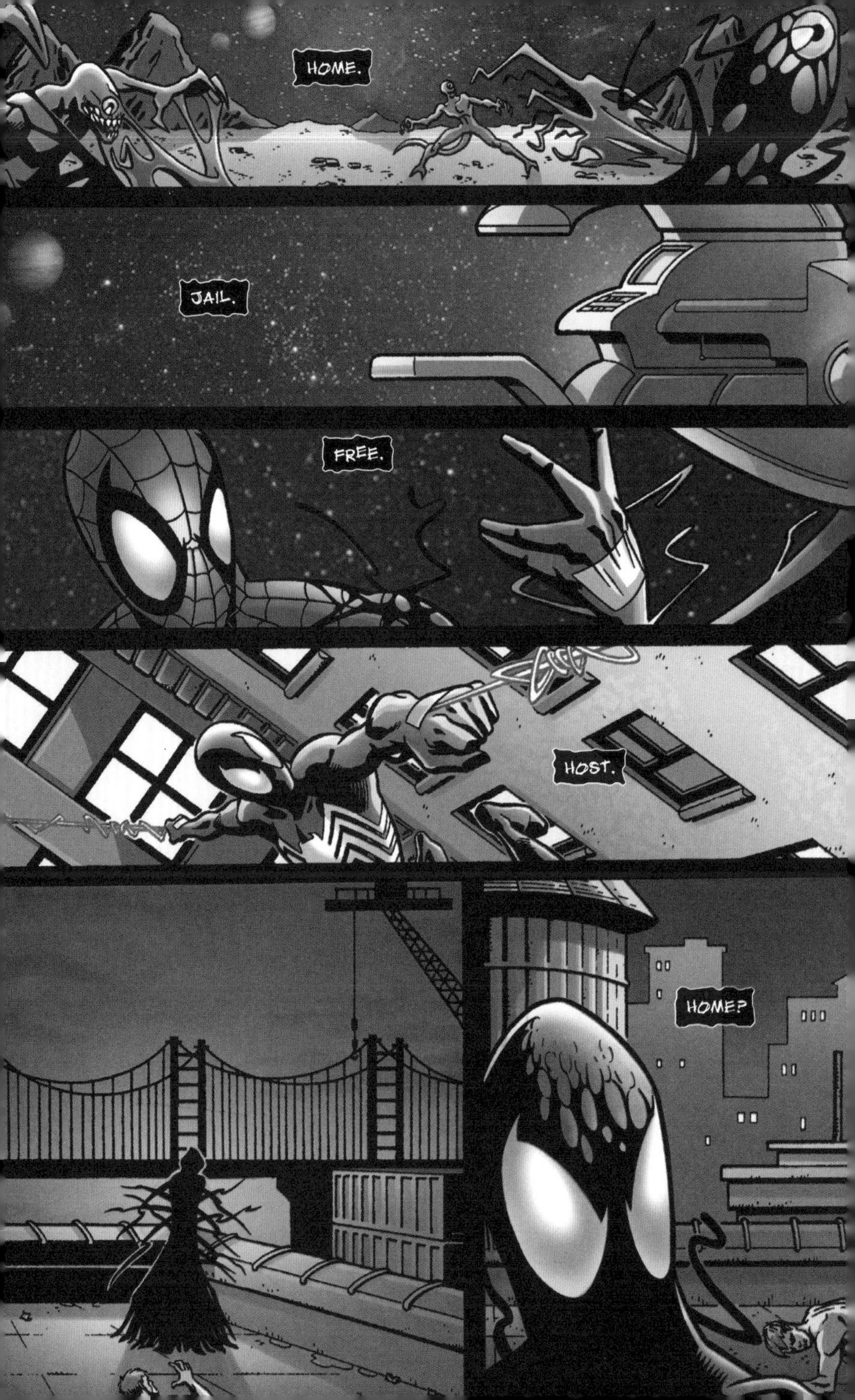
HOME.
JAIL.
FREE.
HOST.
HOME?

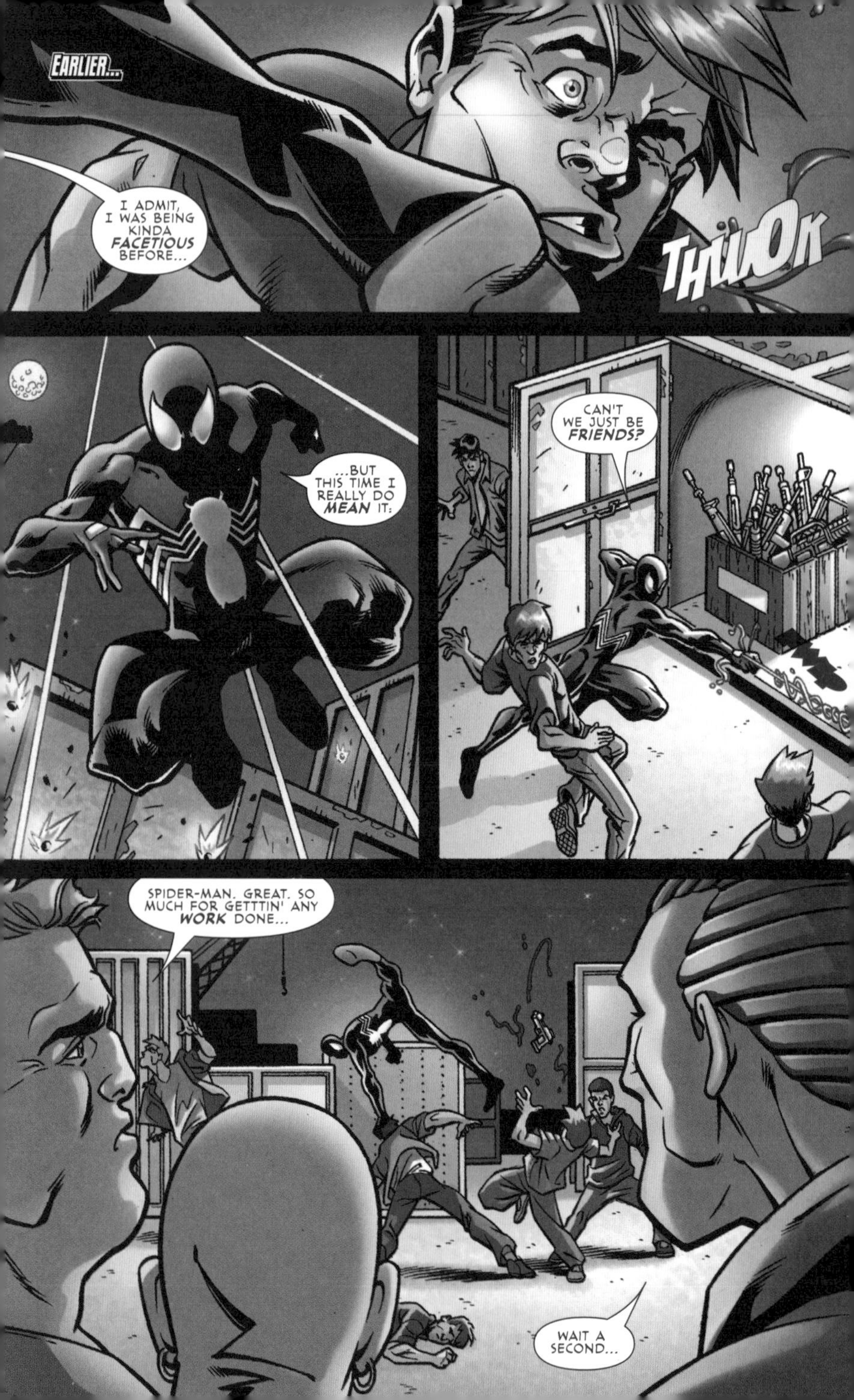
EARLIER...
I ADMIT, I WAS BEING KINDA FACETIOUS BEFORE...
THWOK
...BUT THIS TIME I REALLY DO MEAN IT:
CAN'T WE JUST BE FRIENDS?
SPIDER-MAN. GREAT. SO MUCH FOR GETTTIN' ANY WORK DONE...
WAIT A SECOND...

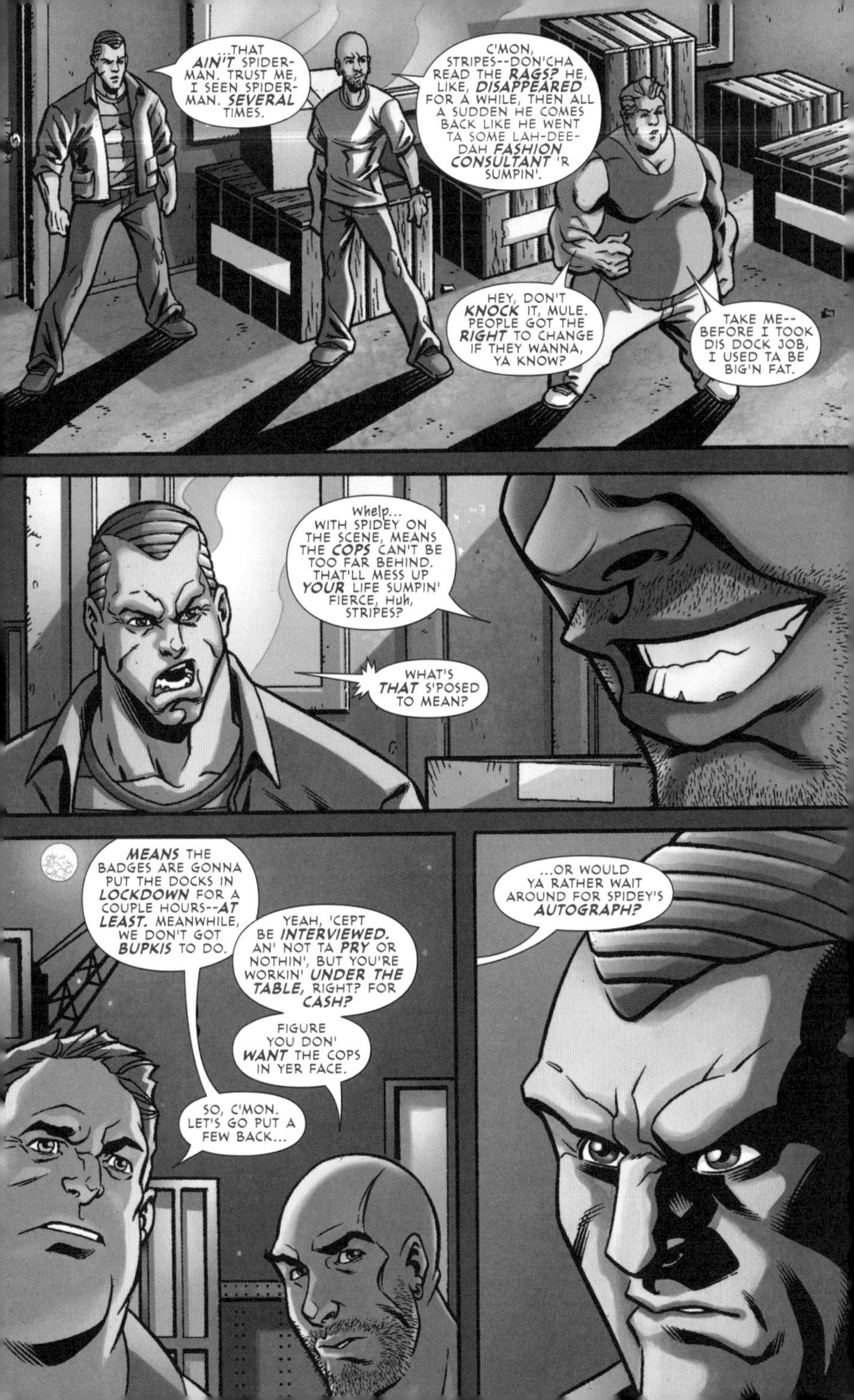
...THAT AIN'T SPIDER-MAN. TRUST ME, I SEEN SPIDER-MAN. SEVERAL TIMES.
C'MON, STRIPES--DON'CHA READ THE RAGS? HE, LIKE, DISAPPEARED FOR A WHILE, THEN ALL A SUDDEN HE COMES BACK LIKE HE WENT TA SOME LAH-DEE-DAH FASHION CONSULTANT 'R SUMPIN'.
HEY, DON'T KNOCK IT, MULE. PEOPLE GOT THE RIGHT TO CHANGE IF THEY WANNA, YA KNOW?
TAKE ME--BEFORE I TOOK DIS DOCK JOB, I USED TA BE BIG'N FAT.
Whelp... WITH SPIDEY ON THE SCENE, MEANS THE COPS CAN'T BE TOO FAR BEHIND. THAT'LL MESS UP YOUR LIFE SUMPIN' FIERCE, Huh, STRIPES?
WHAT'S THAT S'POSED TO MEAN?
MEANS THE BADGES ARE GONNA PUT THE DOCKS IN LOCKDOWN FOR A COUPLE HOURS--AT LEAST. MEANWHILE, WE DON'T GOT BUPKIS TO DO.
YEAH, 'CEPT BE INTERVIEWED. AN' NOT TA PRY OR NOTHIN', BUT YOU'RE WORKIN' UNDER THE TABLE, RIGHT? FOR CASH?
FIGURE YOU DON' WANT THE COPS IN YER FACE.
SO, C'MON. LET'S GO PUT A FEW BACK...
...OR WOULD YA RATHER WAIT AROUND FOR SPIDEY'S AUTOGRAPH?

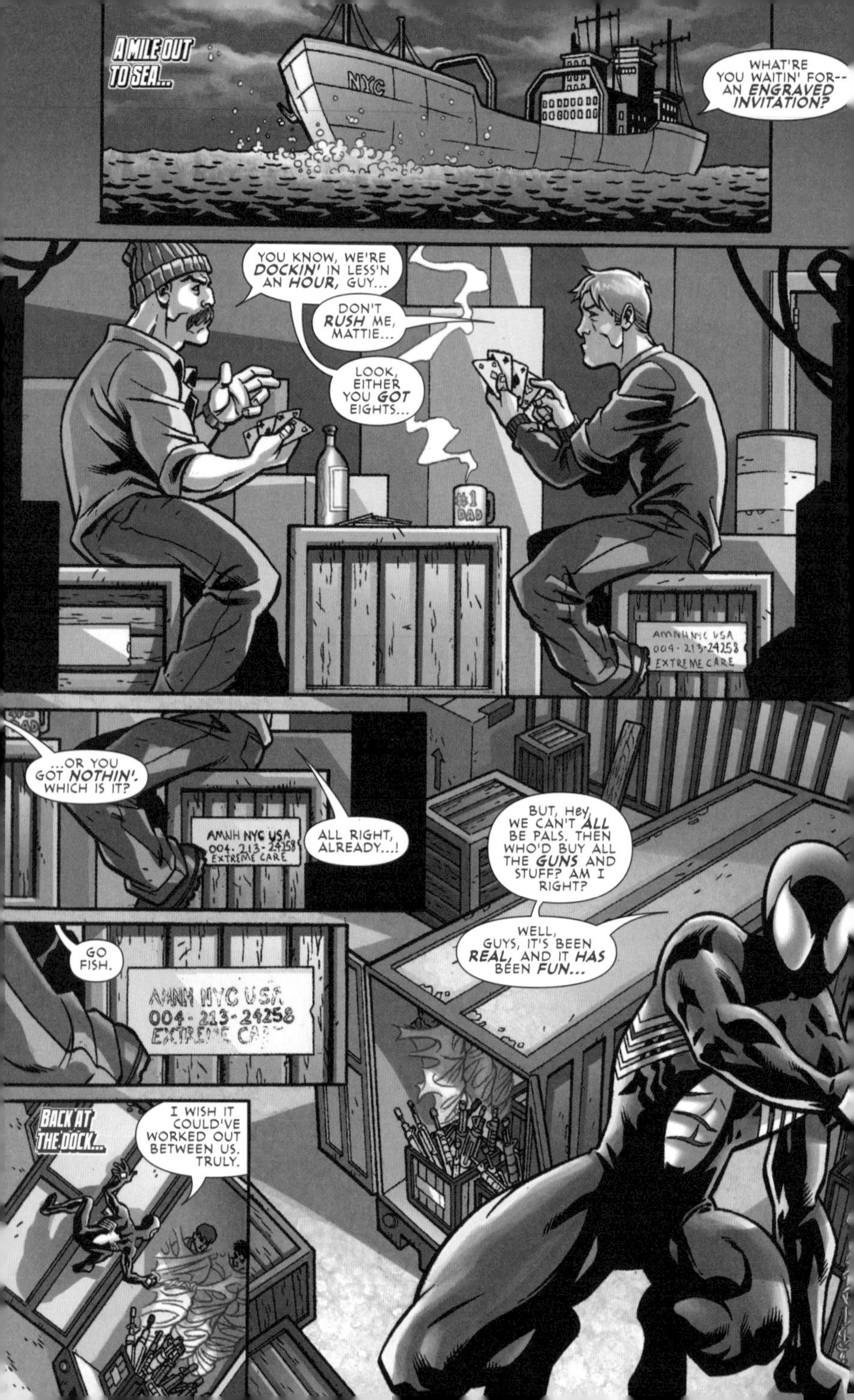
A MILE OUT TO SEA...
WHAT'RE YOU WAITIN' FOR-- AN ENGRAVED INVITATION?
NYC
YOU KNOW, WE'RE DOCKIN' IN LESS'N AN HOUR, GUY...
DON'T RUSH ME, MATTIE...
LOOK, EITHER YOU GOT EIGHTS...
#1 DAD
AMNH NYC USA 004-213-24258 EXTREME CARE
...OR YOU GOT NOTHIN'. WHICH IS IT?
ALL RIGHT, ALREADY...!
AMNH NYC USA 004-213-24258 EXTREME CARE
BUT, HEY, WE CAN'T ALL BE PALS. THEN WHO'D BUY ALL THE GUNS AND STUFF? AM I RIGHT?
GO FISH.
AMNH NYC USA 004-213-24258
WELL, GUYS, IT'S BEEN REAL, AND IT HAS BEEN FUN...
BACK AT THE DOCK...
I WISH IT COULD'VE WORKED OUT BETWEEN US. TRULY.

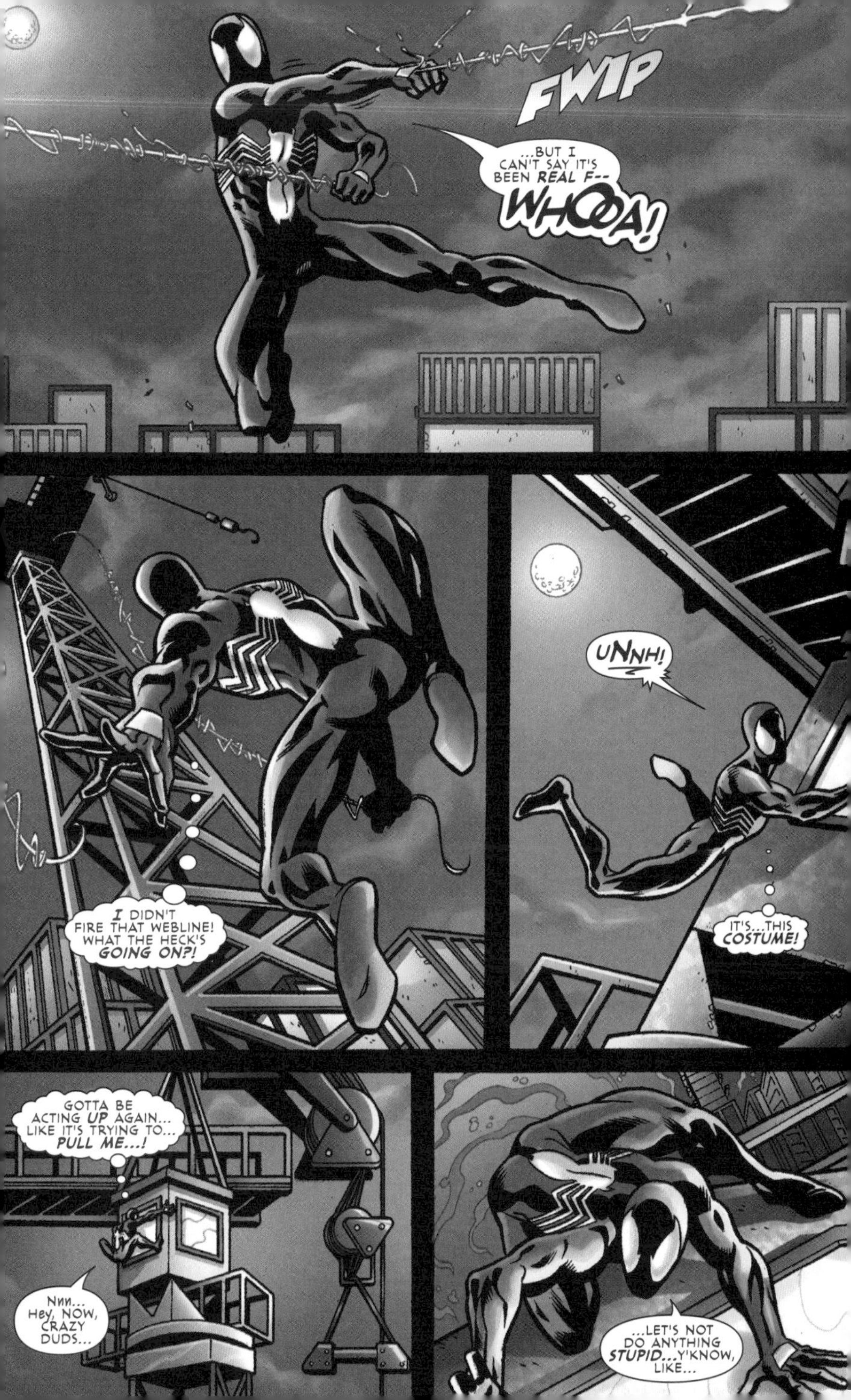
FWIP
...BUT I CAN'T SAY IT'S BEEN REAL F--
WHOOA!
I DIDN'T FIRE THAT WEBLINE! WHAT THE HECK'S GOING ON?!
UNNH!
IT'S...THIS COSTUME!
GOTTA BE ACTING UP AGAIN... LIKE IT'S TRYING TO... PULL ME...!
Nnn... Hey, NOW, CRAZY DUDS...
...LET'S NOT DO ANYTHING STUPID...Y'KNOW, LIKE...

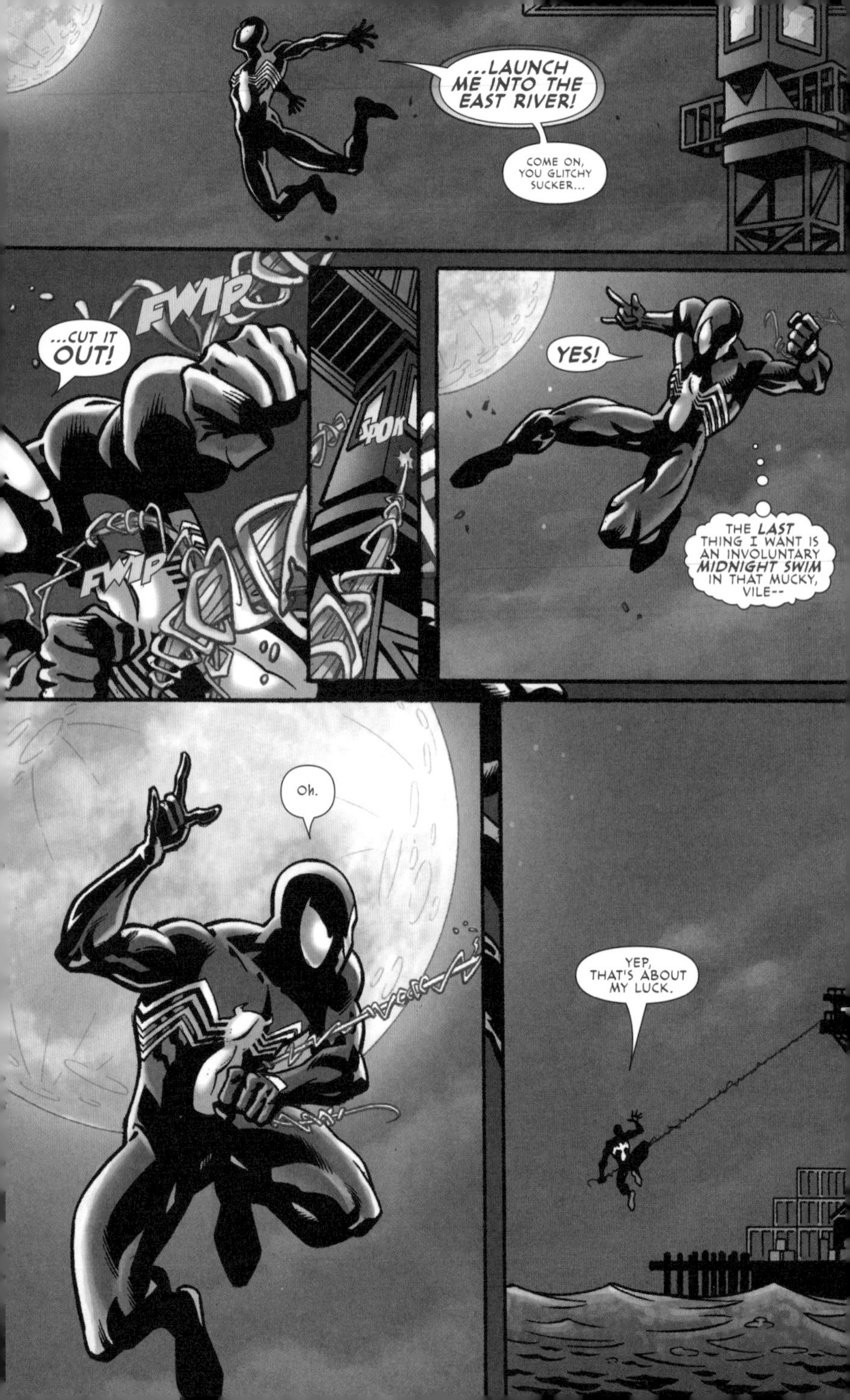
...LAUNCH ME INTO THE EAST RIVER!
COME ON, YOU GLITCHY SUCKER...
FWIP
...CUT IT OUT!
FWIP
SPOK
YES!
THE LAST THING I WANT IS AN INVOLUNTARY MIDNIGHT SWIM IN THAT MUCKY, VILE--
Oh.
YEP, THAT'S ABOUT MY LUCK.

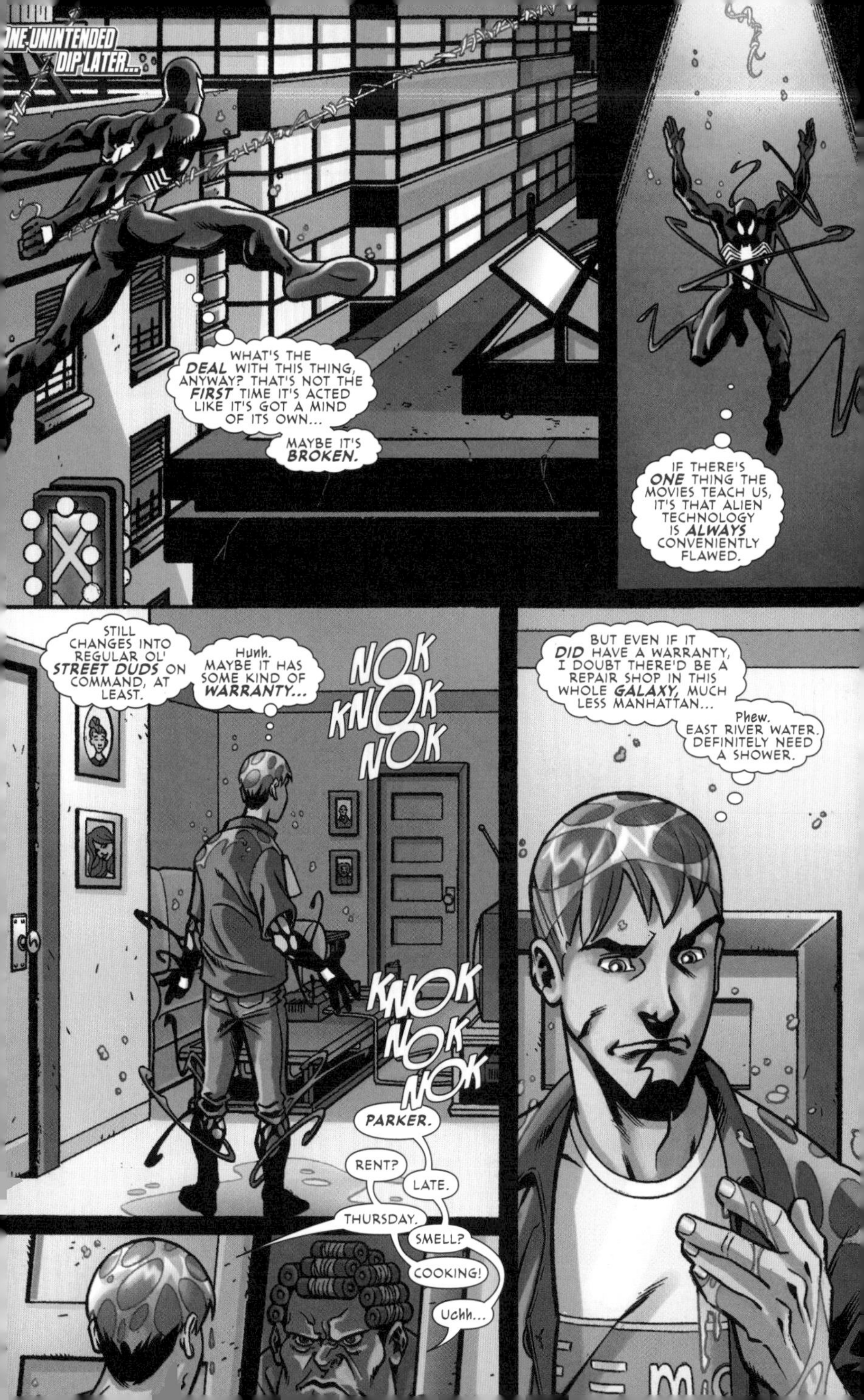
ONE UNINTENDED DIP LATER...
WHAT'S THE DEAL WITH THIS THING, ANYWAY? THAT'S NOT THE FIRST TIME IT'S ACTED LIKE IT'S GOT A MIND OF ITS OWN...
MAYBE IT'S BROKEN.
IF THERE'S ONE THING THE MOVIES TEACH US, IT'S THAT ALIEN TECHNOLOGY IS ALWAYS CONVENIENTLY FLAWED.
STILL CHANGES INTO REGULAR OL' STREET DUDS ON COMMAND, AT LEAST.
Hunh. MAYBE IT HAS SOME KIND OF WARRANTY...
BUT EVEN IF IT DID HAVE A WARRANTY, I DOUBT THERE'D BE A REPAIR SHOP IN THIS WHOLE GALAXY, MUCH LESS MANHATTAN...
Phew. EAST RIVER WATER. DEFINITELY NEED A SHOWER.
NOK KNOK NOK
KNOK NOK NOK
PARKER.
RENT?
LATE.
THURSDAY.
SMELL?
COOKING!
Uchh...

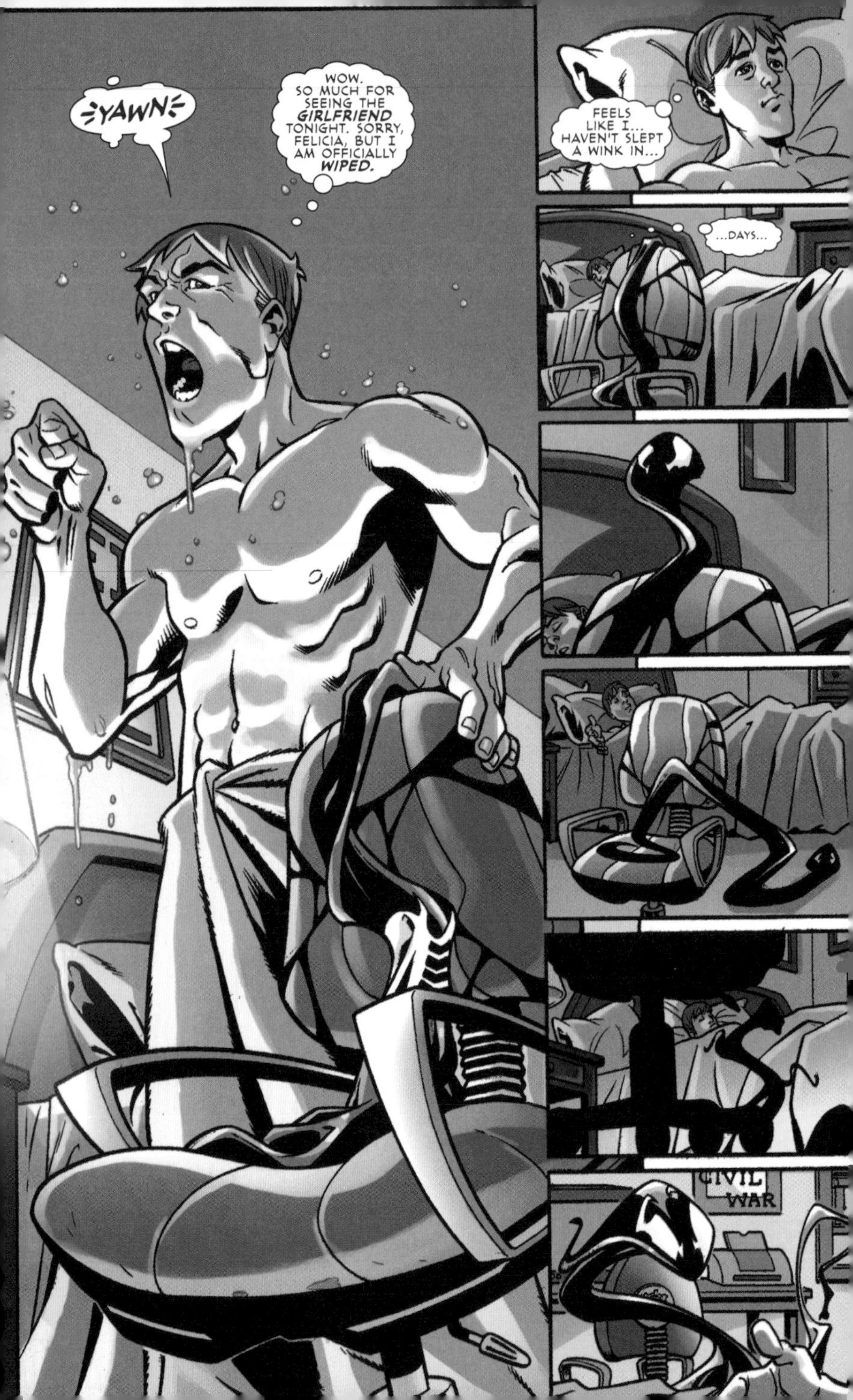
YAWN
WOW. SO MUCH FOR SEEING THE GIRLFRIEND TONIGHT. SORRY, FELICIA, BUT I AM OFFICIALLY WIPED.
FEELS LIKE I... HAVEN'T SLEPT A WINK IN...
...DAYS...
CIVIL WAR

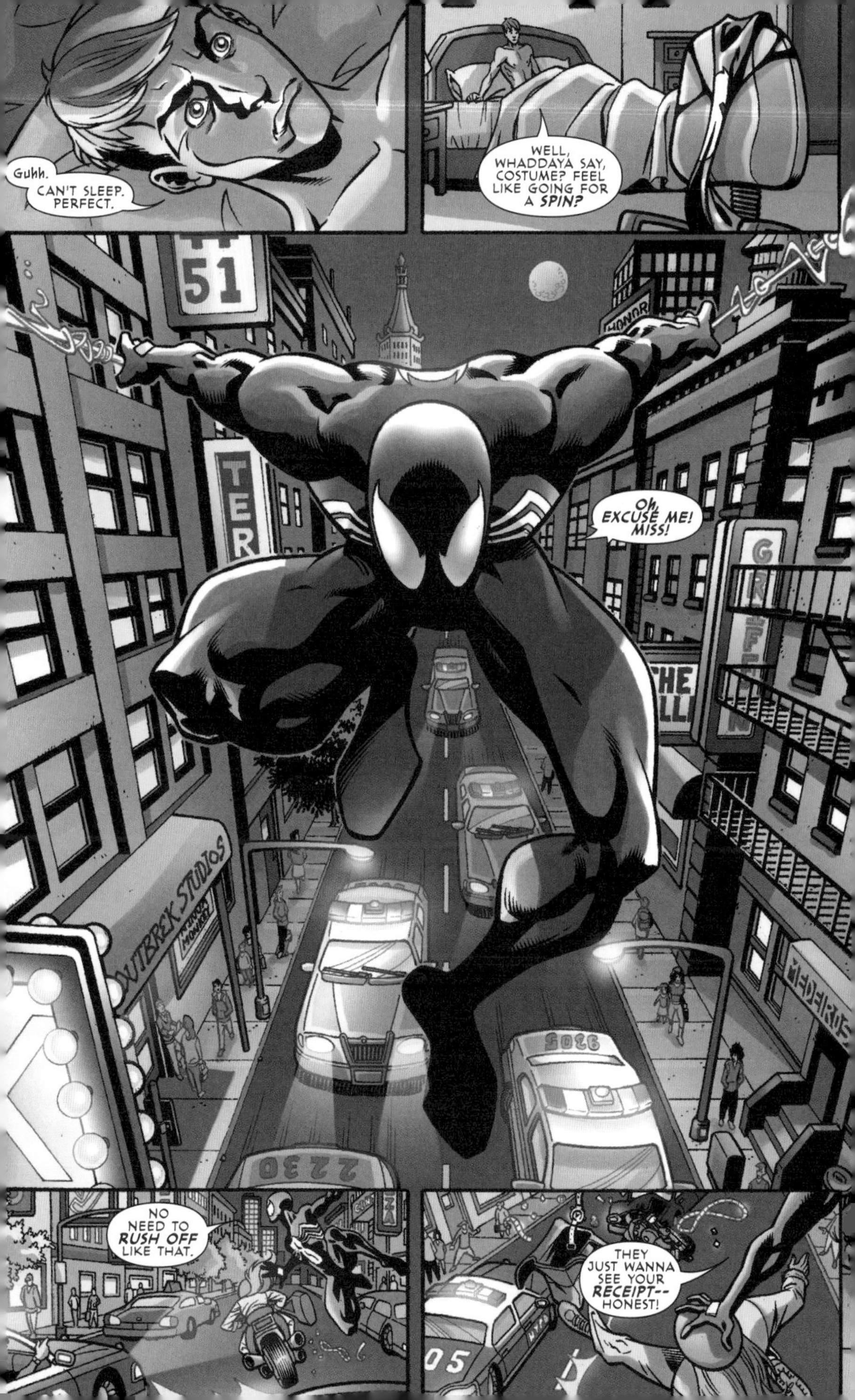

Guhh.
CAN'T SLEEP. PERFECT.
WELL, WHADDAYA SAY, COSTUME? FEEL LIKE GOING FOR A SPIN?
51
Oh, EXCUSE ME! MISS!
NO NEED TO RUSH OFF LIKE THAT.
THEY JUST WANNA SEE YOUR RECEIPT-- HONEST!

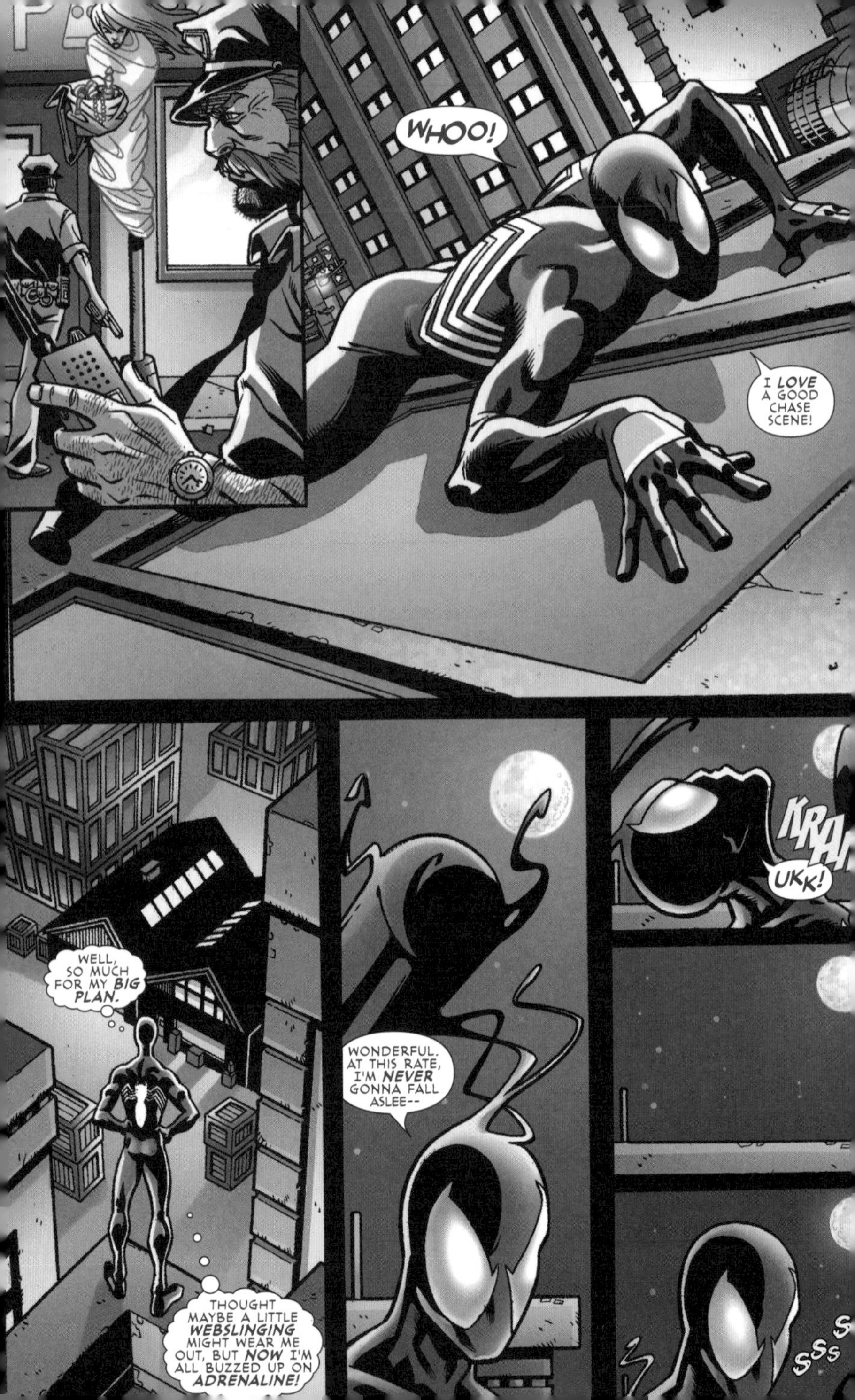
WHOO!
I LOVE A GOOD CHASE SCENE!
WELL, SO MUCH FOR MY BIG PLAN.
THOUGHT MAYBE A LITTLE WEBSLINGING MIGHT WEAR ME OUT, BUT NOW I'M ALL BUZZED UP ON ADRENALINE!
WONDERFUL. AT THIS RATE, I'M NEVER GONNA FALL ASLEE--
UKK!
SSSS

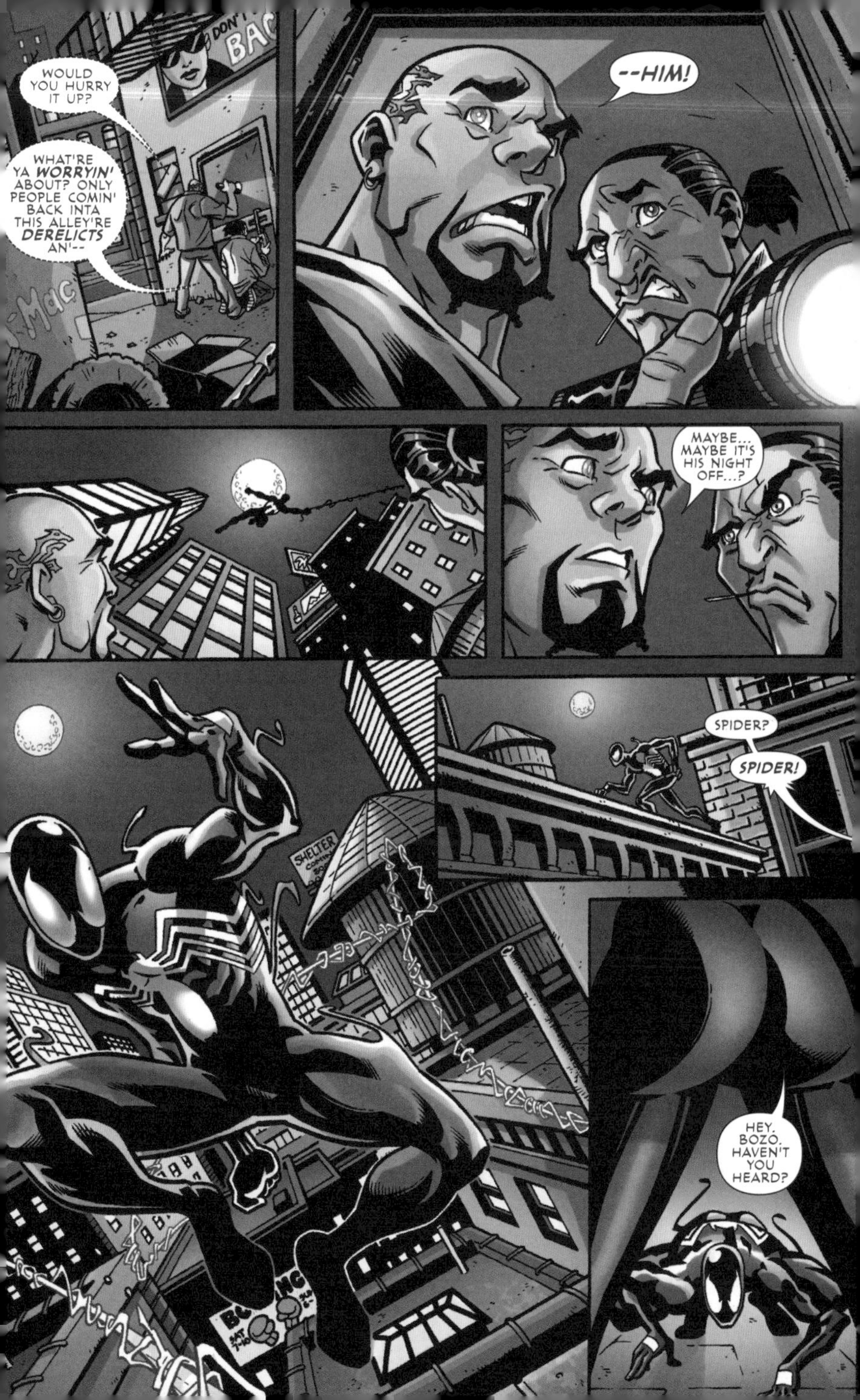
WOULD YOU HURRY IT UP?
WHAT'RE YA WORRYIN' ABOUT? ONLY PEOPLE COMIN' BACK INTA THIS ALLEY'RE DERELICTS AN'--
--HIM!
MAYBE... MAYBE IT'S HIS NIGHT OFF...?
SPIDER?
SPIDER!
HEY. BOZO. HAVEN'T YOU HEARD?

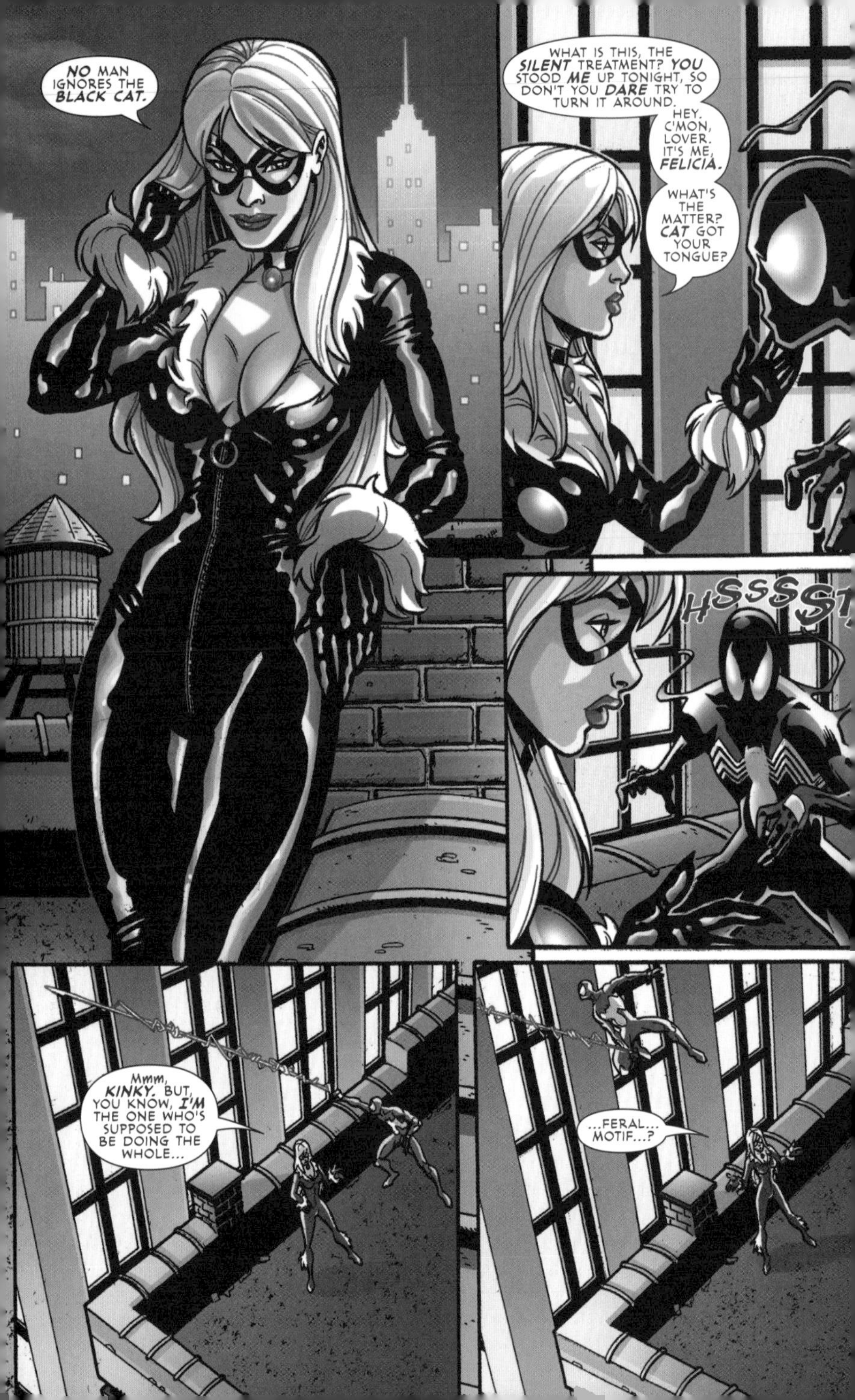
NO MAN IGNORES THE BLACK CAT.
WHAT IS THIS, THE SILENT TREATMENT? YOU STOOD ME UP TONIGHT, SO DON'T YOU DARE TRY TO TURN IT AROUND.
HEY. C'MON, LOVER. IT'S ME, FELICIA.
WHAT'S THE MATTER? CAT GOT YOUR TONGUE?
HSSSST!
Mmm, KINKY. BUT, YOU KNOW, I'M THE ONE WHO'S SUPPOSED TO BE DOING THE WHOLE...
...FERAL... MOTIF...?

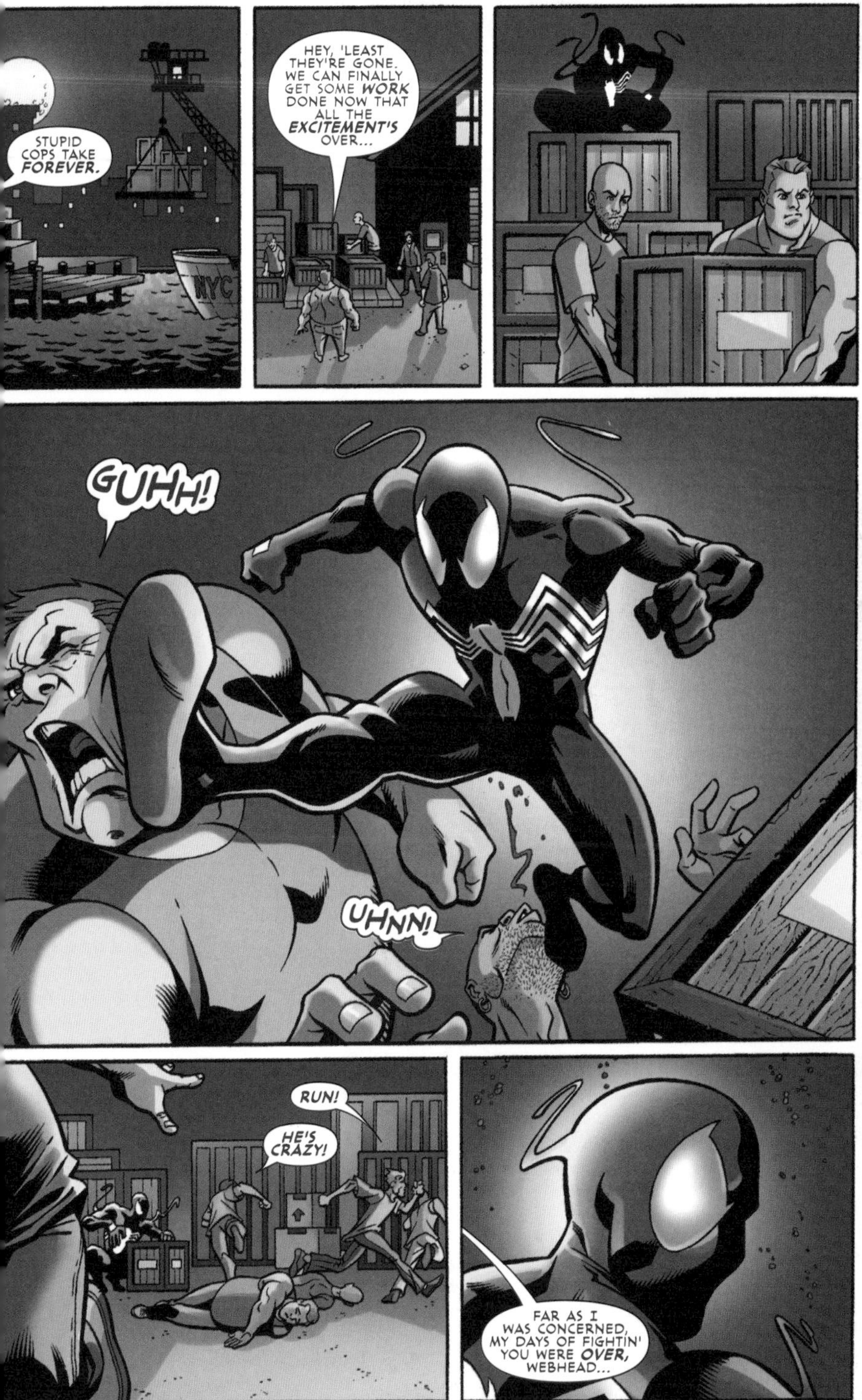
STUPID COPS TAKE FOREVER.
HEY, 'LEAST THEY'RE GONE. WE CAN FINALLY GET SOME WORK DONE NOW THAT ALL THE EXCITEMENT'S OVER...
NYC
GUHH!
UHNN!
RUN!
HE'S CRAZY!
FAR AS I WAS CONCERNED, MY DAYS OF FIGHTIN' YOU WERE OVER, WEBHEAD...

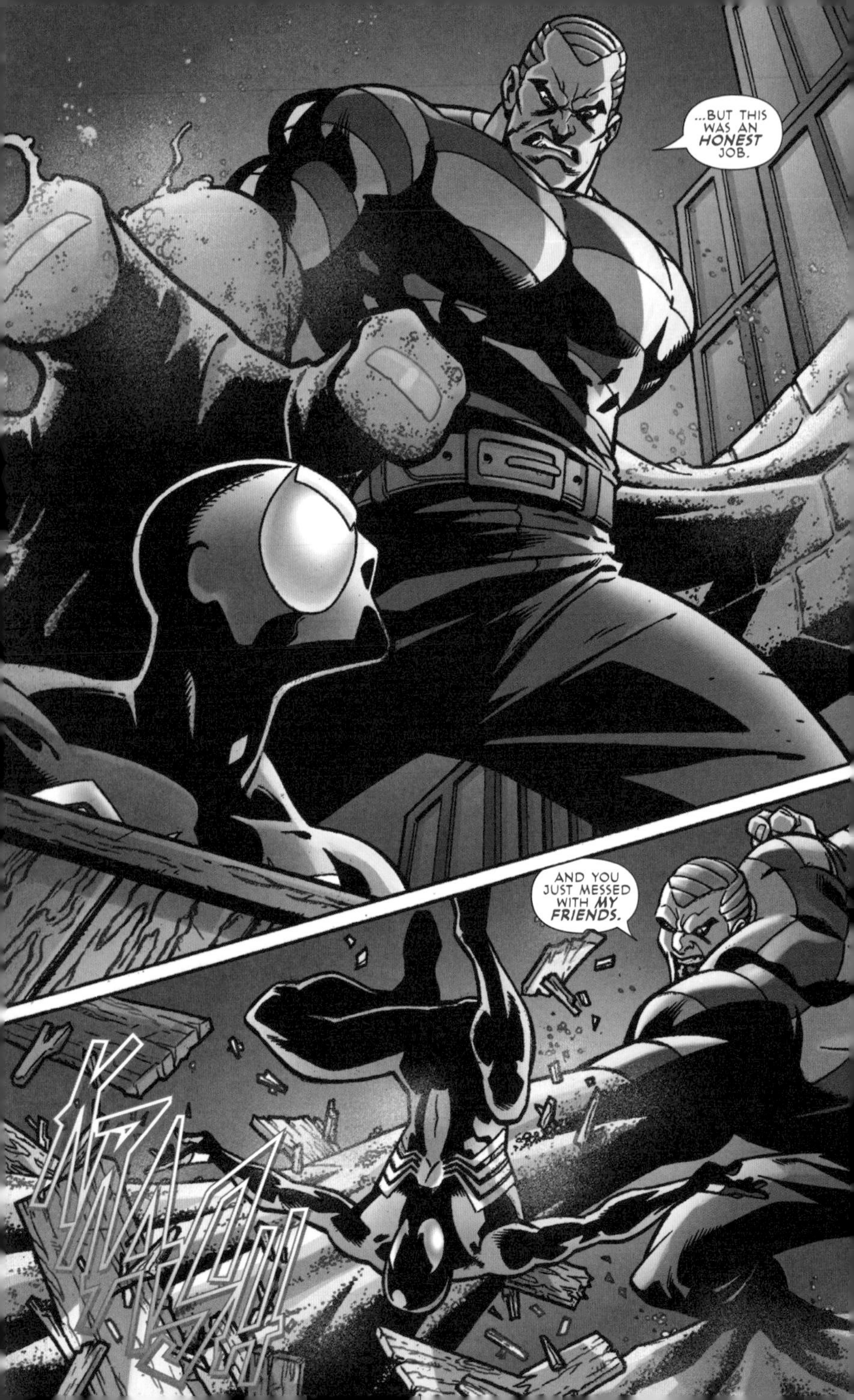
...BUT THIS WAS AN HONEST JOB.
AND YOU JUST MESSED WITH MY FRIENDS.
KRAK!!

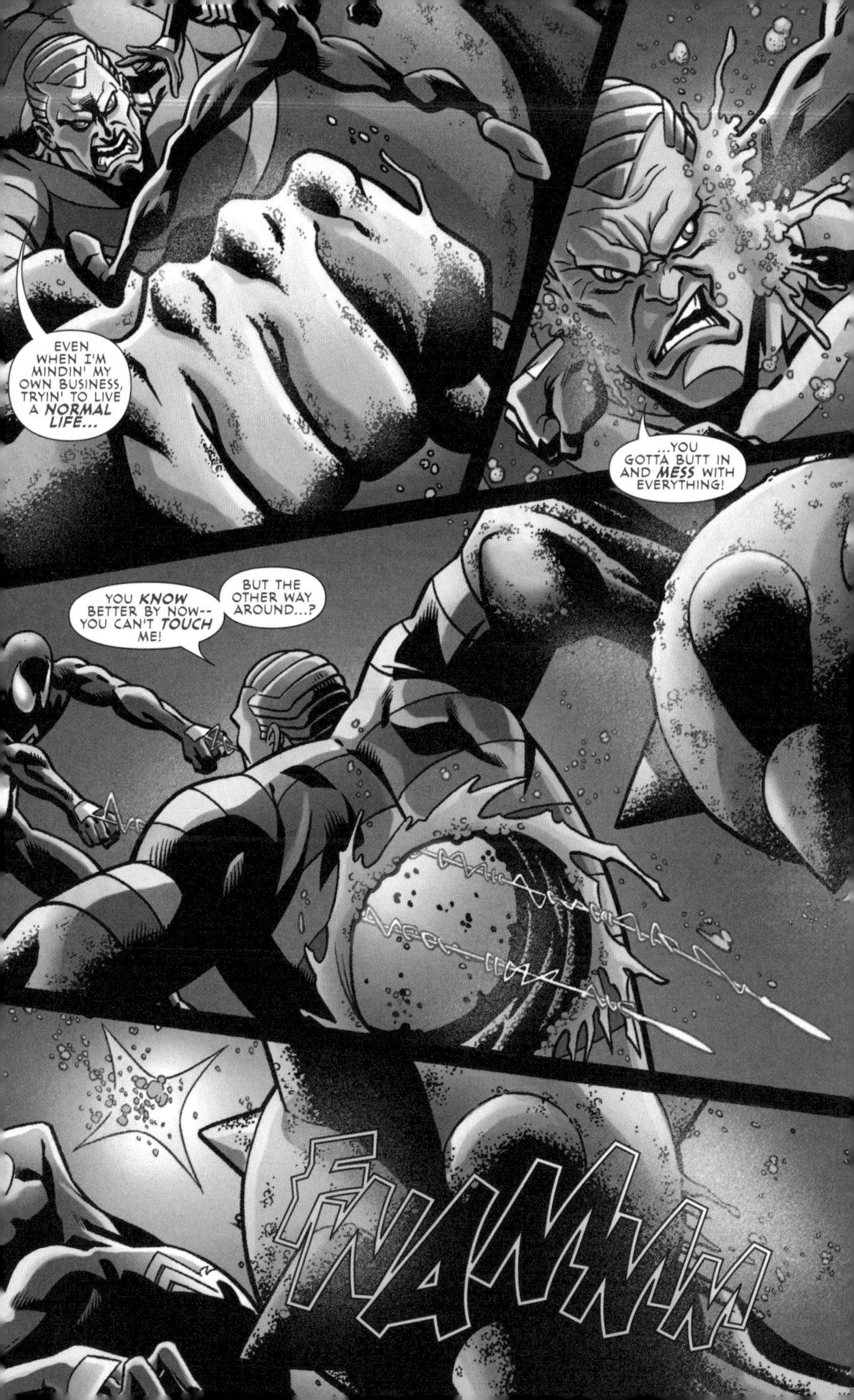
EVEN WHEN I'M MINDIN' MY OWN BUSINESS, TRYIN' TO LIVE A **NORMAL LIFE...**
...YOU GOTTA BUTT IN AND **MESS** WITH EVERYTHING!
YOU **KNOW** BETTER BY NOW-- YOU CAN'T **TOUCH** ME!
BUT THE OTHER WAY AROUND...?
FWAMMM

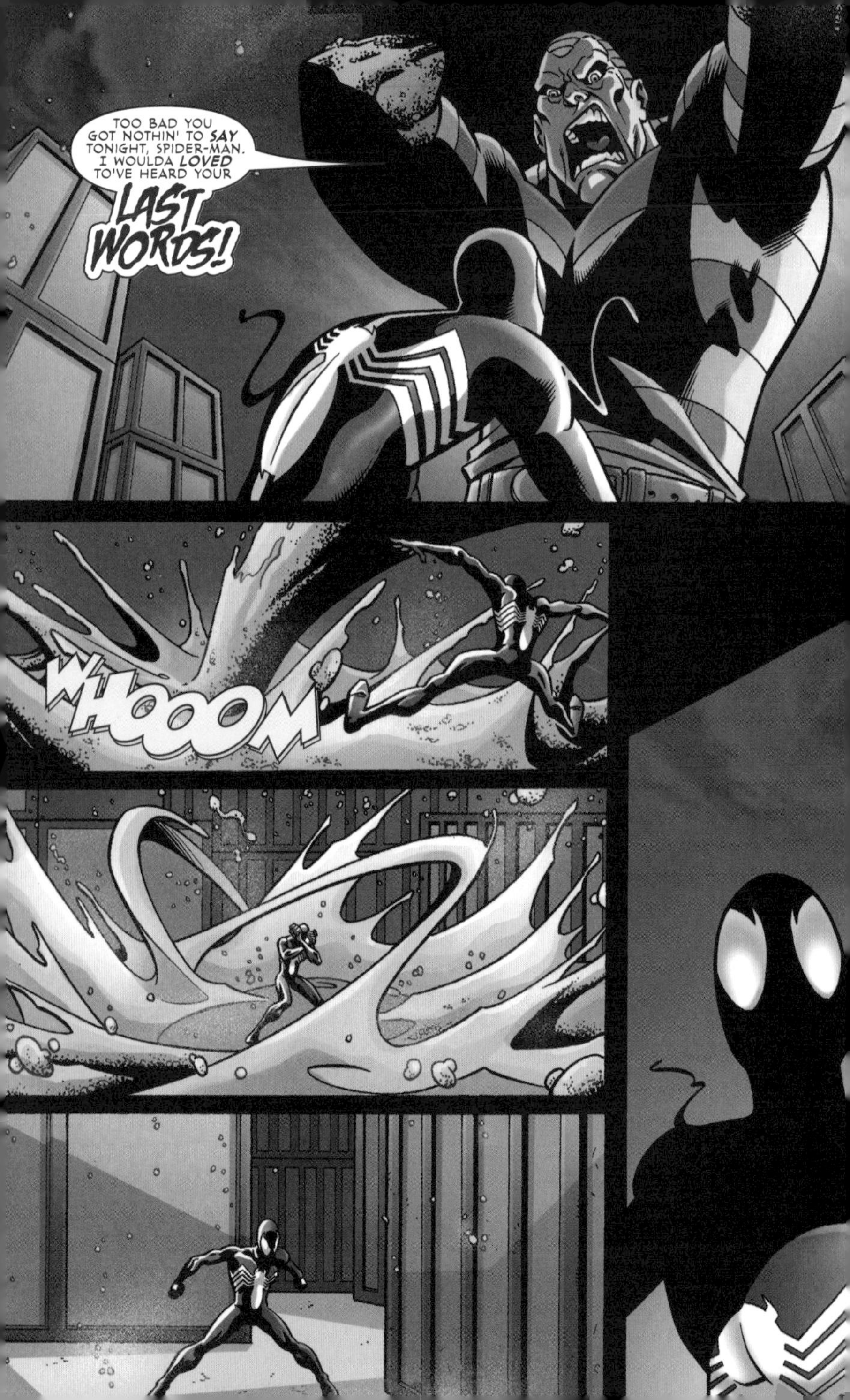
TOO BAD YOU GOT NOTHIN' TO SAY TONIGHT, SPIDER-MAN. I WOULDA LOVED TO'VE HEARD YOUR LAST WORDS!
WHOOOM

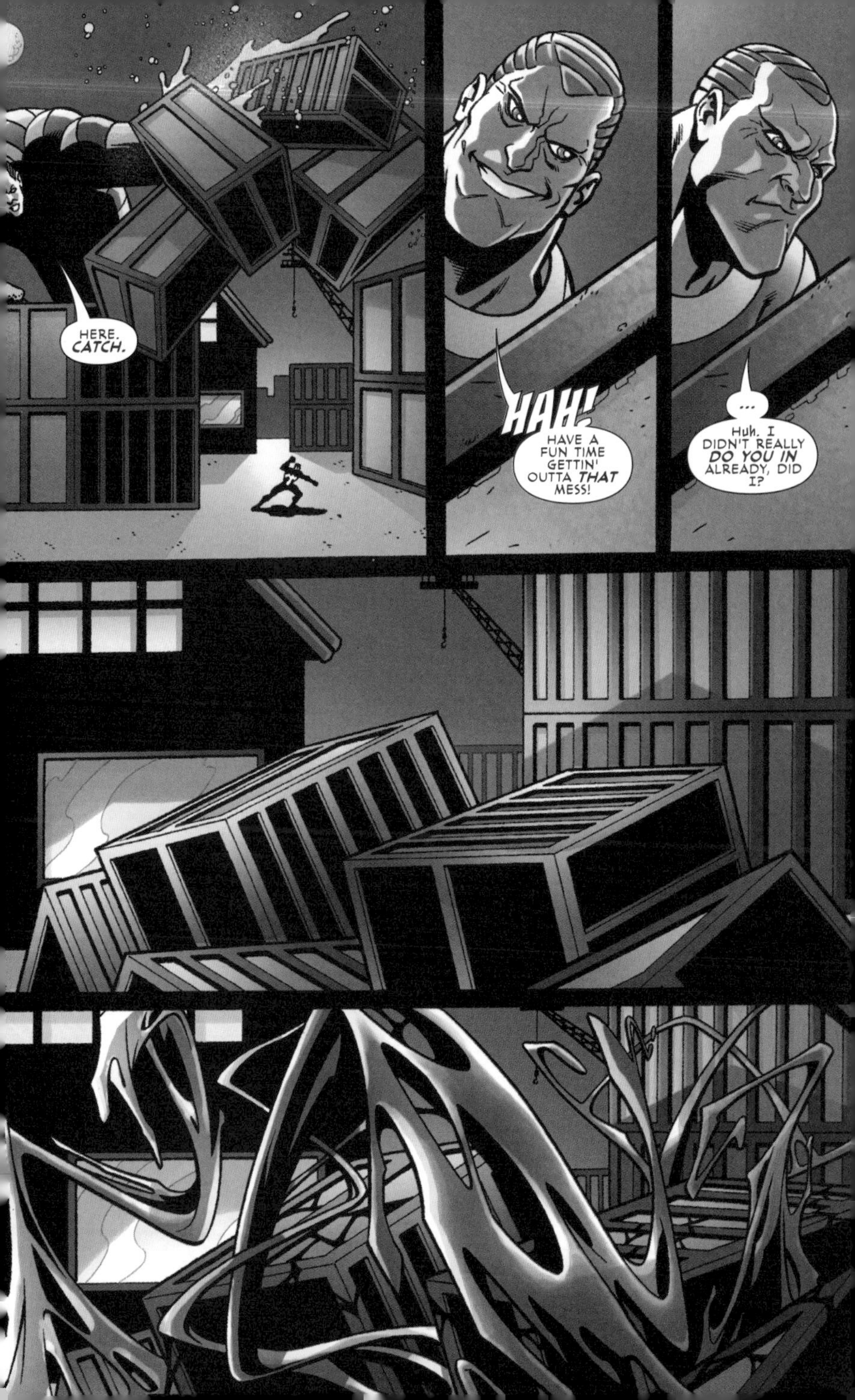
HERE. CATCH.
HAH!
HAVE A FUN TIME GETTIN' OUTTA THAT MESS!
...
Huh. I DIDN'T REALLY DO YOU IN ALREADY, DID I?

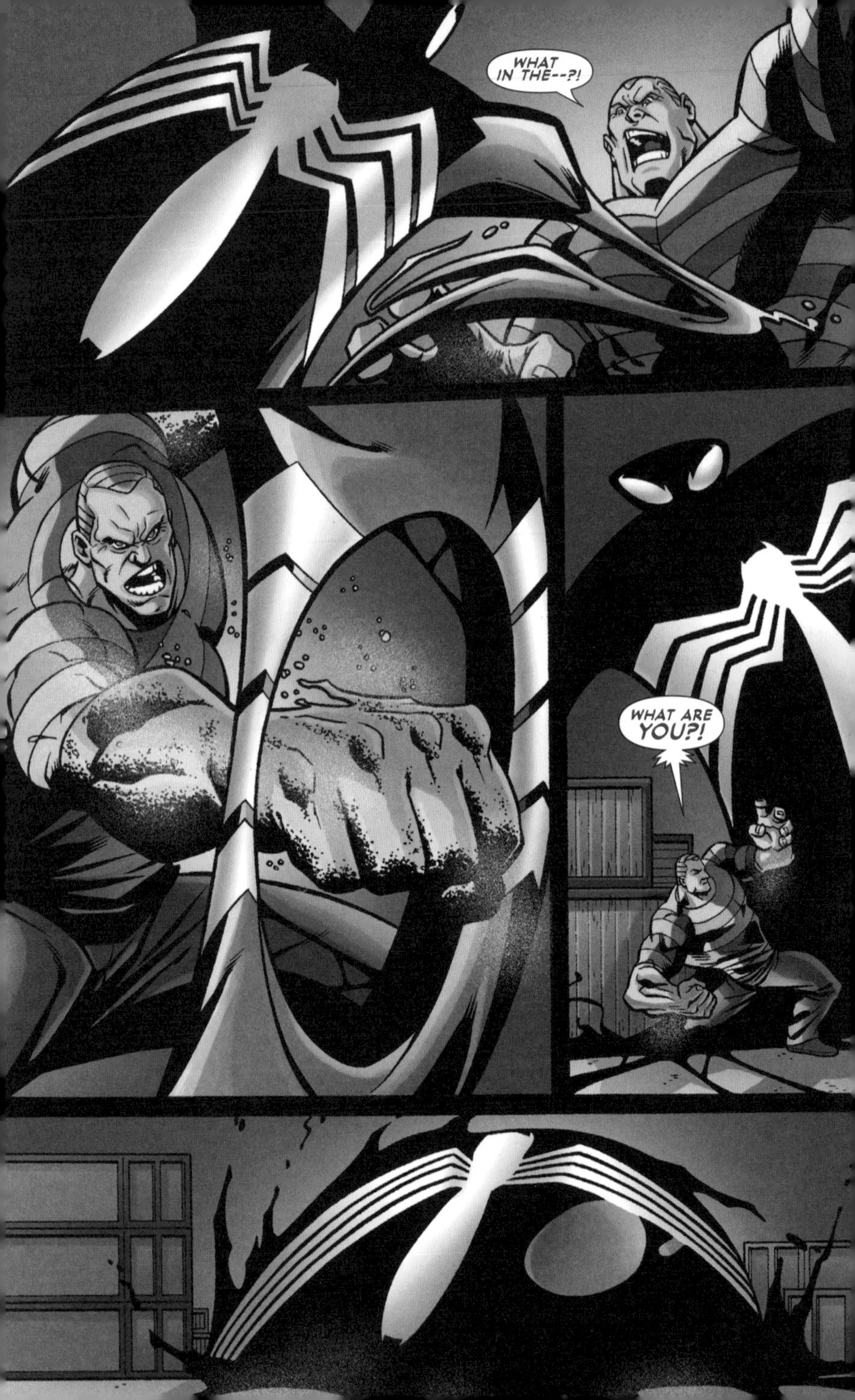
WHAT IN THE--?!
WHAT ARE YOU?!

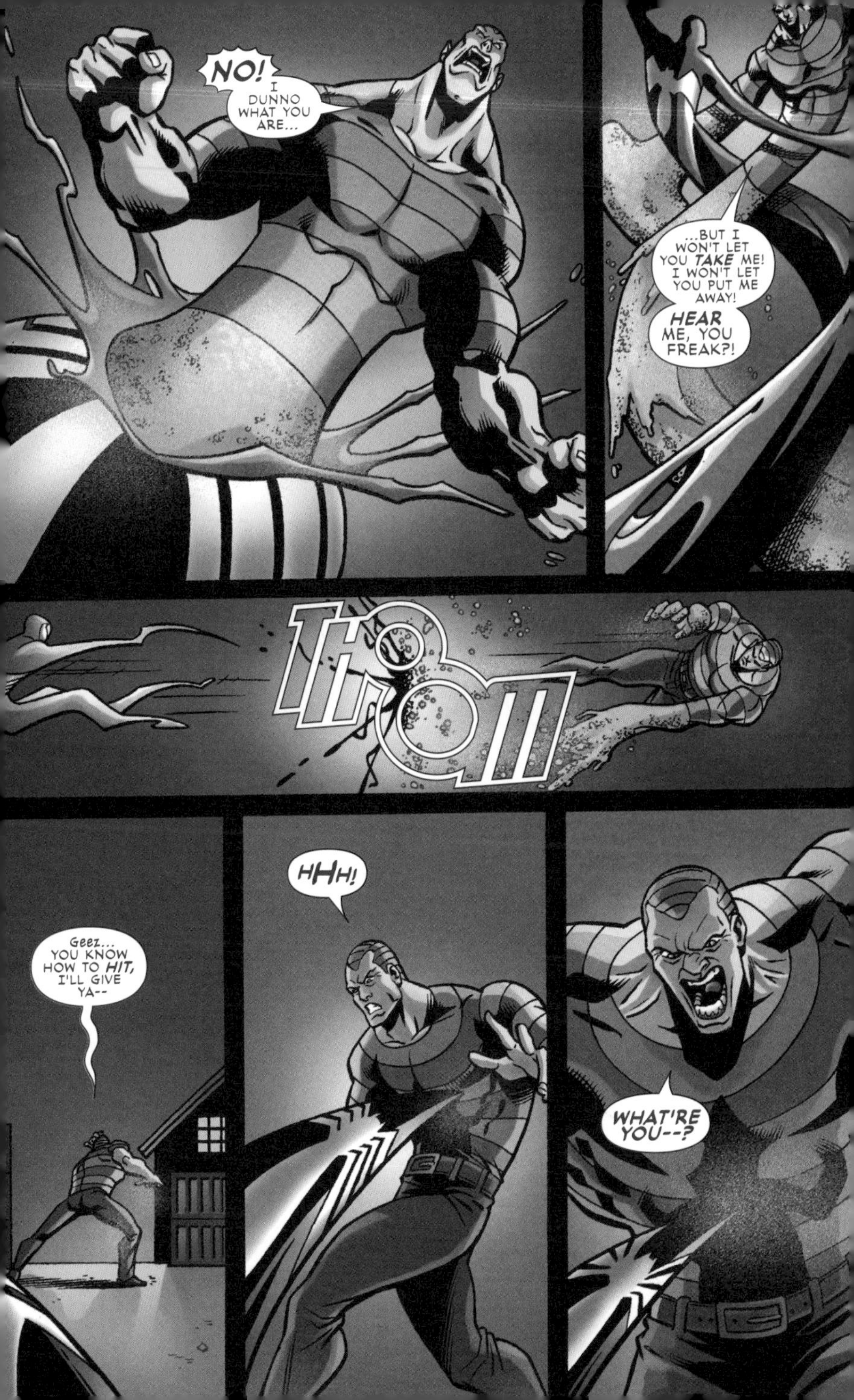
NO!
I DUNNO WHAT YOU ARE...
...BUT I WON'T LET YOU TAKE ME! I WON'T LET YOU PUT ME AWAY!
HEAR ME, YOU FREAK?!
THOOM
Geez... YOU KNOW HOW TO HIT, I'LL GIVE YA--
HHH!
WHAT'RE YOU--?

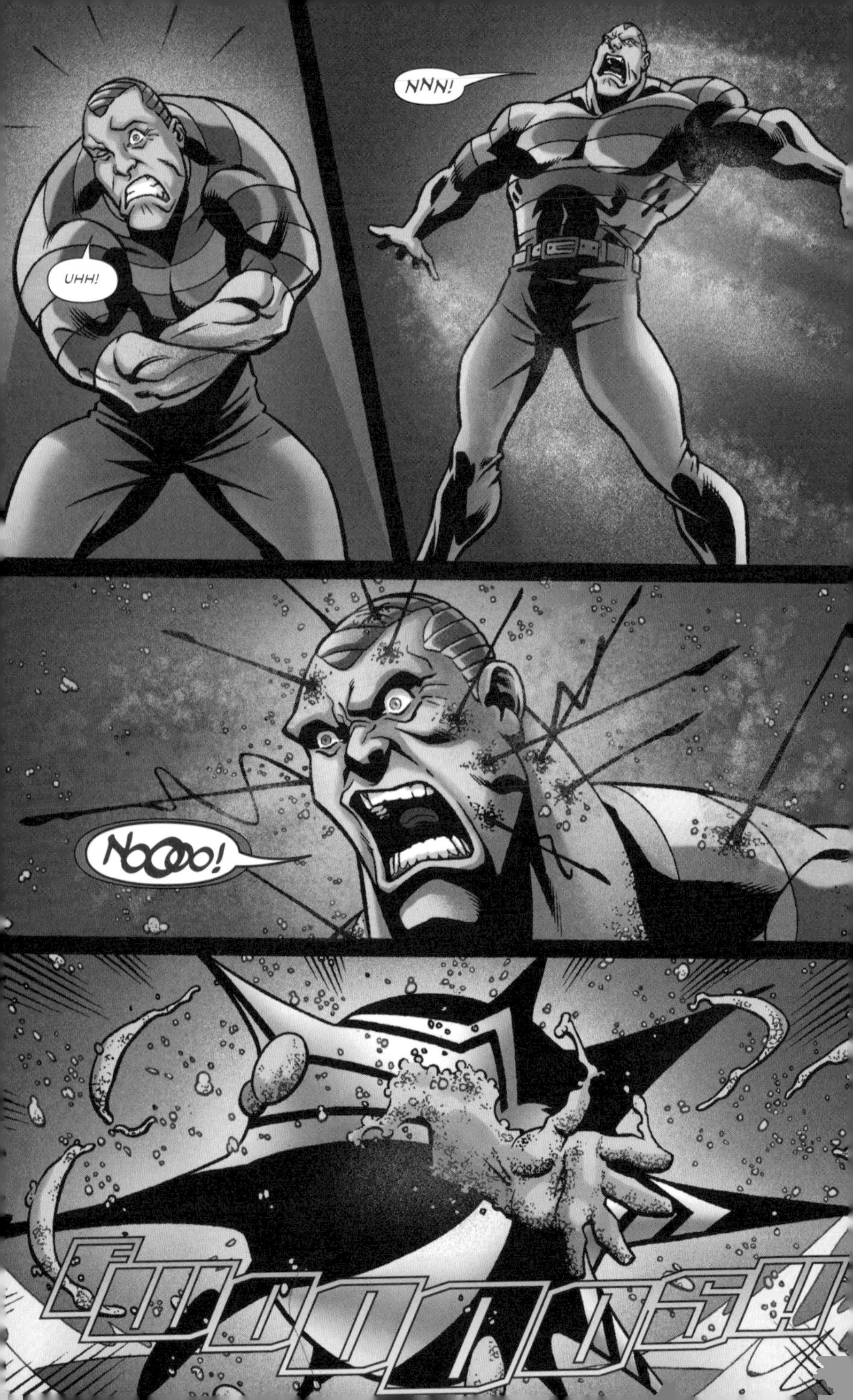
UHH!
NNN!
NOOOO!

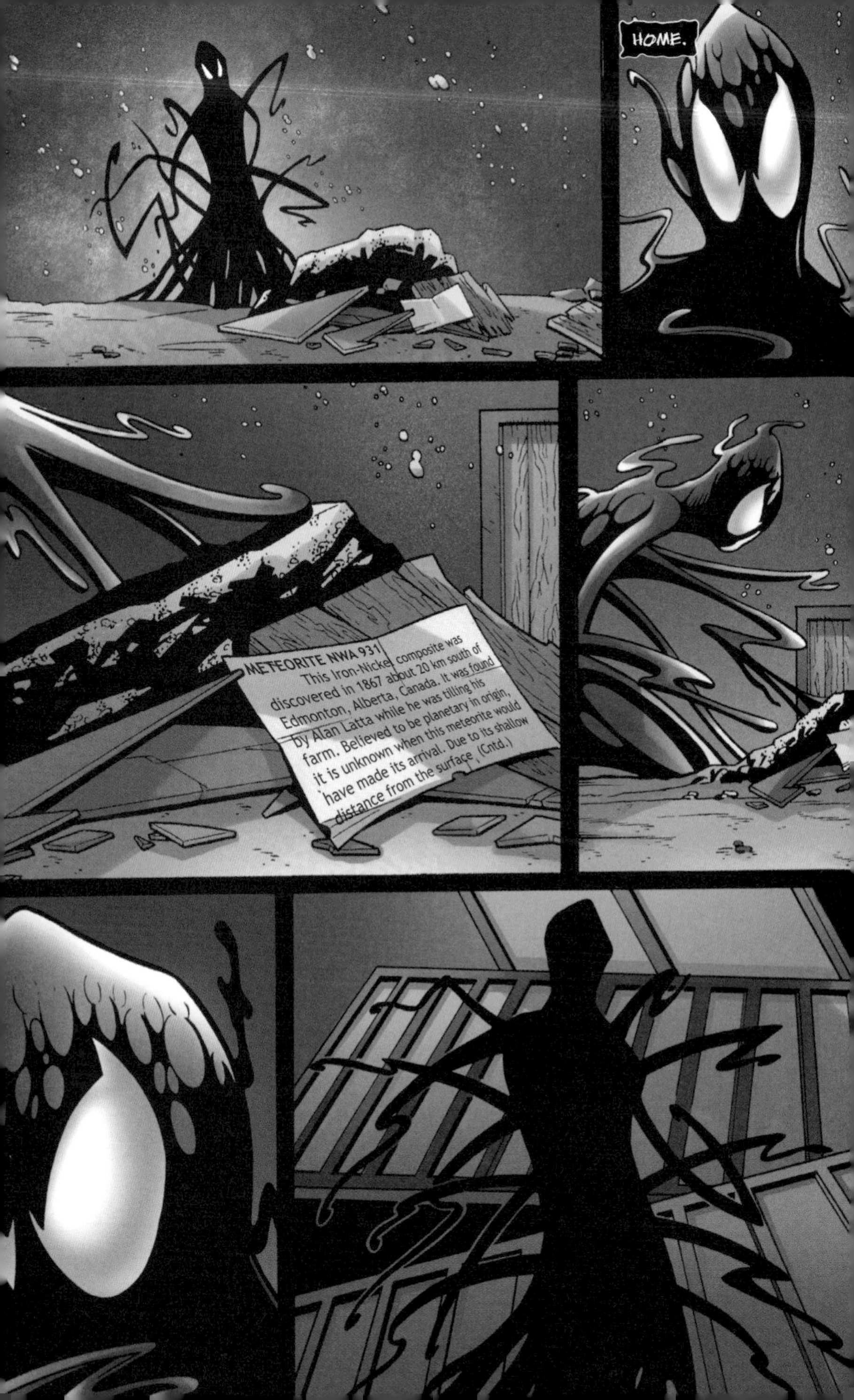
HOME.
METEORITE NWA 931
This Iron-Nickel composite was discovered in 1867 about 20 km south of Edmonton, Alberta, Canada. It was found by Alan Latta while he was tilling his farm. Believed to be planetary in origin, it is unknown when this meteorite would have made its arrival. Due to its shallow distance from the surface (Cntd.)

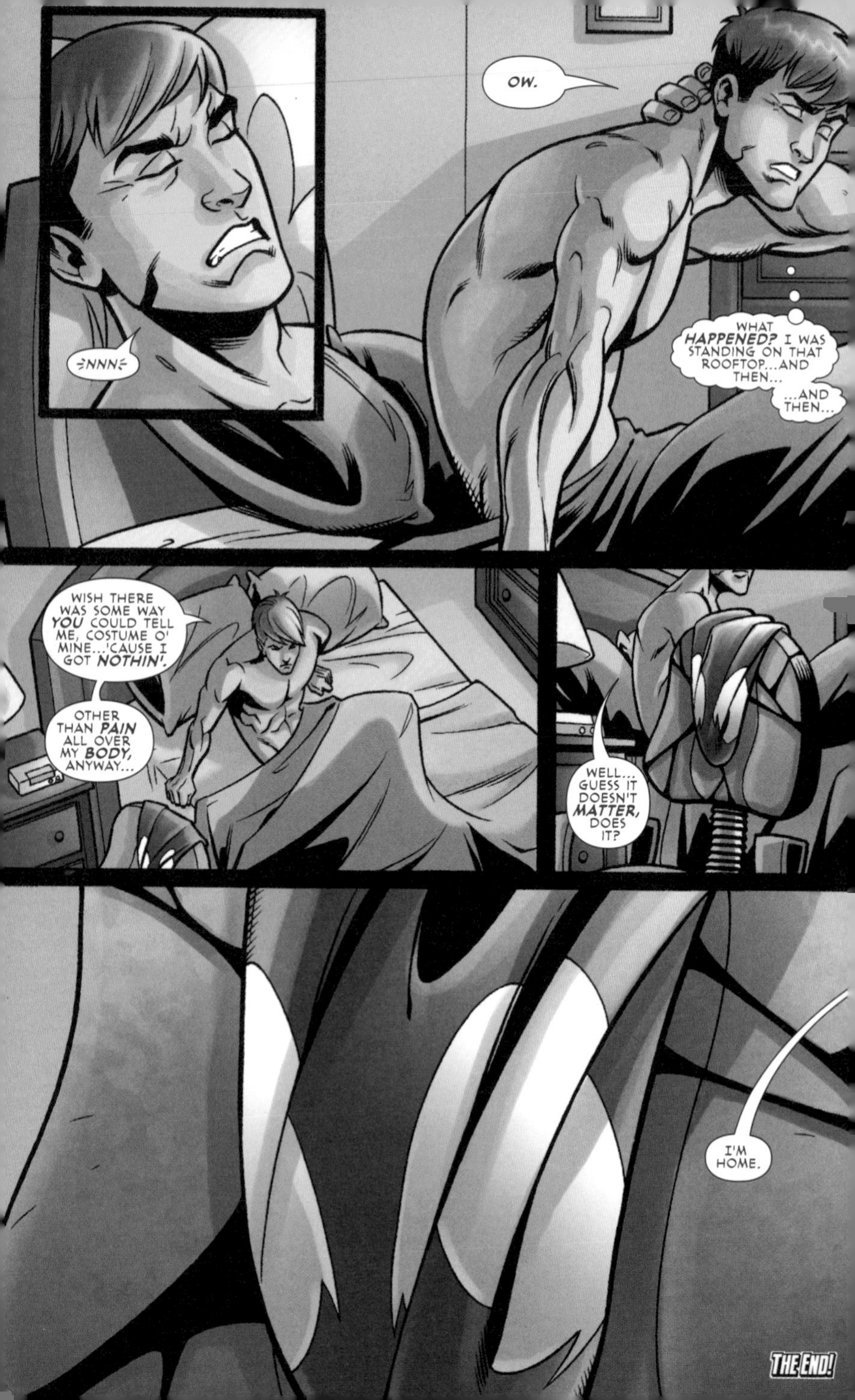
NNN
OW.
WHAT HAPPENED? I WAS STANDING ON THAT ROOFTOP...AND THEN...
...AND THEN...
WISH THERE WAS SOME WAY YOU COULD TELL ME, COSTUME O' MINE...'CAUSE I GOT NOTHIN'.
OTHER THAN PAIN ALL OVER MY BODY, ANYWAY...
WELL... GUESS IT DOESN'T MATTER, DOES IT?
I'M HOME.
THE END!

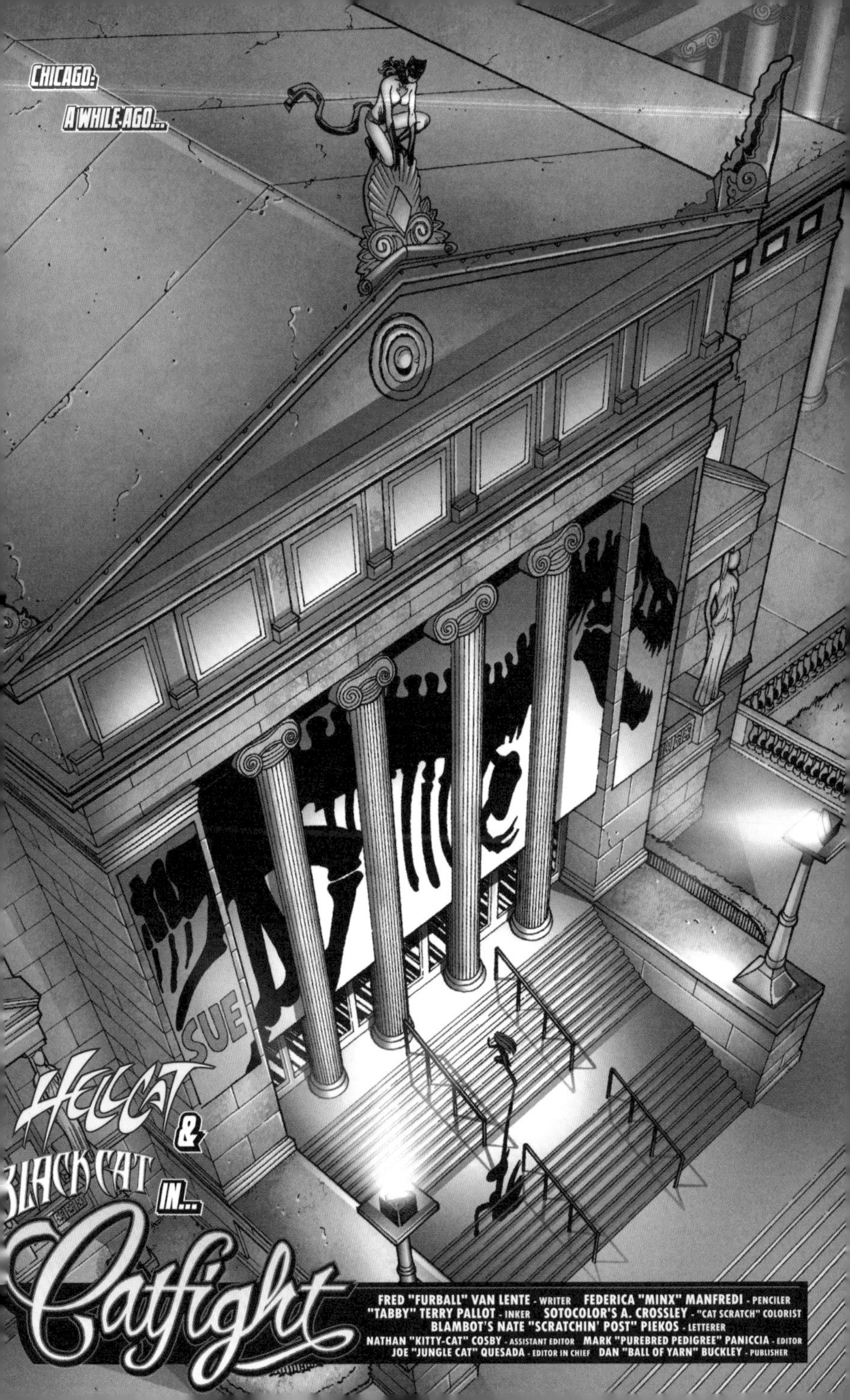

CHICAGO:
A WHILE AGO...
SUE
HELLCAT & BLACK CAT IN...
Catfight
FRED "FURBALL" VAN LENTE - WRITER FEDERICA "MINX" MANFREDI - PENCILER
"TABBY" TERRY PALLOT - INKER SOTOCOLOR'S A. CROSSLEY - "CAT SCRATCH" COLORIST
BLAMBOT'S NATE "SCRATCHIN' POST" PIEKOS - LETTERER
NATHAN "KITTY-CAT" COSBY - ASSISTANT EDITOR MARK "PUREBRED PEDIGREE" PANICCIA - EDITOR
JOE "JUNGLE CAT" QUESADA - EDITOR IN CHIEF DAN "BALL OF YARN" BUCKLEY - PUBLISHER

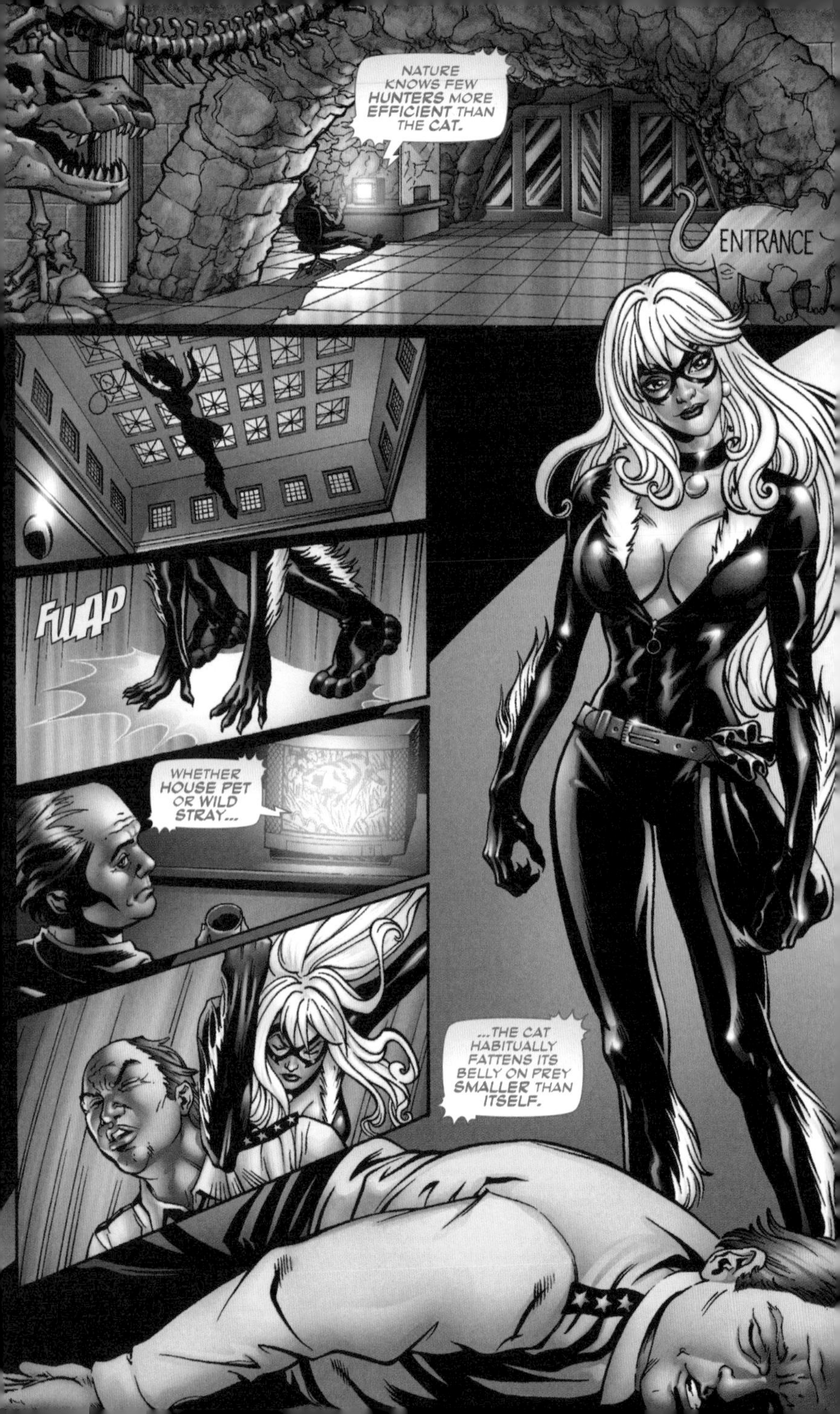
NATURE KNOWS FEW HUNTERS MORE EFFICIENT THAN THE CAT.
ENTRANCE
FWAP
WHETHER HOUSE PET OR WILD STRAY...
...THE CAT HABITUALLY FATTENS ITS BELLY ON PREY SMALLER THAN ITSELF.

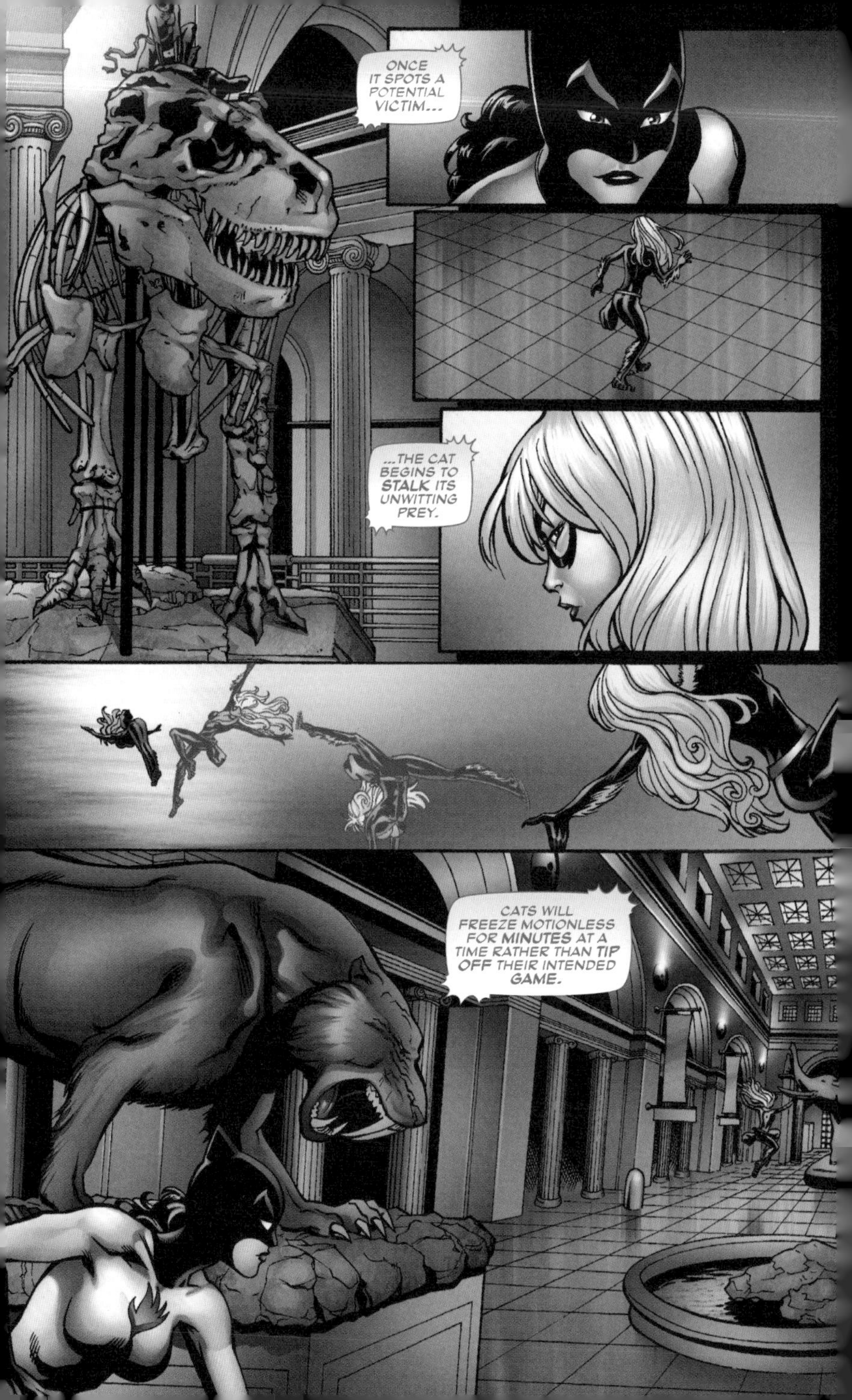
ONCE IT SPOTS A POTENTIAL VICTIM...
...THE CAT BEGINS TO STALK ITS UNWITTING PREY.
CATS WILL FREEZE MOTIONLESS FOR MINUTES AT A TIME RATHER THAN TIP OFF THEIR INTENDED GAME.

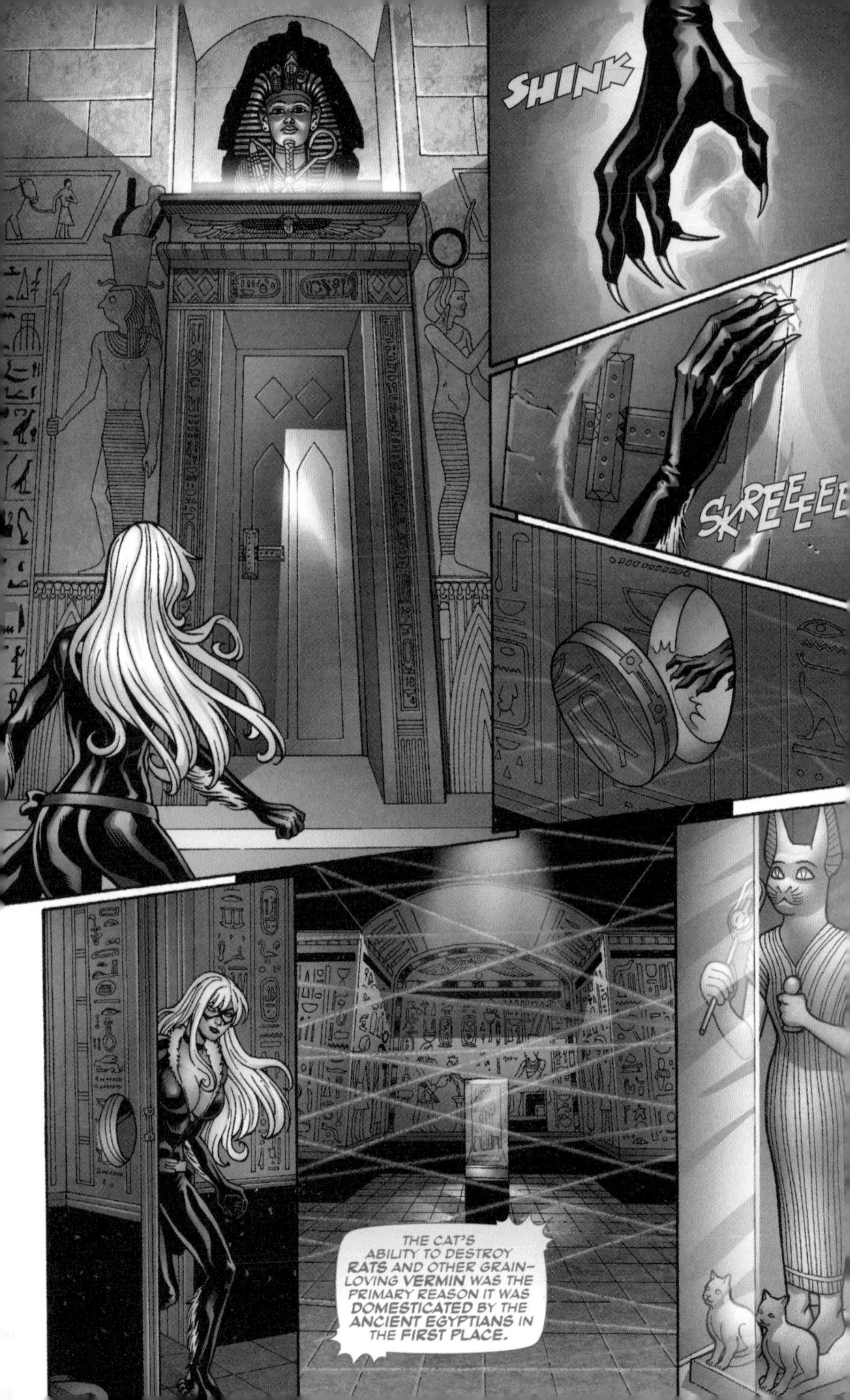
SHINK
SKREEEEEE
THE CAT'S ABILITY TO DESTROY RATS AND OTHER GRAIN-LOVING VERMIN WAS THE PRIMARY REASON IT WAS DOMESTICATED BY THE ANCIENT EGYPTIANS IN THE FIRST PLACE.

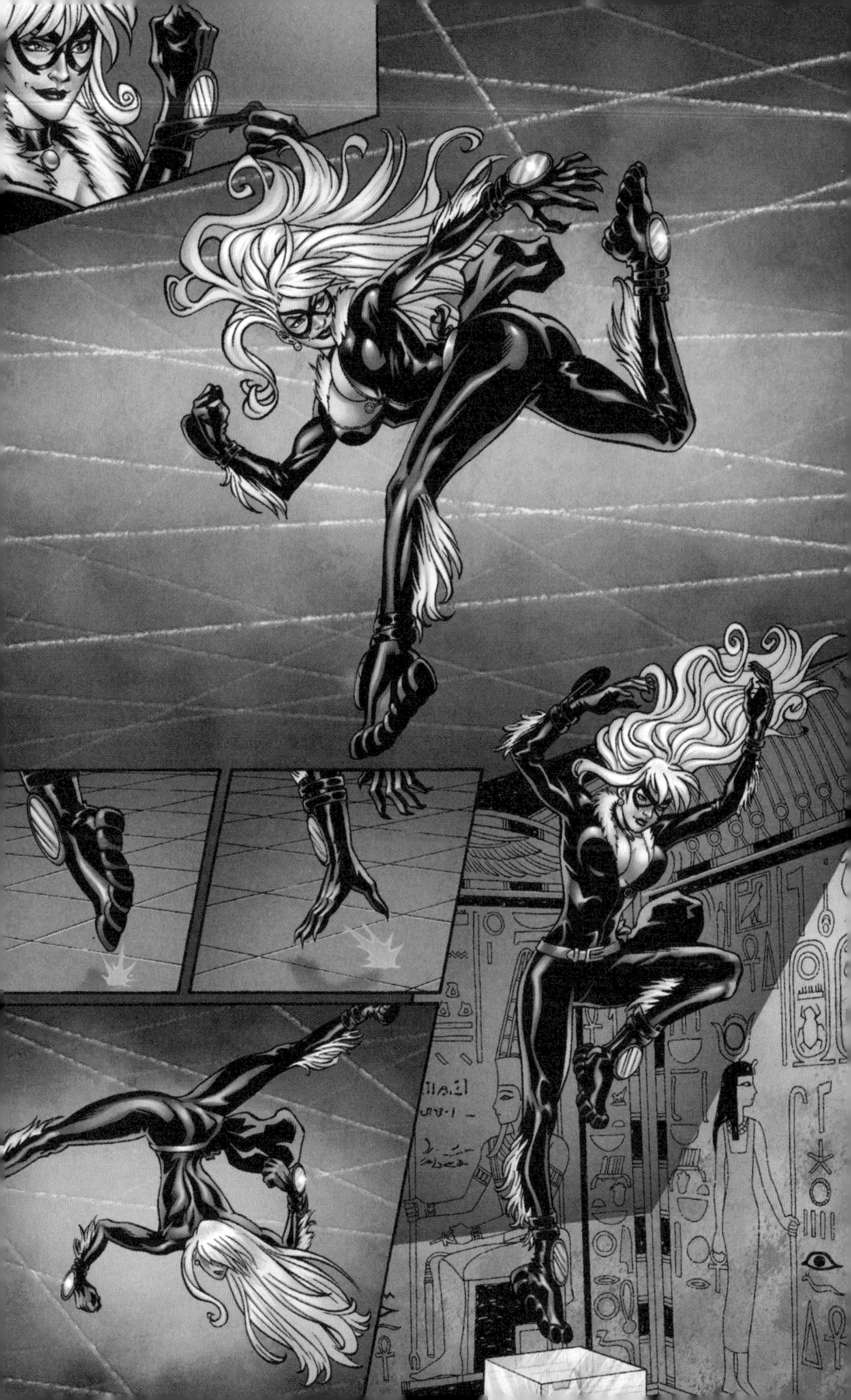

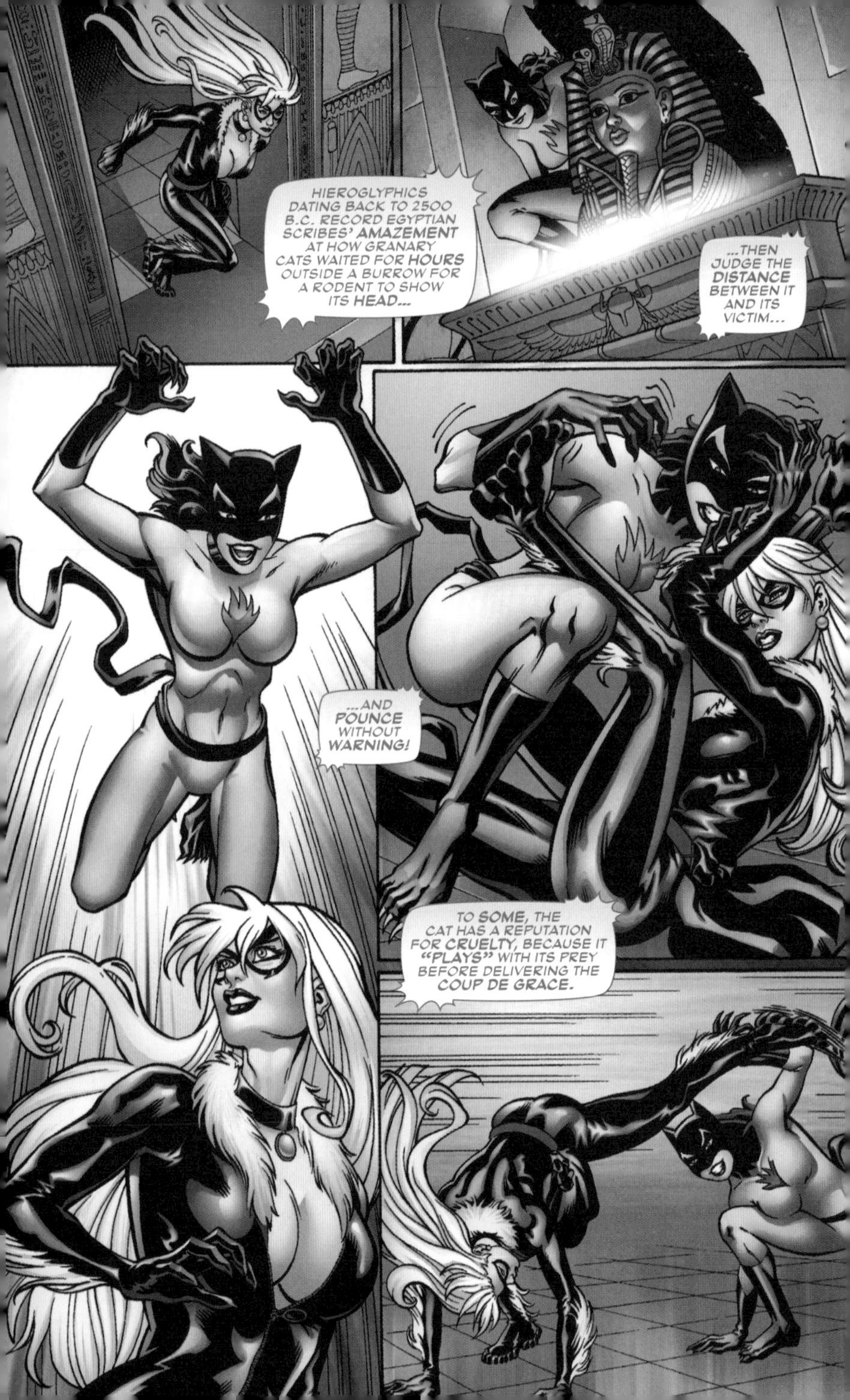
HIEROGLYPHICS DATING BACK TO 2500 B.C. RECORD EGYPTIAN SCRIBES' AMAZEMENT AT HOW GRANARY CATS WAITED FOR HOURS OUTSIDE A BURROW FOR A RODENT TO SHOW ITS HEAD...
...THEN JUDGE THE DISTANCE BETWEEN IT AND ITS VICTIM...
...AND POUNCE WITHOUT WARNING!
TO SOME, THE CAT HAS A REPUTATION FOR CRUELTY, BECAUSE IT "PLAYS" WITH ITS PREY BEFORE DELIVERING THE COUP DE GRACE.

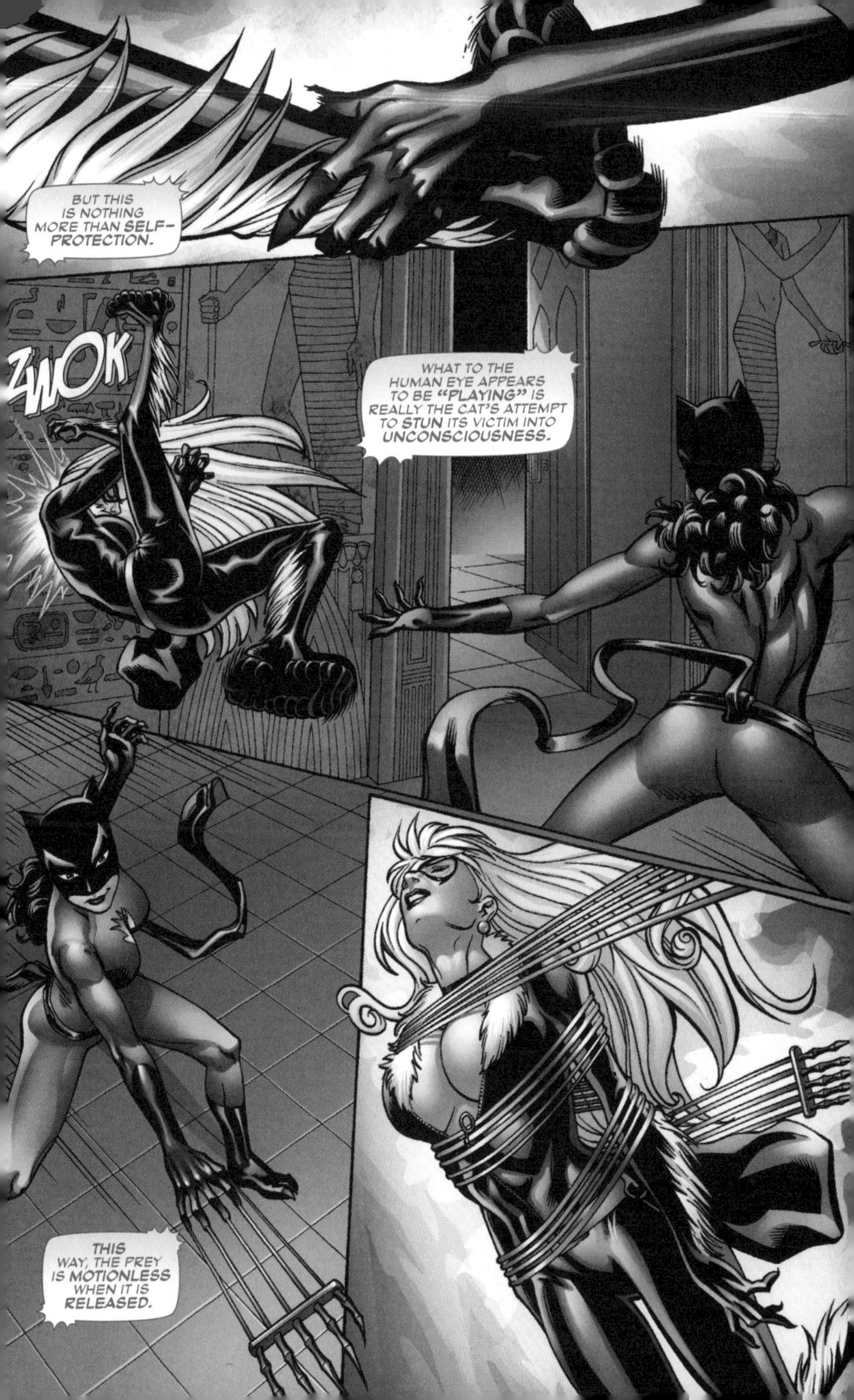

BUT THIS IS NOTHING MORE THAN SELF-PROTECTION.
ZWOK
WHAT TO THE HUMAN EYE APPEARS TO BE "PLAYING" IS REALLY THE CAT'S ATTEMPT TO STUN ITS VICTIM INTO UNCONSCIOUSNESS.
THIS WAY, THE PREY IS MOTIONLESS WHEN IT IS RELEASED.

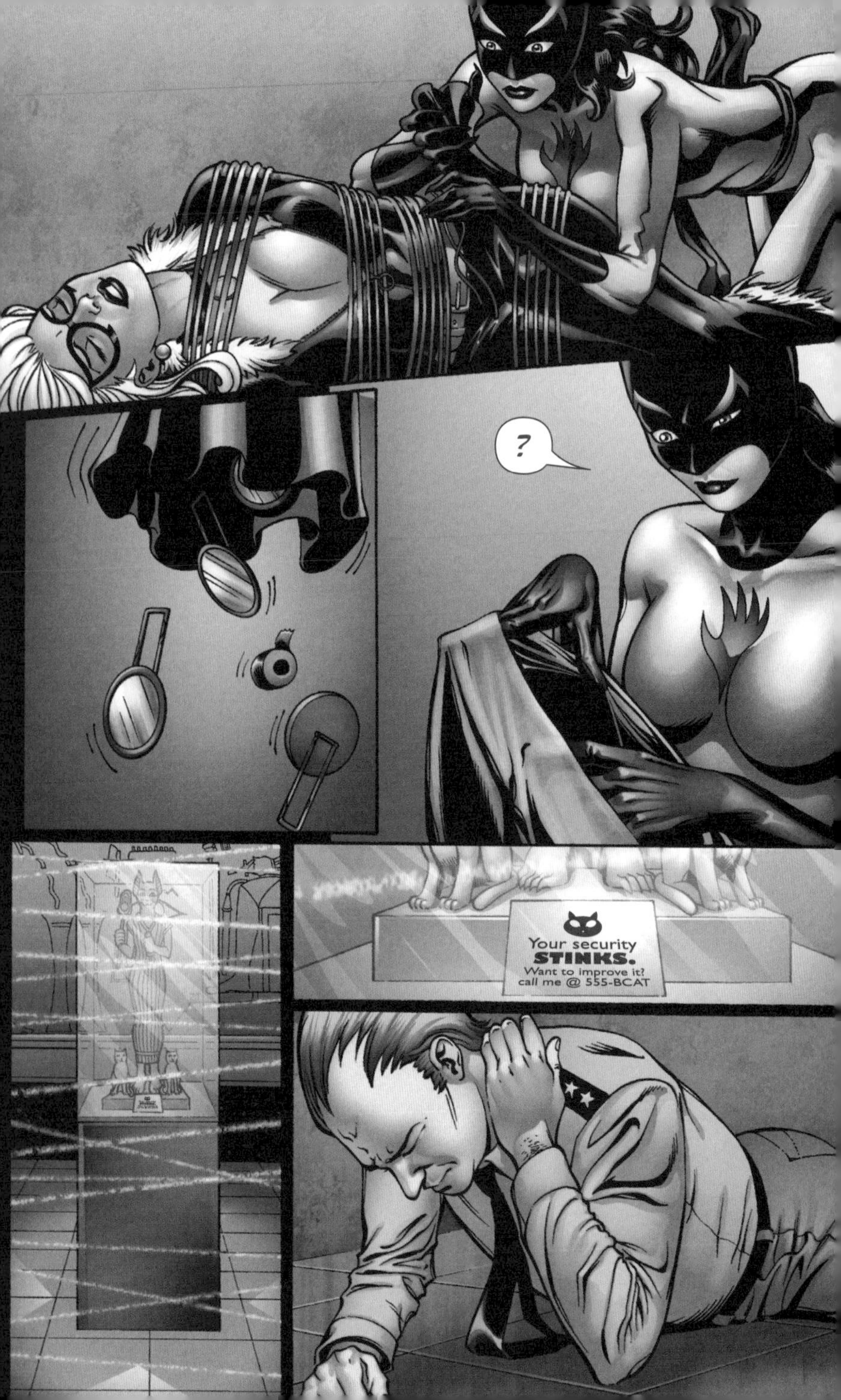
?
Your security
STINKS.
Want to improve it?
call me @ 555-BCAT

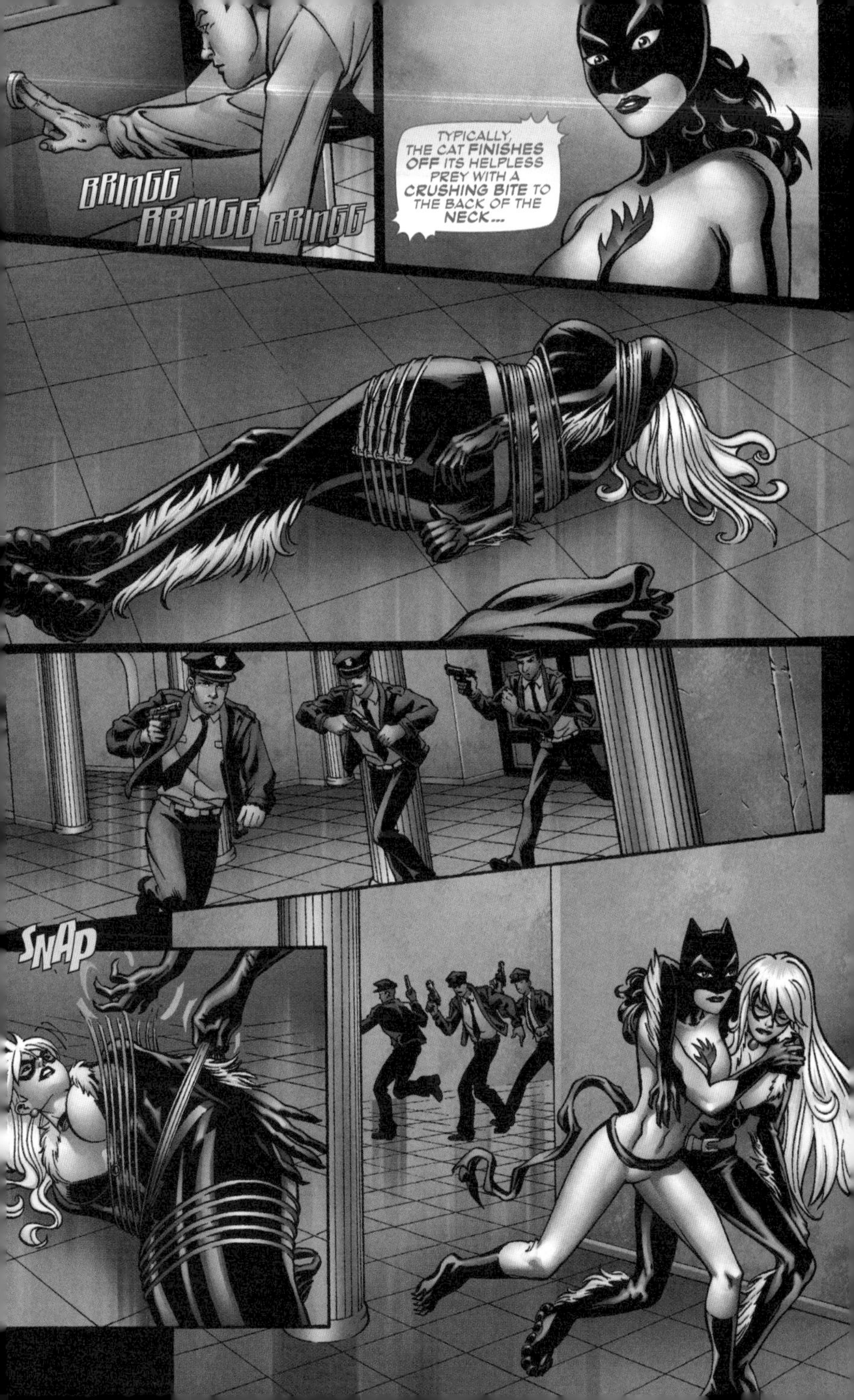
BRINGG BRINGG BRINGG
TYPICALLY, THE CAT FINISHES OFF ITS HELPLESS PREY WITH A CRUSHING BITE TO THE BACK OF THE NECK...
SNAP

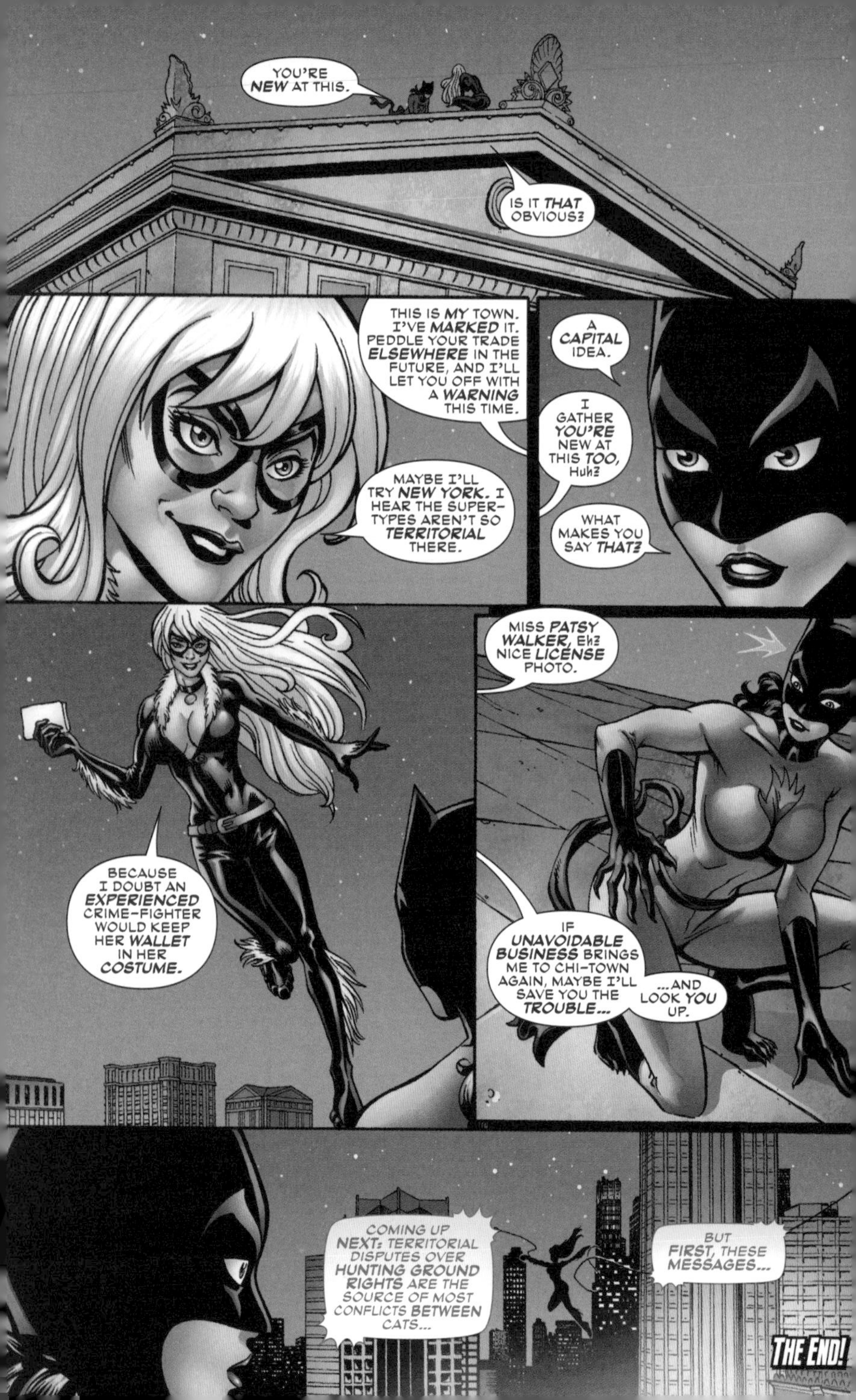
YOU'RE NEW AT THIS.
IS IT THAT OBVIOUS?
THIS IS MY TOWN. I'VE MARKED IT. PEDDLE YOUR TRADE ELSEWHERE IN THE FUTURE, AND I'LL LET YOU OFF WITH A WARNING THIS TIME.
A CAPITAL IDEA.
I GATHER YOU'RE NEW AT THIS TOO, HUH?
MAYBE I'LL TRY NEW YORK. I HEAR THE SUPER-TYPES AREN'T SO TERRITORIAL THERE.
WHAT MAKES YOU SAY THAT?
BECAUSE I DOUBT AN EXPERIENCED CRIME-FIGHTER WOULD KEEP HER WALLET IN HER COSTUME.
MISS PATSY WALKER, EH? NICE LICENSE PHOTO.
IF UNAVOIDABLE BUSINESS BRINGS ME TO CHI-TOWN AGAIN, MAYBE I'LL SAVE YOU THE TROUBLE...
...AND LOOK YOU UP.
COMING UP NEXT: TERRITORIAL DISPUTES OVER HUNTING GROUND RIGHTS ARE THE SOURCE OF MOST CONFLICTS BETWEEN CATS...
BUT FIRST, THESE MESSAGES...
THE END!

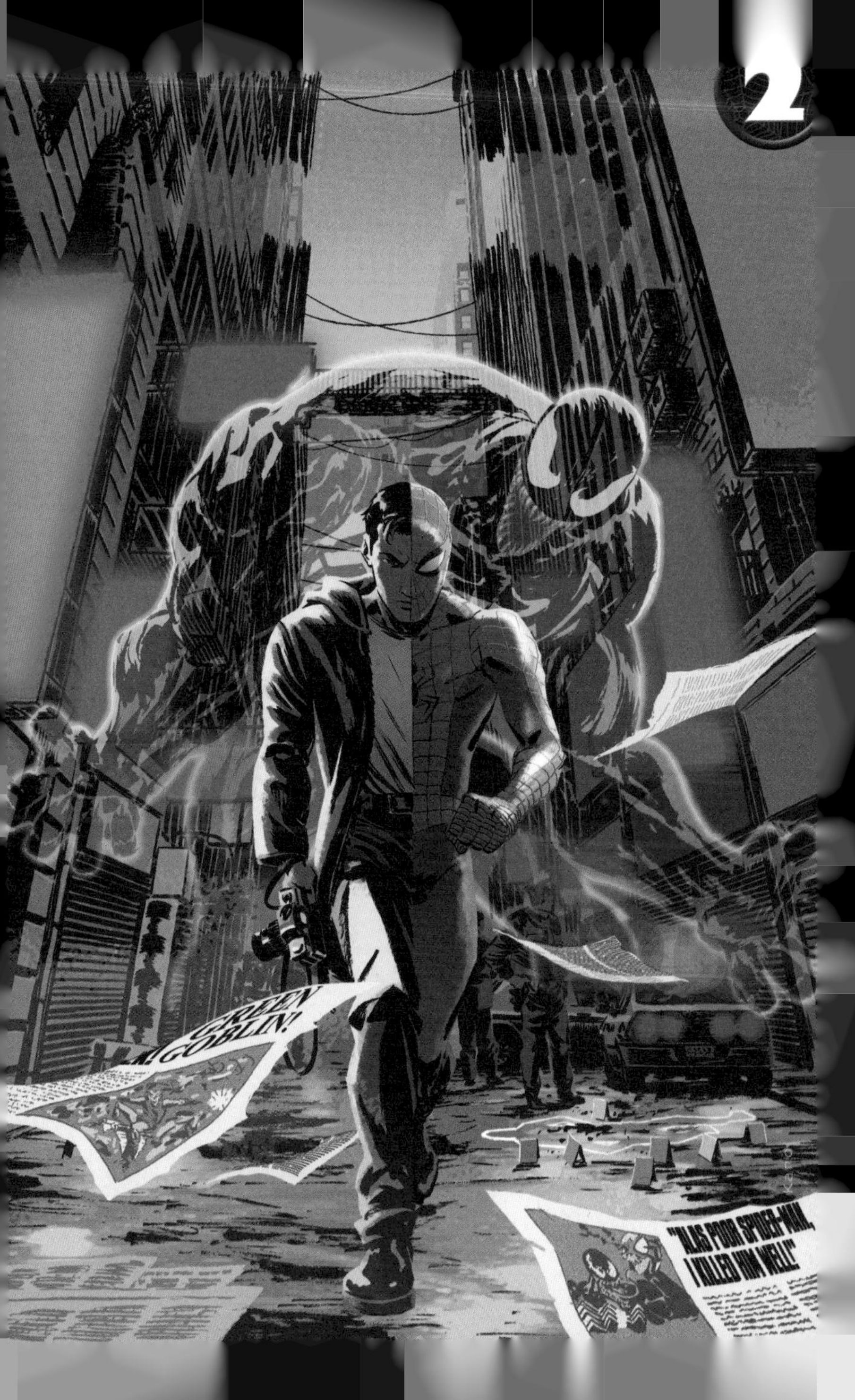
2
GREEN
GOBLIN!
"ALAS POOR SPIDER-MAN, I KILLED HIM WELL!"

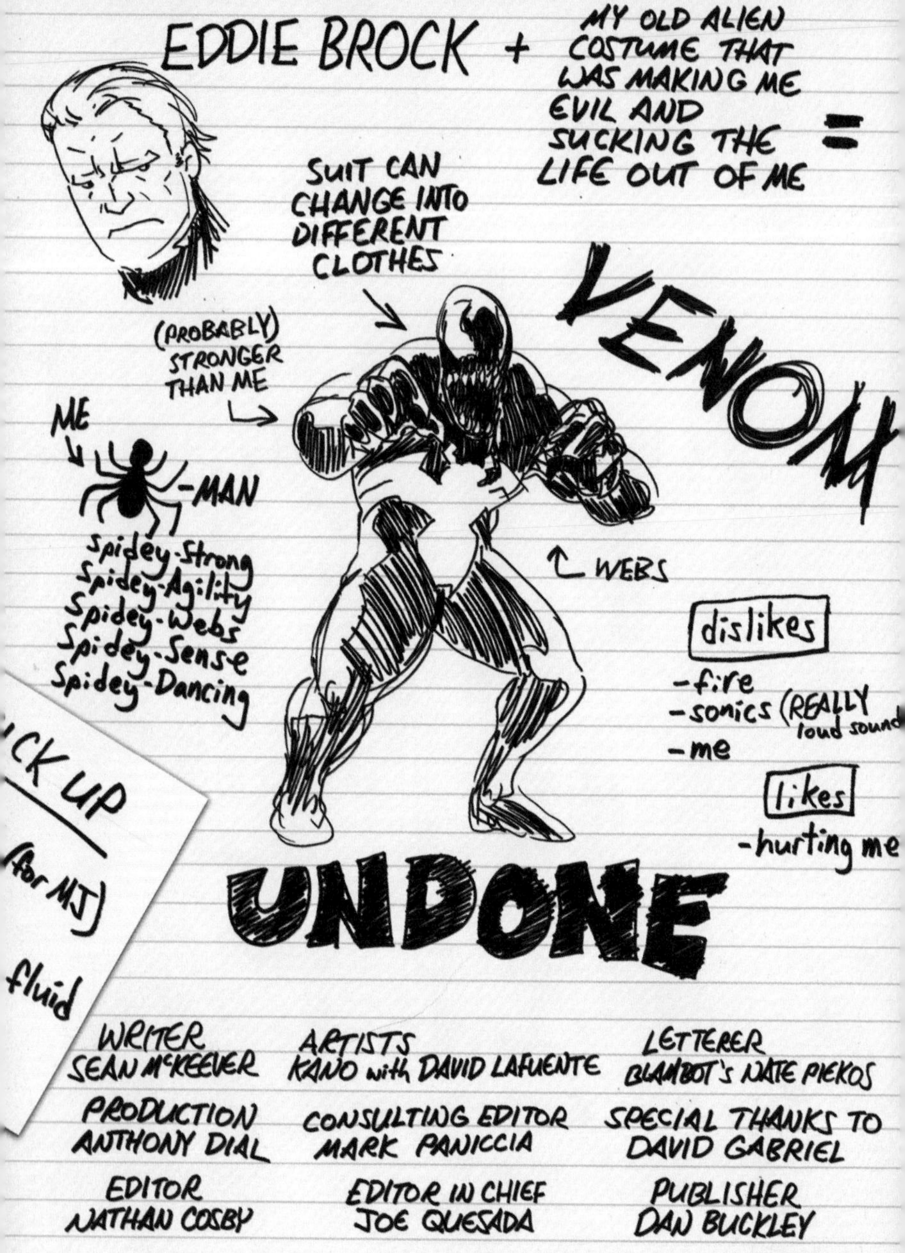
EDDIE BROCK + MY OLD ALIEN COSTUME THAT WAS MAKING ME EVIL AND SUCKING THE LIFE OUT OF ME =
SUIT CAN CHANGE INTO DIFFERENT CLOTHES
VENOM
(PROBABLY) STRONGER THAN ME
ME
-MAN
Spidey-Strong
Spidey-Agility
Spidey-Webs
Spidey-Sense
Spidey-Dancing
WEBS
dislikes
-fire
-sonics (REALLY loud sound
-me
likes
-hurting me
CK UP
(for MJ)
fluid
UNDONE

WRITER
SEAN McKEEVER

ARTISTS
KANO with DAVID LAFUENTE

LETTERER
BLAMBOT'S NATE PIEKOS

PRODUCTION
ANTHONY DIAL

CONSULTING EDITOR
MARK PANICCIA

SPECIAL THANKS TO
DAVID GABRIEL

EDITOR
NATHAN COSBY

EDITOR IN CHIEF
JOE QUESADA

PUBLISHER
DAN BUCKLEY

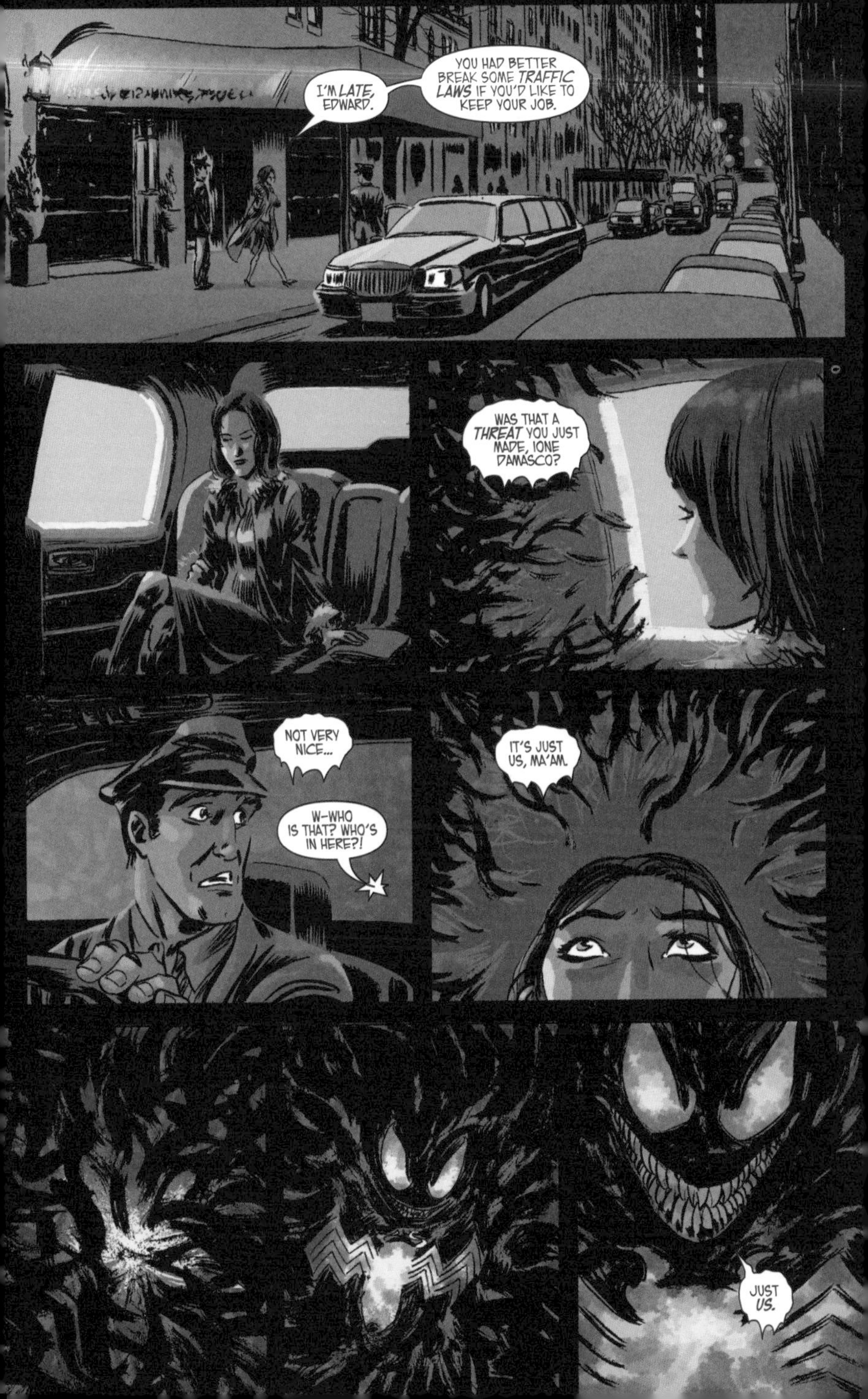
I'M LATE, EDWARD.
YOU HAD BETTER BREAK SOME TRAFFIC LAWS IF YOU'D LIKE TO KEEP YOUR JOB.
WAS THAT A THREAT YOU JUST MADE, IONE DAMASCO?
NOT VERY NICE...
W-WHO IS THAT? WHO'S IN HERE?!
IT'S JUST US, MA'AM.
JUST US.

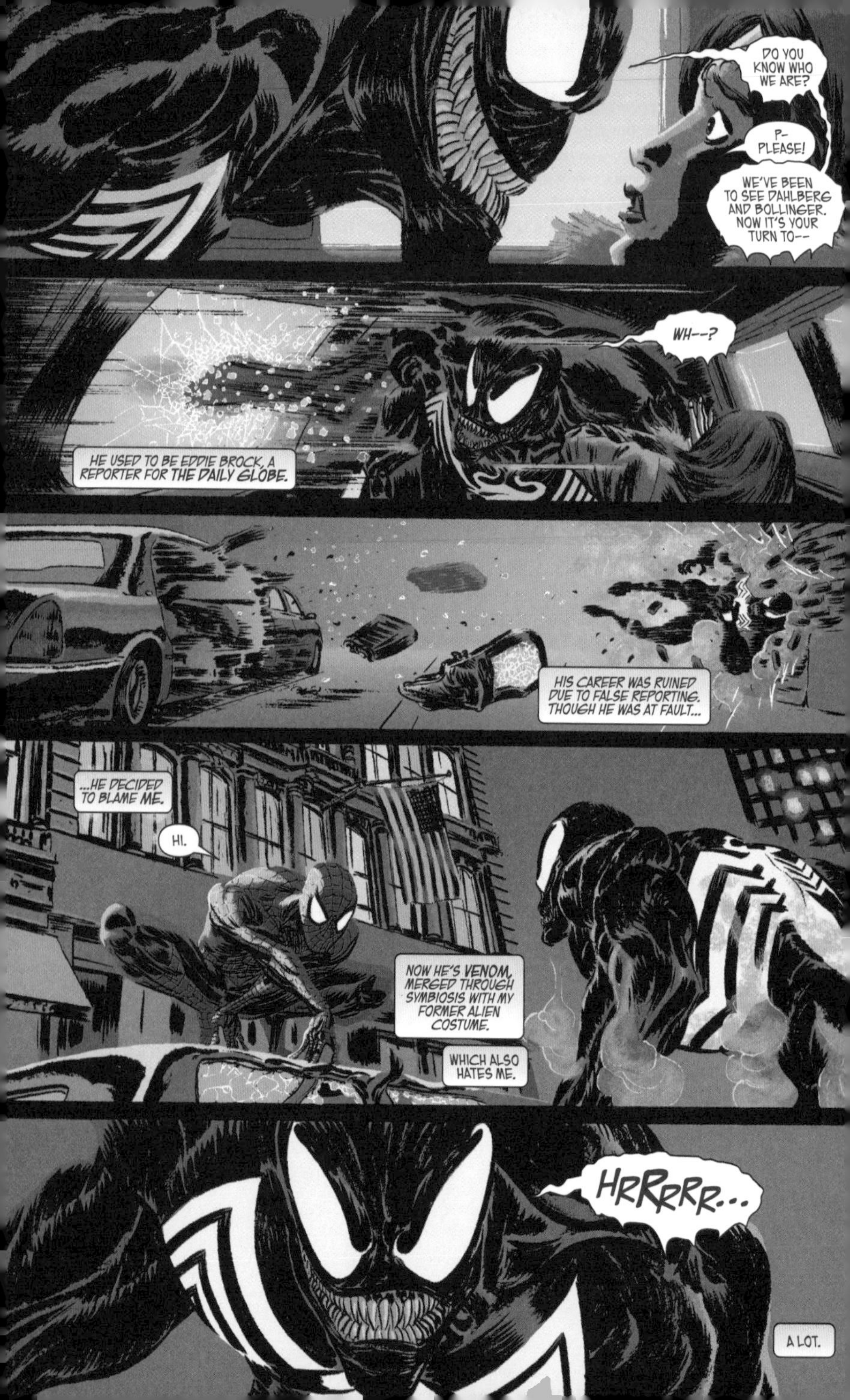
DO YOU KNOW WHO WE ARE?
P-PLEASE!
WE'VE BEEN TO SEE DAHLBERG AND BOLLINGER. NOW IT'S YOUR TURN TO--
WH--?
HE USED TO BE EDDIE BROCK, A REPORTER FOR THE DAILY GLOBE.
HIS CAREER WAS RUINED DUE TO FALSE REPORTING. THOUGH HE WAS AT FAULT...
...HE DECIDED TO BLAME ME.
HI.
NOW HE'S VENOM, MERGED THROUGH SYMBIOSIS WITH MY FORMER ALIEN COSTUME.
WHICH ALSO HATES ME.
HRRRRR...
A LOT.

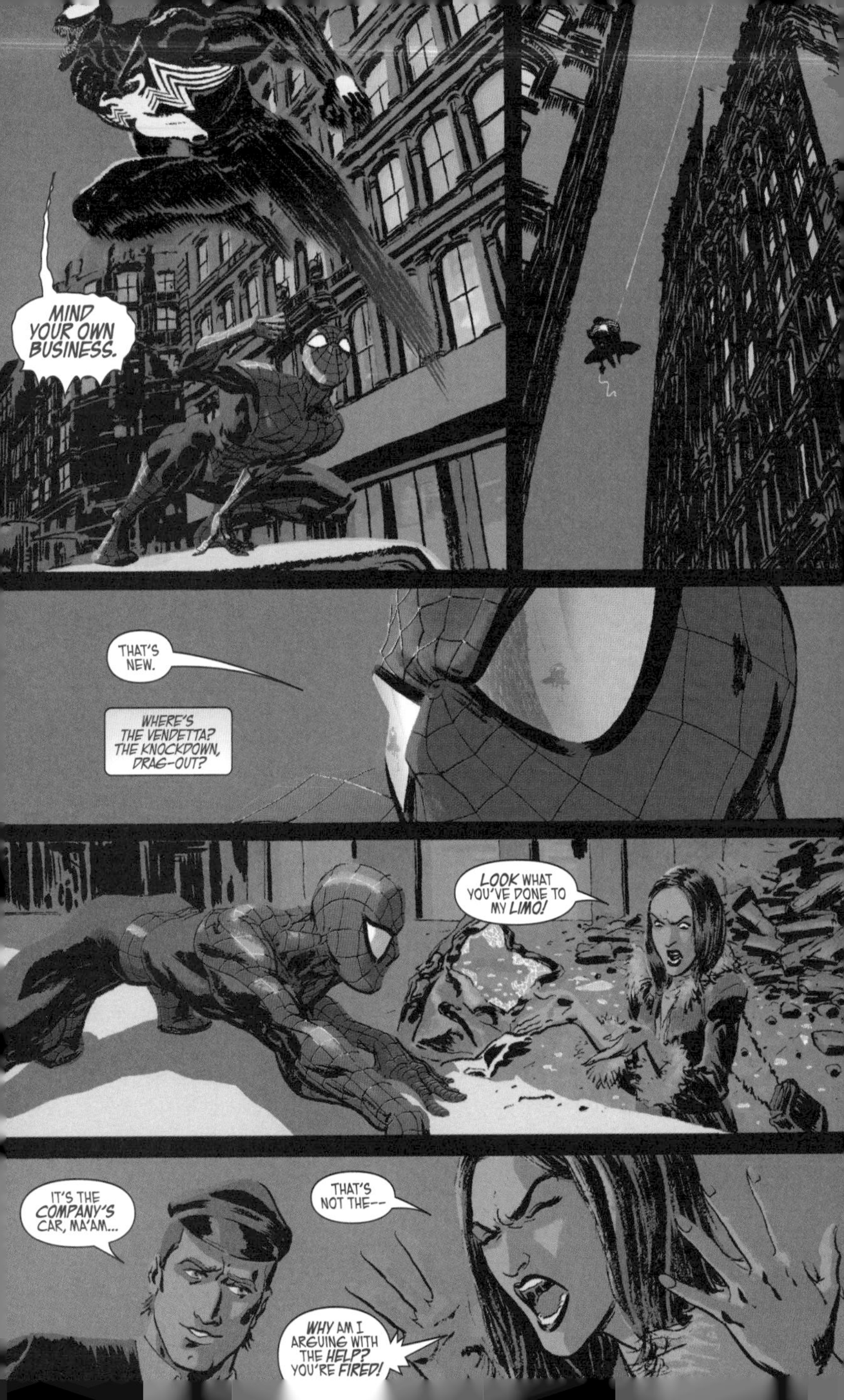
MIND YOUR OWN BUSINESS.
THAT'S NEW.
WHERE'S THE VENDETTA? THE KNOCKDOWN, DRAG-OUT?
LOOK WHAT YOU'VE DONE TO MY LIMO!
IT'S THE COMPANY'S CAR, MA'AM...
THAT'S NOT THE--
WHY AM I ARGUING WITH THE HELP? YOU'RE FIRED!

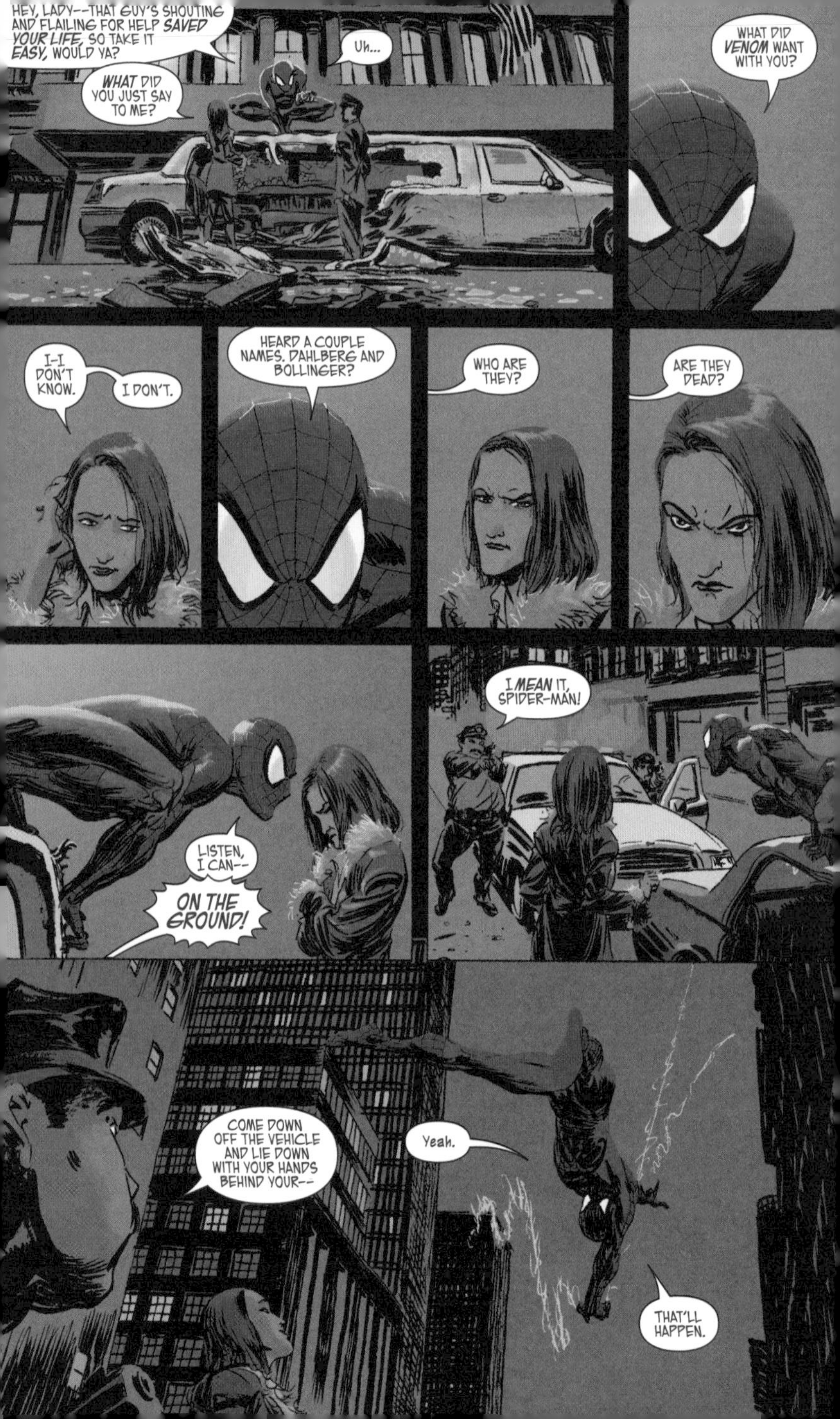
HEY, LADY--THAT GUY'S SHOUTING AND FLAILING FOR HELP SAVED YOUR LIFE, SO TAKE IT EASY, WOULD YA?
Uh...
WHAT DID YOU JUST SAY TO ME?
WHAT DID VENOM WANT WITH YOU?
I-I DON'T KNOW.
I DON'T.
HEARD A COUPLE NAMES. DAHLBERG AND BOLLINGER?
WHO ARE THEY?
ARE THEY DEAD?
LISTEN, I CAN--
ON THE GROUND!
I MEAN IT, SPIDER-MAN!
COME DOWN OFF THE VEHICLE AND LIE DOWN WITH YOUR HANDS BEHIND YOUR--
Yeah.
THAT'LL HAPPEN.

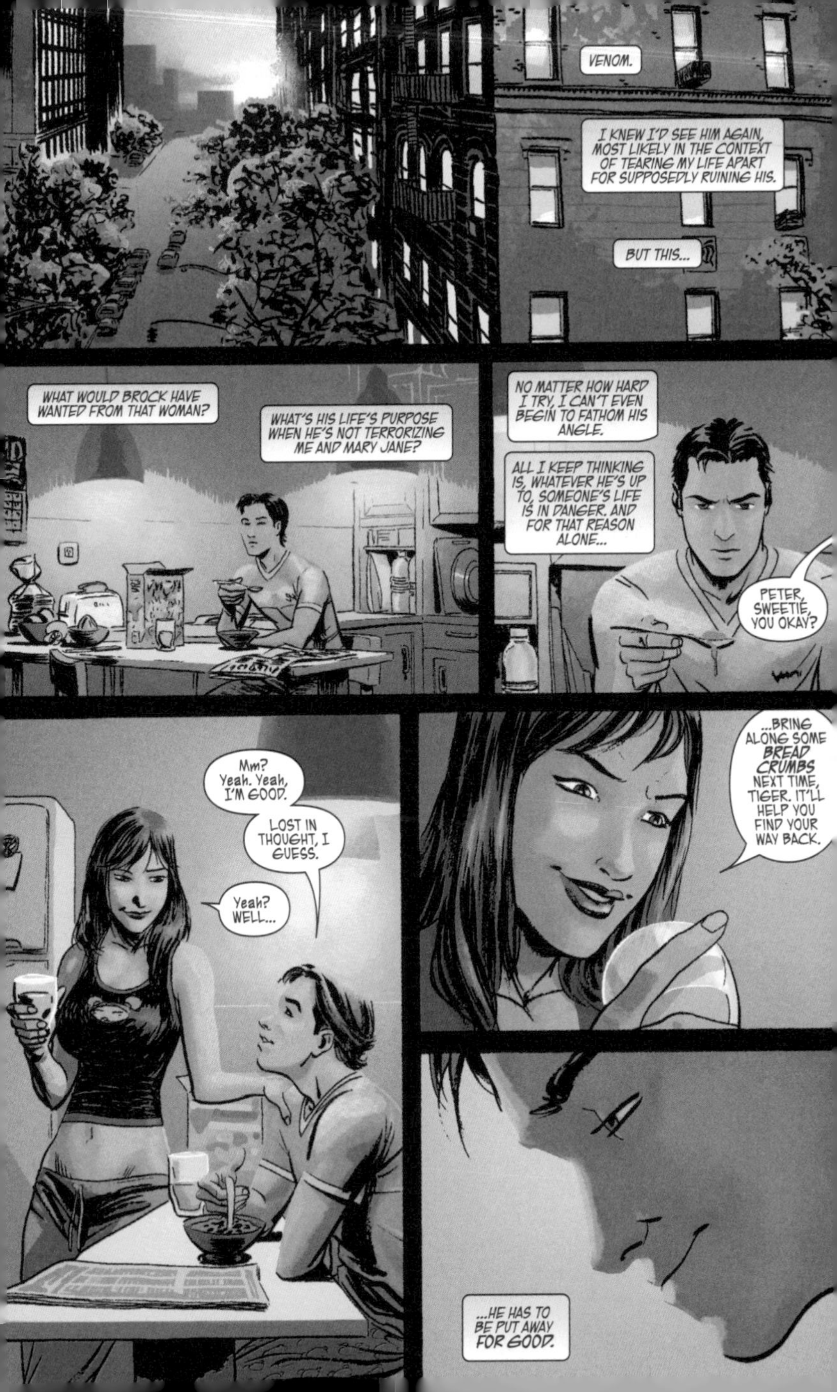
VENOM.
I KNEW I'D SEE HIM AGAIN, MOST LIKELY IN THE CONTEXT OF TEARING MY LIFE APART FOR SUPPOSEDLY RUINING HIS.
BUT THIS...
WHAT WOULD BROCK HAVE WANTED FROM THAT WOMAN?
WHAT'S HIS LIFE'S PURPOSE WHEN HE'S NOT TERRORIZING ME AND MARY JANE?
NO MATTER HOW HARD I TRY, I CAN'T EVEN BEGIN TO FATHOM HIS ANGLE.
ALL I KEEP THINKING IS, WHATEVER HE'S UP TO, SOMEONE'S LIFE IS IN DANGER. AND FOR THAT REASON ALONE...
PETER, SWEETIE, YOU OKAY?
Mm? Yeah. Yeah, I'M GOOD.
LOST IN THOUGHT, I GUESS.
Yeah? WELL...
...BRING ALONG SOME BREAD CRUMBS NEXT TIME, TIGER. IT'LL HELP YOU FIND YOUR WAY BACK.
...HE HAS TO BE PUT AWAY FOR GOOD.

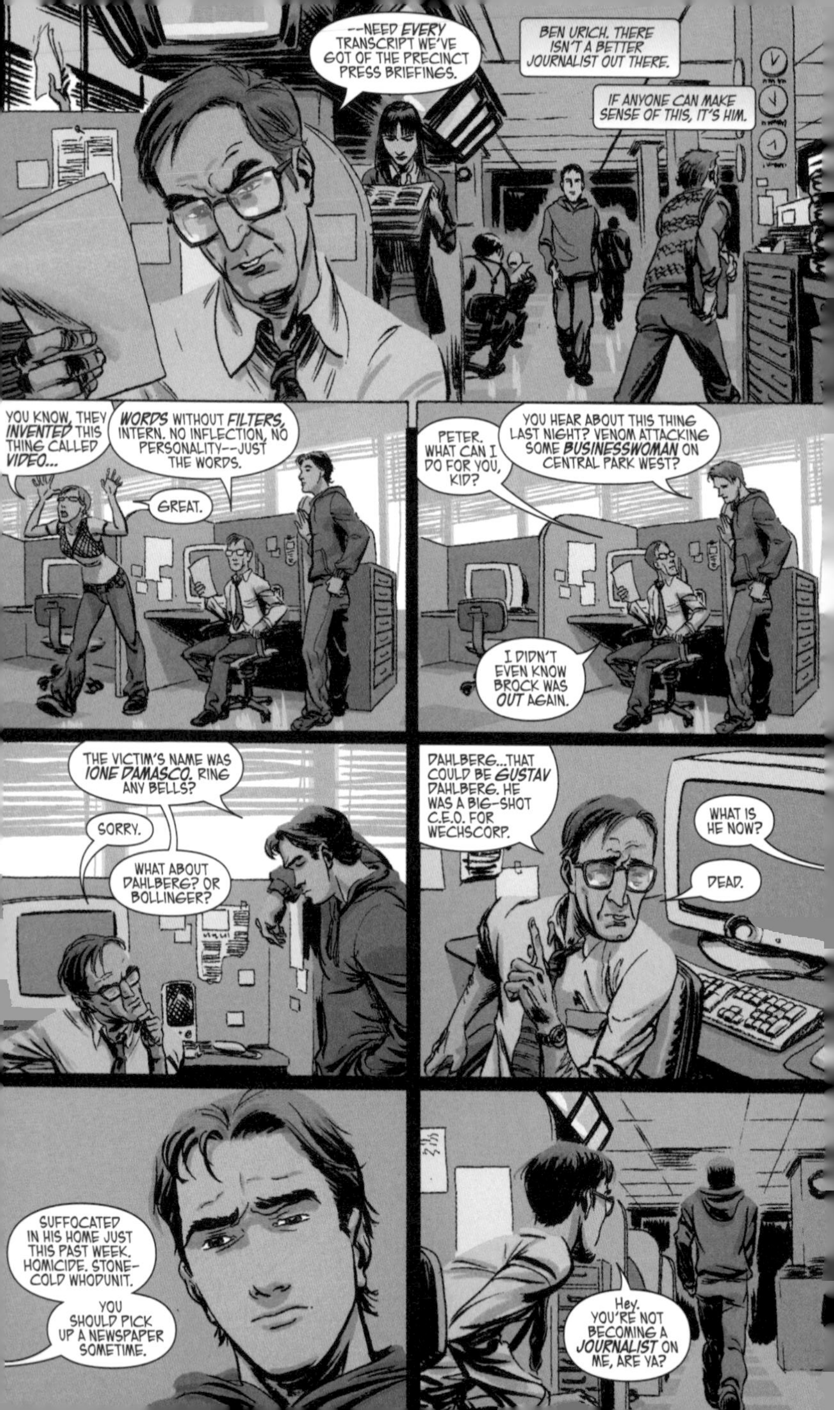
--NEED EVERY TRANSCRIPT WE'VE GOT OF THE PRECINCT PRESS BRIEFINGS.
BEN URICH. THERE ISN'T A BETTER JOURNALIST OUT THERE.
IF ANYONE CAN MAKE SENSE OF THIS, IT'S HIM.
YOU KNOW, THEY INVENTED THIS THING CALLED VIDEO...
WORDS WITHOUT FILTERS, INTERN. NO INFLECTION, NO PERSONALITY--JUST THE WORDS.
GREAT.
PETER. WHAT CAN I DO FOR YOU, KID?
YOU HEAR ABOUT THIS THING LAST NIGHT? VENOM ATTACKING SOME BUSINESSWOMAN ON CENTRAL PARK WEST?
I DIDN'T EVEN KNOW BROCK WAS OUT AGAIN.
THE VICTIM'S NAME WAS IONE DAMASCO. RING ANY BELLS?
SORRY.
WHAT ABOUT DAHLBERG? OR BOLLINGER?
DAHLBERG...THAT COULD BE GUSTAV DAHLBERG. HE WAS A BIG-SHOT C.E.O. FOR WECHSCORP.
WHAT IS HE NOW?
DEAD.
SUFFOCATED IN HIS HOME JUST THIS PAST WEEK. HOMICIDE. STONE-COLD WHODUNIT.
YOU SHOULD PICK UP A NEWSPAPER SOMETIME.
Hey. YOU'RE NOT BECOMING A JOURNALIST ON ME, ARE YA?

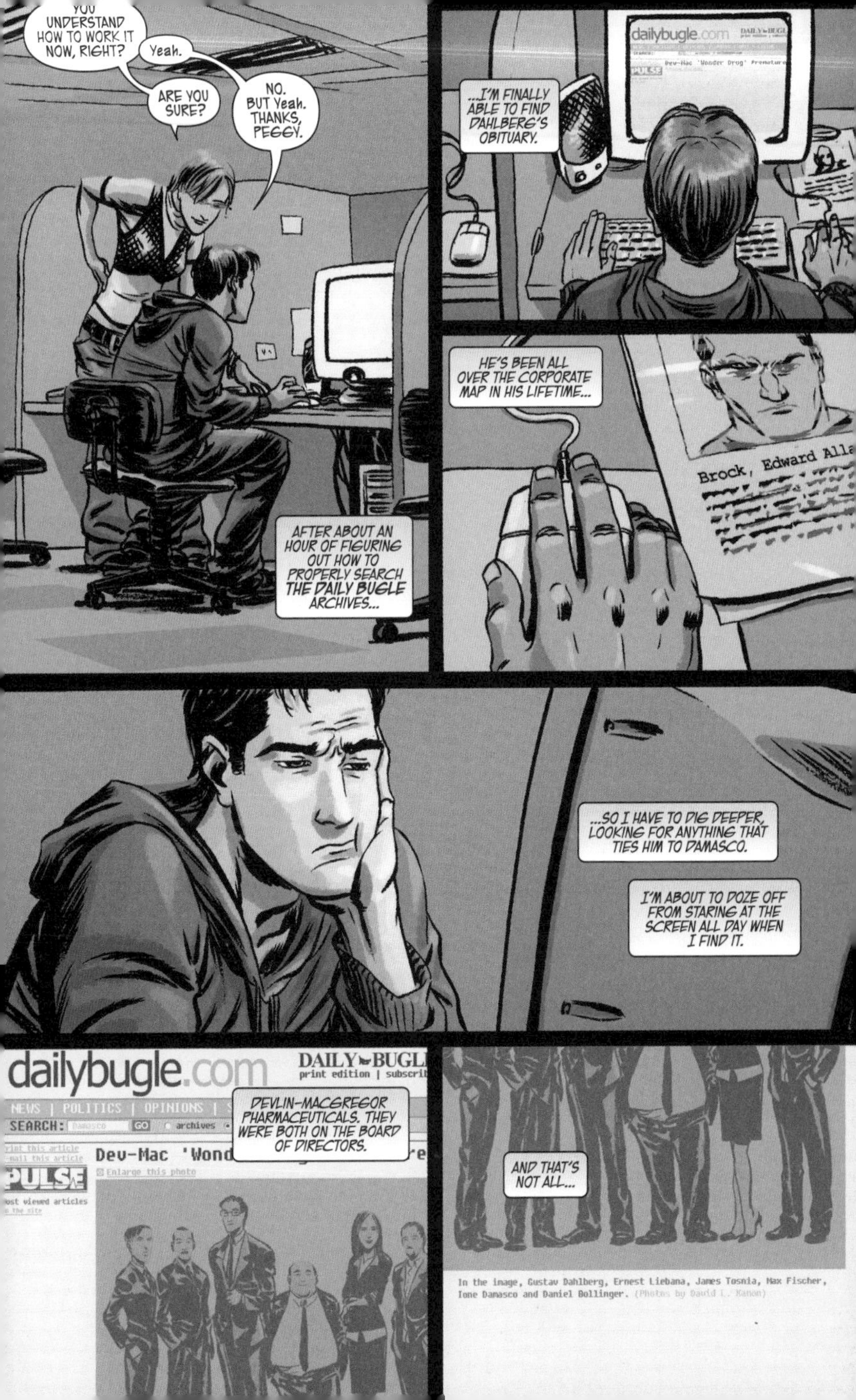

YOU UNDERSTAND HOW TO WORK IT NOW, RIGHT?
Yeah.
ARE YOU SURE?
NO. BUT Yeah. THANKS, PEGGY.
AFTER ABOUT AN HOUR OF FIGURING OUT HOW TO PROPERLY SEARCH THE DAILY BUGLE ARCHIVES...
dailybugle.com
...I'M FINALLY ABLE TO FIND DAHLBERG'S OBITUARY.
HE'S BEEN ALL OVER THE CORPORATE MAP IN HIS LIFETIME...
Brock, Edward Alla
...SO I HAVE TO DIG DEEPER, LOOKING FOR ANYTHING THAT TIES HIM TO DAMASCO.
I'M ABOUT TO DOZE OFF FROM STARING AT THE SCREEN ALL DAY WHEN I FIND IT.
dailybugle.com
DAILY BUGL
print edition | subscrib
NEWS | POLITICS | OPINIONS
SEARCH:
archives
PULSE
Dev-Mac 'Wond
Enlarge this photo
DEVLIN-MACGREGOR PHARMACEUTICALS. THEY WERE BOTH ON THE BOARD OF DIRECTORS.
AND THAT'S NOT ALL...
In the image, Gustav Dahlberg, Ernest Liebana, James Tosnia, Max Fischer, Ione Damasco and Daniel Bollinger.

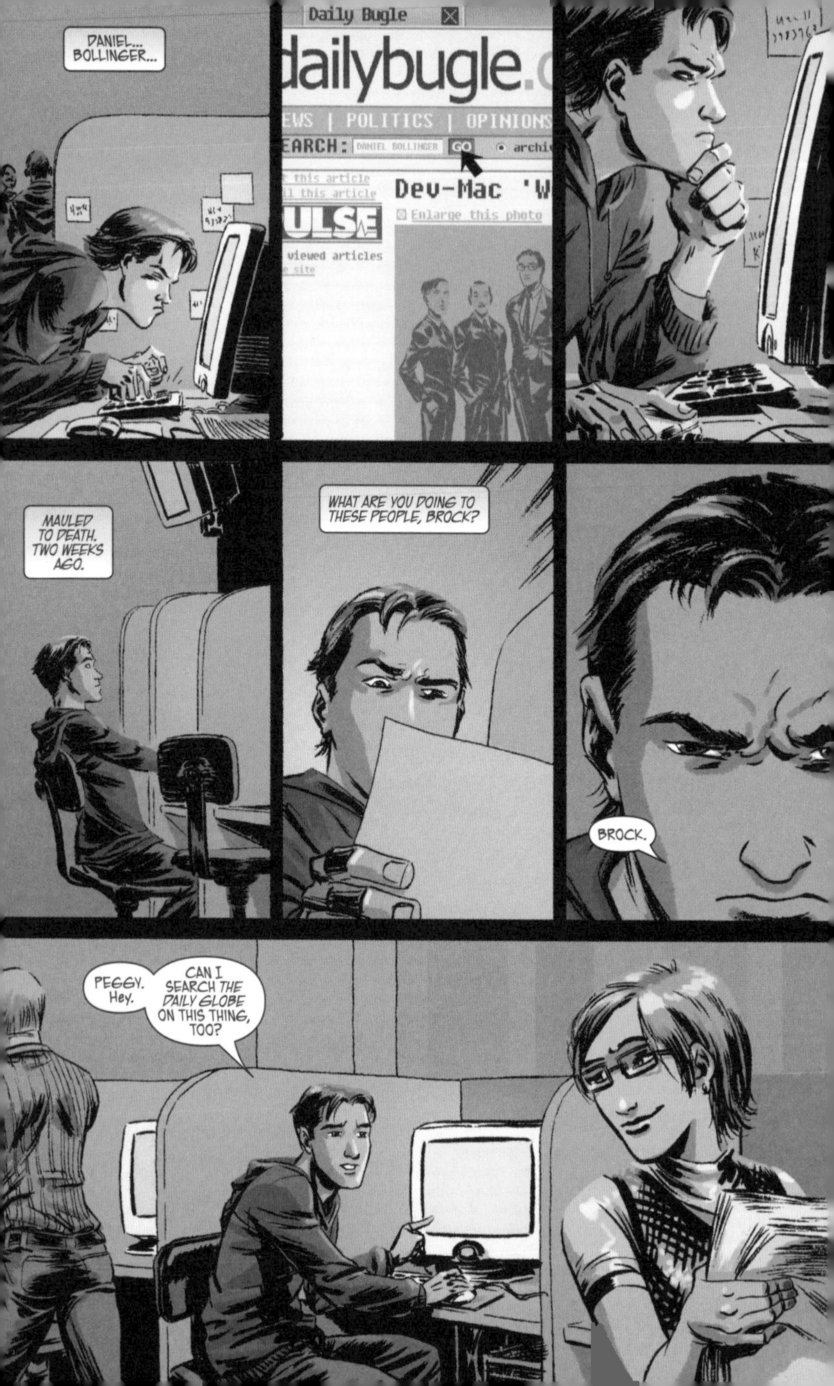
DANIEL... BOLLINGER...
Daily Bugle
dailybugle.
EWS | POLITICS | OPINIONS
EARCH: DANIEL BOLLINGER GO
Dev-Mac 'W
Enlarge this photo
viewed articles
MAULED TO DEATH. TWO WEEKS AGO.
WHAT ARE YOU DOING TO THESE PEOPLE, BROCK?
BROCK.
PEGGY. Hey.
CAN I SEARCH THE DAILY GLOBE ON THIS THING, TOO?

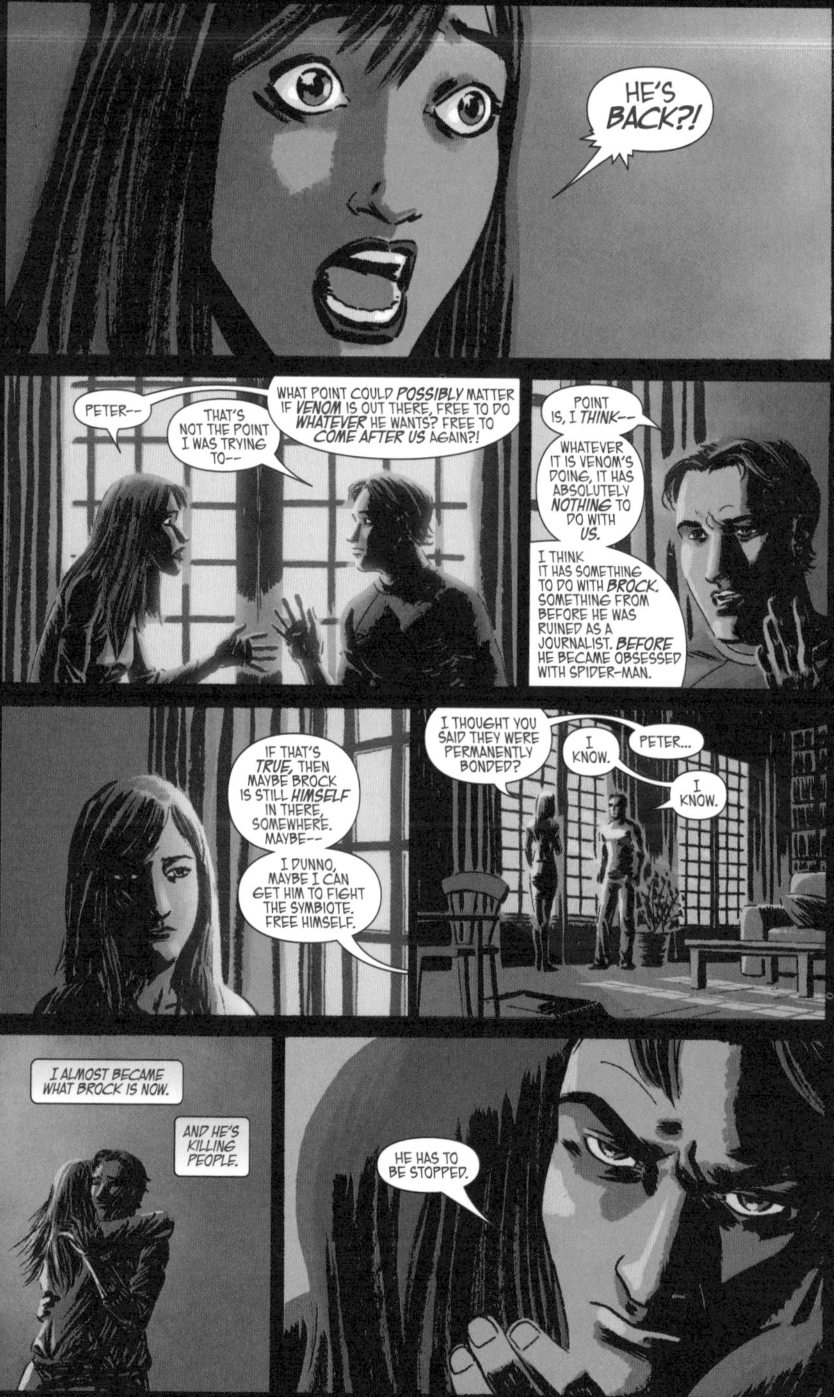
HE'S BACK?!
PETER--
THAT'S NOT THE POINT I WAS TRYING TO--
WHAT POINT COULD POSSIBLY MATTER IF VENOM IS OUT THERE, FREE TO DO WHATEVER HE WANTS? FREE TO COME AFTER US AGAIN?!
POINT IS, I THINK--
WHATEVER IT IS VENOM'S DOING, IT HAS ABSOLUTELY NOTHING TO DO WITH US.
I THINK IT HAS SOMETHING TO DO WITH BROCK. SOMETHING FROM BEFORE HE WAS RUINED AS A JOURNALIST. BEFORE HE BECAME OBSESSED WITH SPIDER-MAN.
IF THAT'S TRUE, THEN MAYBE BROCK IS STILL HIMSELF IN THERE, SOMEWHERE. MAYBE--
I DUNNO, MAYBE I CAN GET HIM TO FIGHT THE SYMBIOTE. FREE HIMSELF.
I THOUGHT YOU SAID THEY WERE PERMANENTLY BONDED?
I KNOW.
PETER...
I KNOW.
I ALMOST BECAME WHAT BROCK IS NOW.
AND HE'S KILLING PEOPLE.
HE HAS TO BE STOPPED.

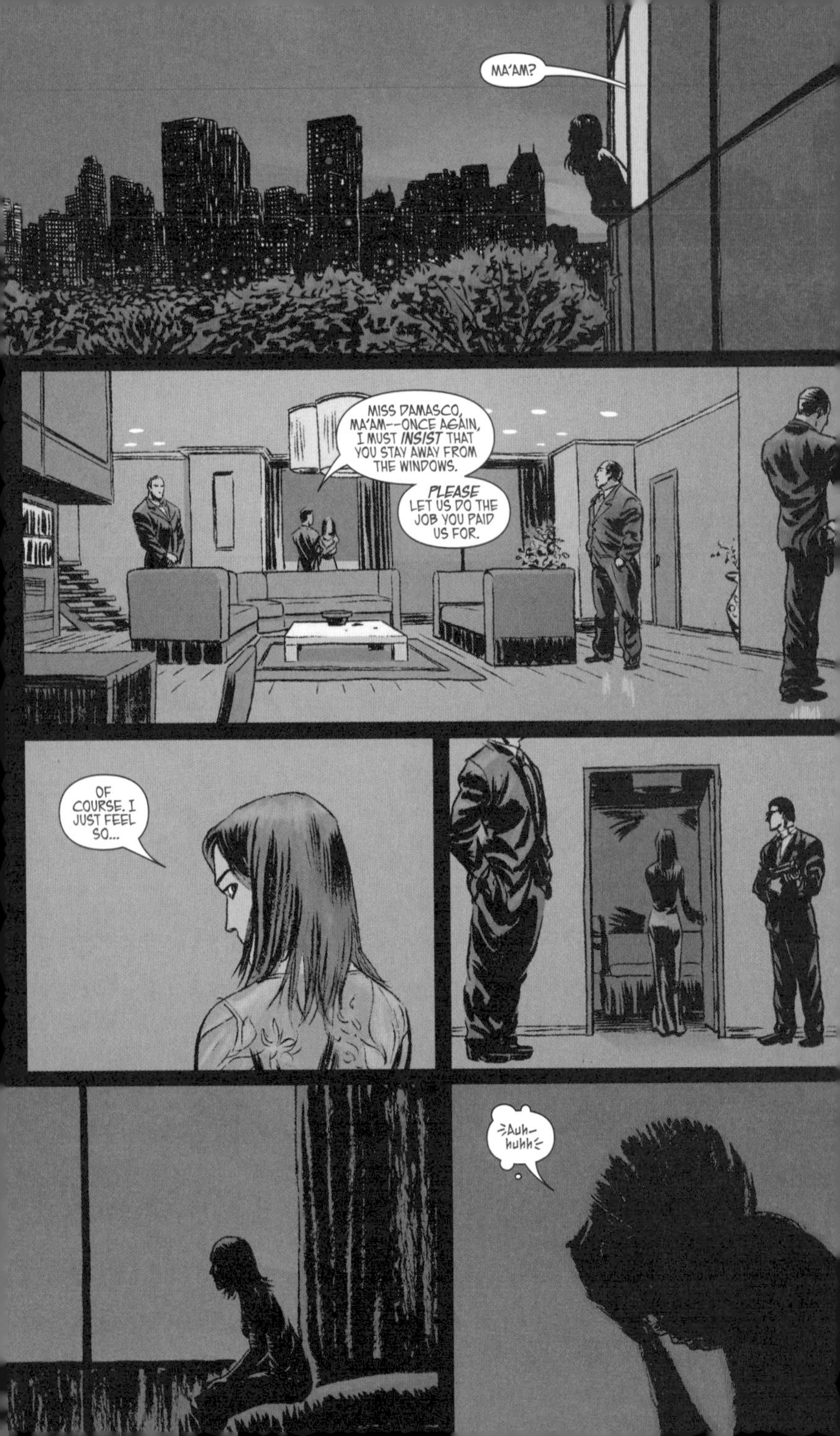
MA'AM?
MISS DAMASCO, MA'AM--ONCE AGAIN, I MUST INSIST THAT YOU STAY AWAY FROM THE WINDOWS.
PLEASE LET US DO THE JOB YOU PAID US FOR.
OF COURSE. I JUST FEEL SO...
Auh-huhh

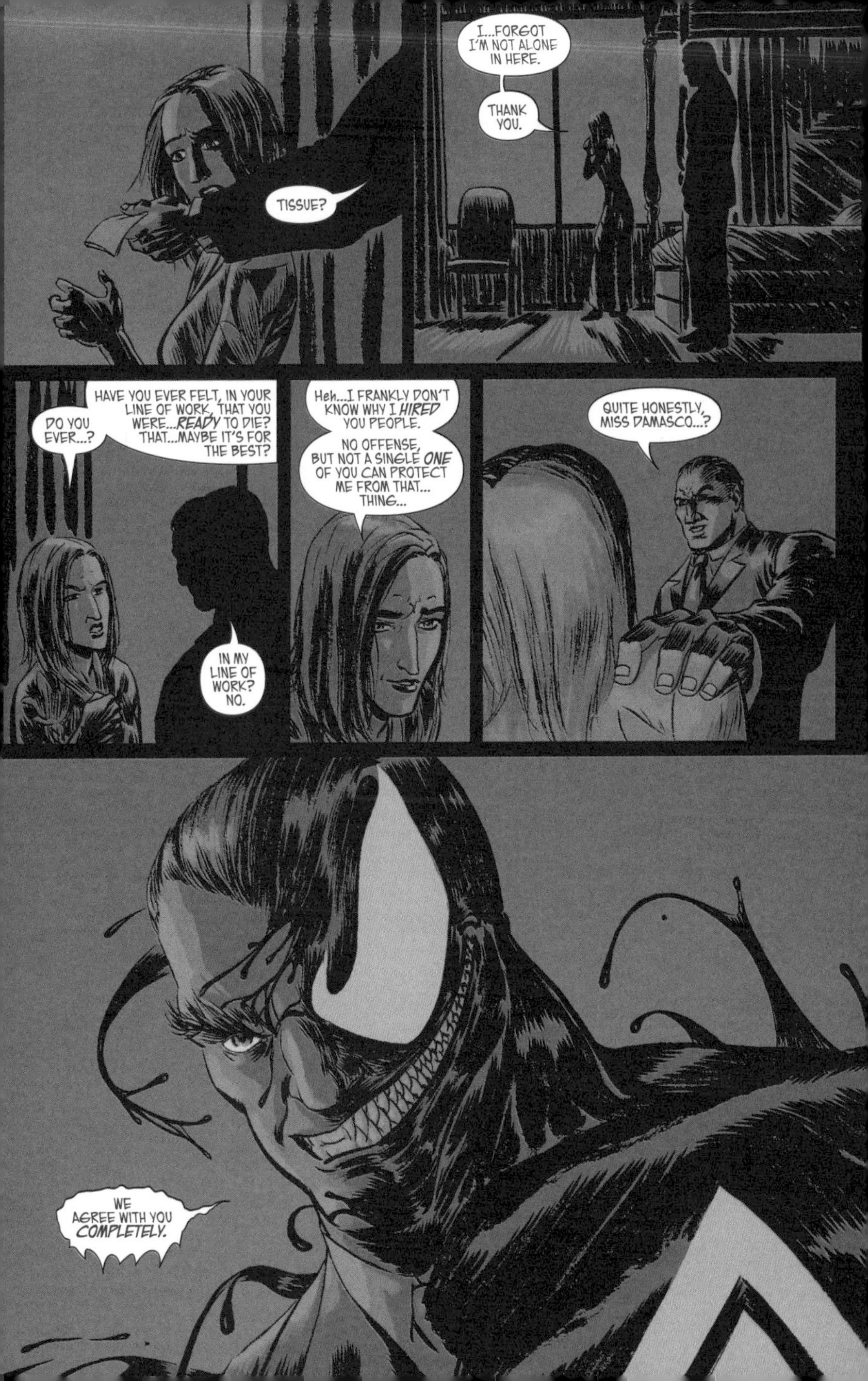
TISSUE?
I...FORGOT I'M NOT ALONE IN HERE.
THANK YOU.
DO YOU EVER...?
HAVE YOU EVER FELT, IN YOUR LINE OF WORK, THAT YOU WERE...READY TO DIE? THAT...MAYBE IT'S FOR THE BEST?
IN MY LINE OF WORK? NO.
Heh...I FRANKLY DON'T KNOW WHY I HIRED YOU PEOPLE.
NO OFFENSE, BUT NOT A SINGLE ONE OF YOU CAN PROTECT ME FROM THAT... THING...
QUITE HONESTLY, MISS DAMASCO...?
WE AGREE WITH YOU COMPLETELY.

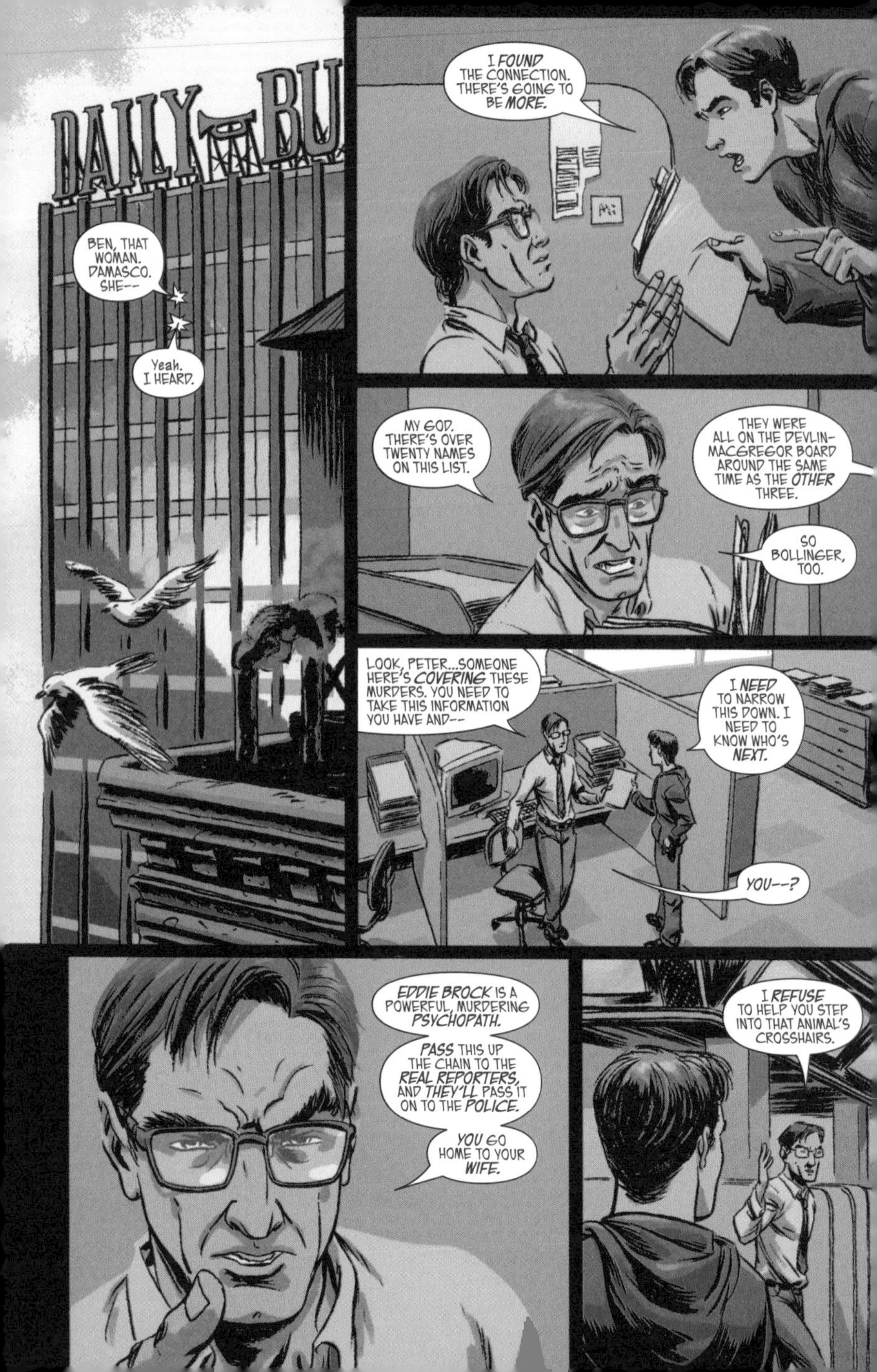
DAILY BU
BEN, THAT WOMAN. DAMASCO. SHE--
Yeah. I HEARD.
I FOUND THE CONNECTION. THERE'S GOING TO BE MORE.
MY GOD. THERE'S OVER TWENTY NAMES ON THIS LIST.
THEY WERE ALL ON THE DEVLIN-MACGREGOR BOARD AROUND THE SAME TIME AS THE OTHER THREE.
SO BOLLINGER, TOO.
LOOK, PETER...SOMEONE HERE'S COVERING THESE MURDERS. YOU NEED TO TAKE THIS INFORMATION YOU HAVE AND--
I NEED TO NARROW THIS DOWN. I NEED TO KNOW WHO'S NEXT.
YOU--?
EDDIE BROCK IS A POWERFUL, MURDERING PSYCHOPATH.
PASS THIS UP THE CHAIN TO THE REAL REPORTERS, AND THEY'LL PASS IT ON TO THE POLICE.
YOU GO HOME TO YOUR WIFE.
I REFUSE TO HELP YOU STEP INTO THAT ANIMAL'S CROSSHAIRS.

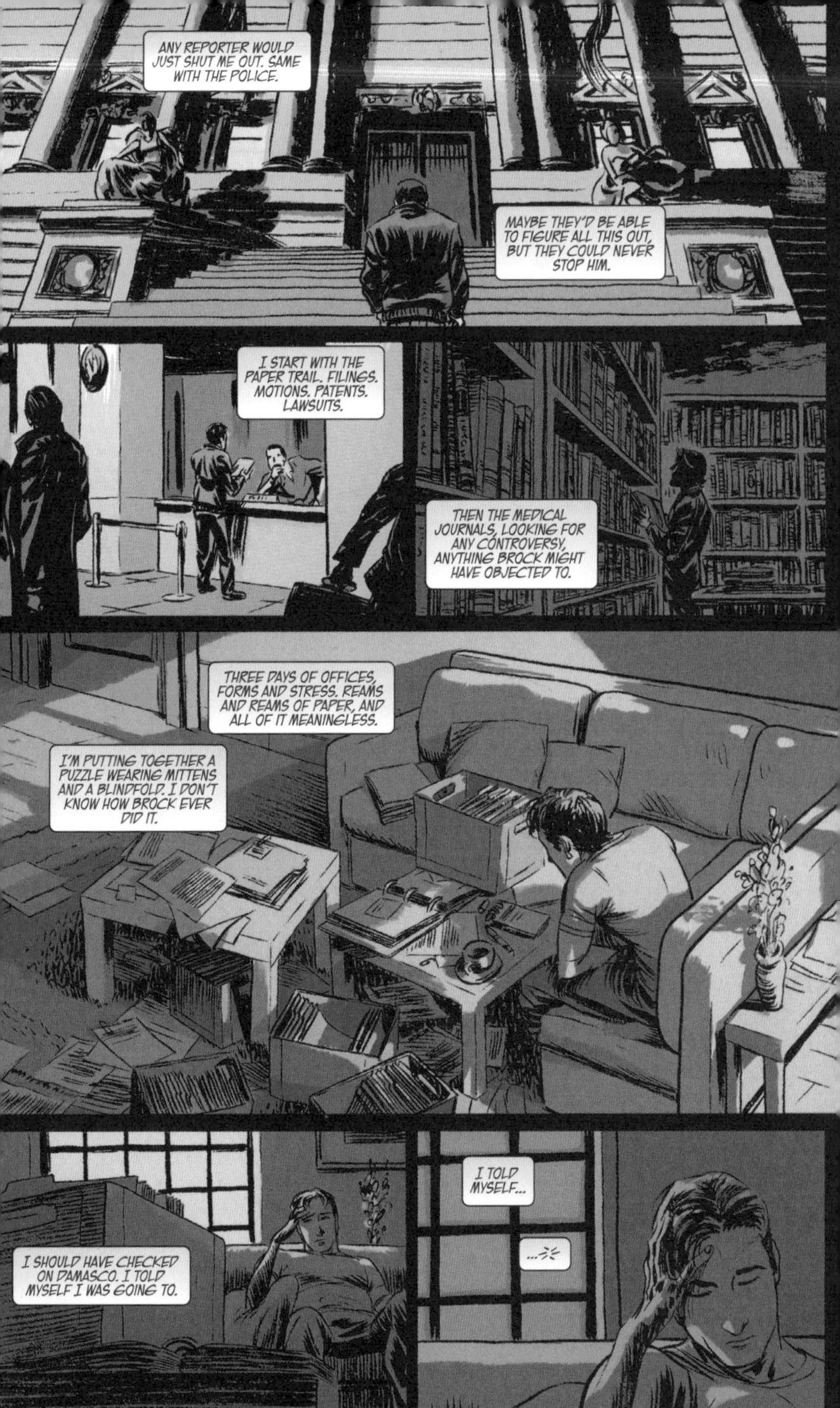
ANY REPORTER WOULD JUST SHUT ME OUT. SAME WITH THE POLICE.
MAYBE THEY'D BE ABLE TO FIGURE ALL THIS OUT, BUT THEY COULD NEVER STOP HIM.
I START WITH THE PAPER TRAIL. FILINGS. MOTIONS. PATENTS. LAWSUITS.
THEN THE MEDICAL JOURNALS, LOOKING FOR ANY CONTROVERSY, ANYTHING BROCK MIGHT HAVE OBJECTED TO.
THREE DAYS OF OFFICES, FORMS AND STRESS. REAMS AND REAMS OF PAPER, AND ALL OF IT MEANINGLESS.
I'M PUTTING TOGETHER A PUZZLE WEARING MITTENS AND A BLINDFOLD. I DON'T KNOW HOW BROCK EVER DID IT.
I SHOULD HAVE CHECKED ON DAMASCO. I TOLD MYSELF I WAS GOING TO.
I TOLD MYSELF...
...

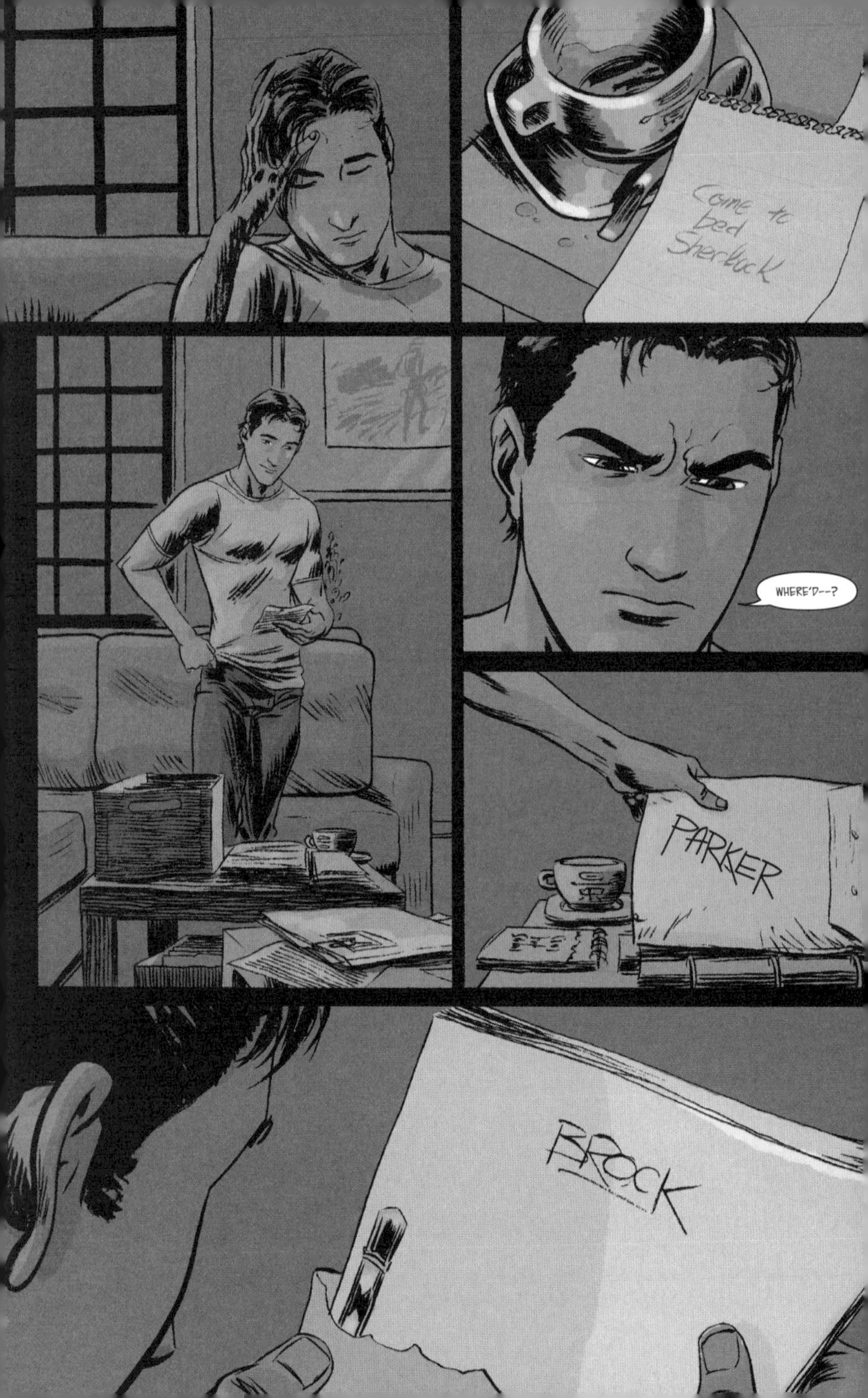
Come to bed Sherlock
WHERE'D--?
PARKER
BROCK

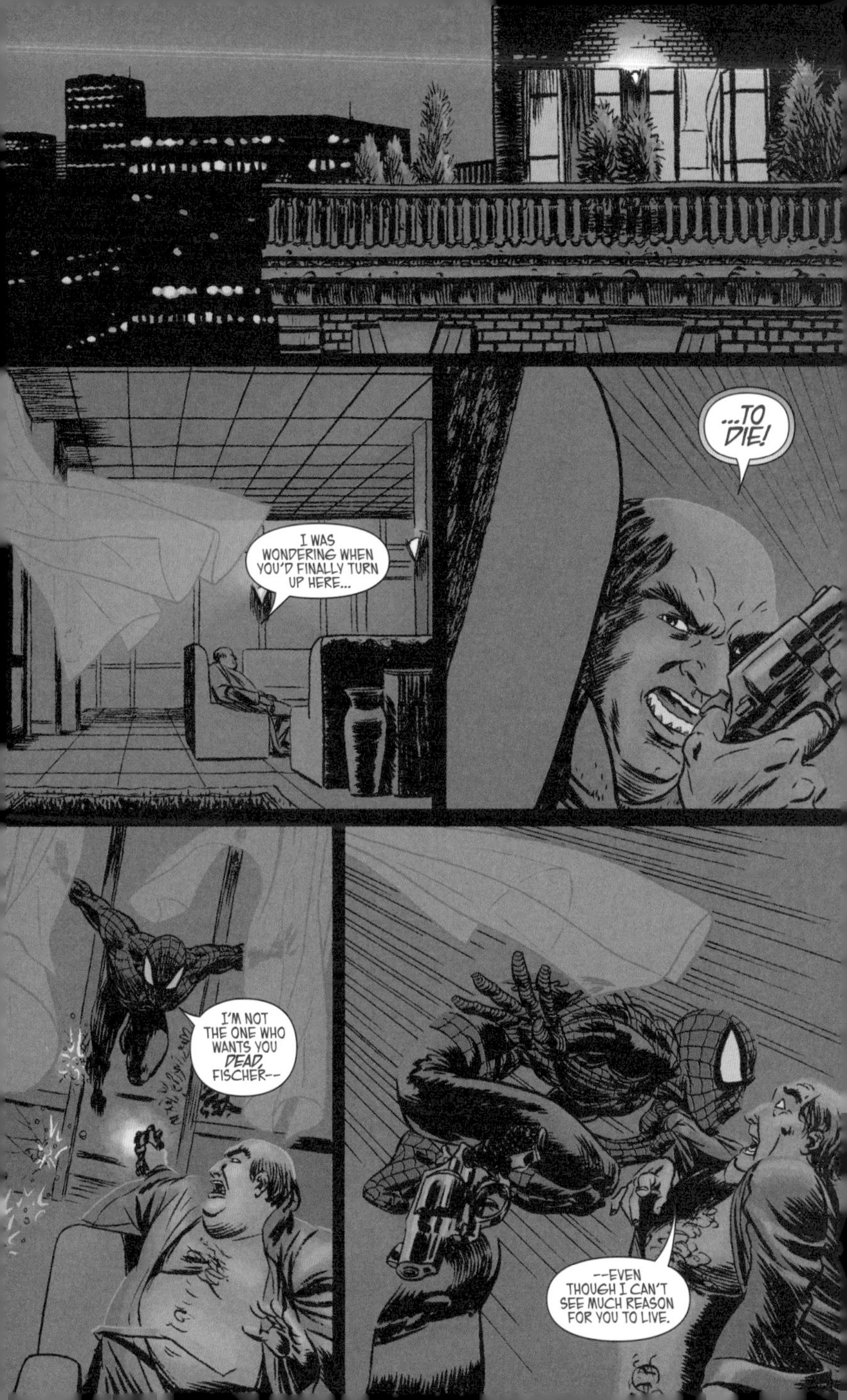
I WAS WONDERING WHEN YOU'D FINALLY TURN UP HERE...
...TO DIE!
I'M NOT THE ONE WHO WANTS YOU *DEAD*, FISCHER--
--EVEN THOUGH I CAN'T SEE MUCH REASON FOR YOU TO LIVE.

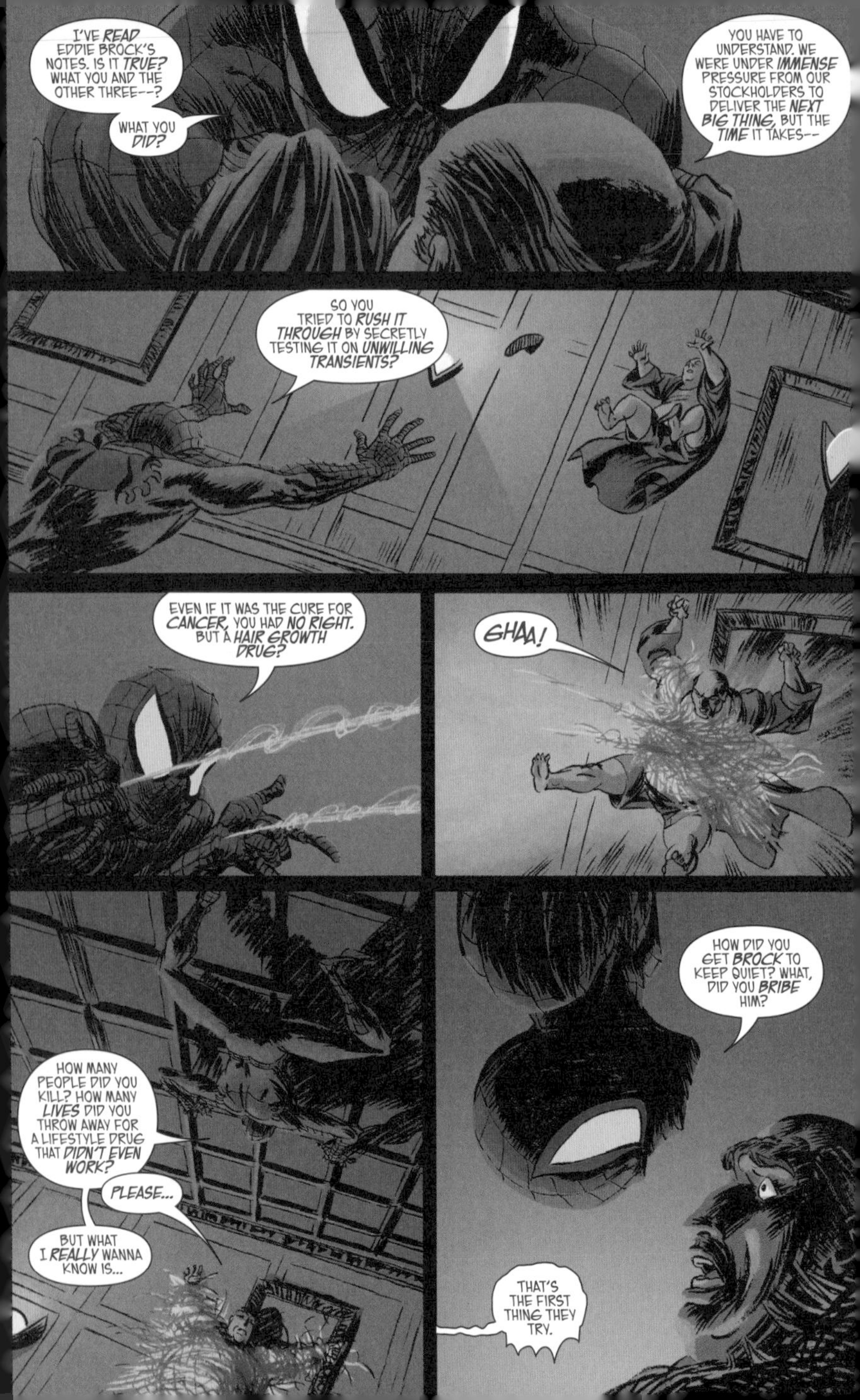
I'VE READ EDDIE BROCK'S NOTES. IS IT TRUE? WHAT YOU AND THE OTHER THREE--?
WHAT YOU DID?
YOU HAVE TO UNDERSTAND. WE WERE UNDER IMMENSE PRESSURE FROM OUR STOCKHOLDERS TO DELIVER THE NEXT BIG THING, BUT THE TIME IT TAKES--
SO YOU TRIED TO RUSH IT THROUGH BY SECRETLY TESTING IT ON UNWILLING TRANSIENTS?
EVEN IF IT WAS THE CURE FOR CANCER, YOU HAD NO RIGHT. BUT A HAIR GROWTH DRUG?
GHAA!
HOW MANY PEOPLE DID YOU KILL? HOW MANY LIVES DID YOU THROW AWAY FOR A LIFESTYLE DRUG THAT DIDN'T EVEN WORK?
PLEASE...
BUT WHAT I REALLY WANNA KNOW IS...
HOW DID YOU GET BROCK TO KEEP QUIET? WHAT, DID YOU BRIBE HIM?
THAT'S THE FIRST THING THEY TRY.

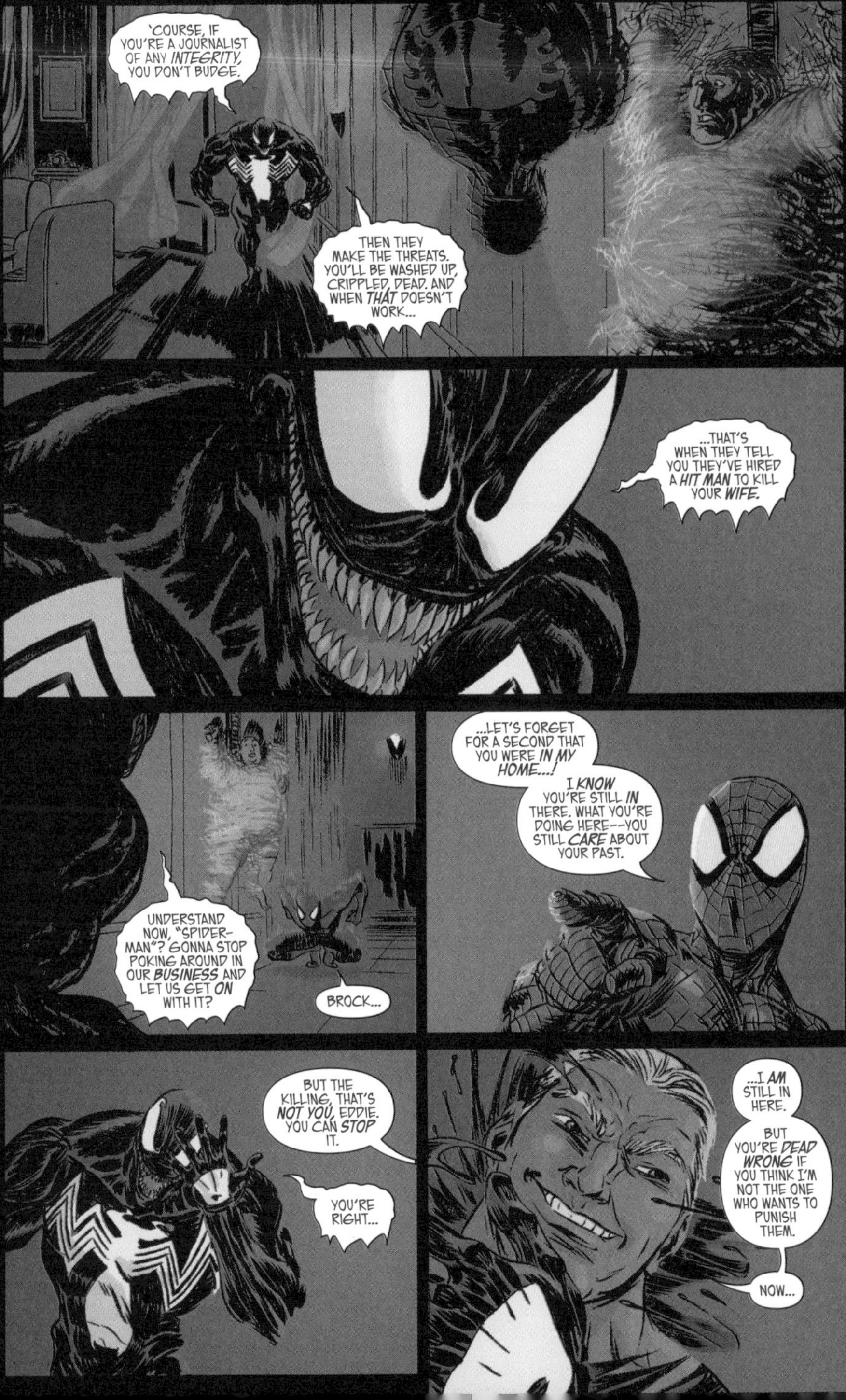
'COURSE, IF YOU'RE A JOURNALIST OF ANY *INTEGRITY,* YOU DON'T BUDGE.
THEN THEY MAKE THE THREATS. YOU'LL BE WASHED UP, CRIPPLED, DEAD. AND WHEN *THAT* DOESN'T WORK...
...THAT'S WHEN THEY TELL YOU THEY'VE HIRED A ***HIT MAN*** TO KILL YOUR ***WIFE.***
UNDERSTAND NOW, "SPIDER-MAN"? GONNA STOP POKING AROUND IN OUR ***BUSINESS*** AND LET US GET ***ON*** WITH IT?
BROCK...
...LET'S FORGET FOR A SECOND THAT YOU WERE ***IN MY HOME...!***
I *KNOW* YOU'RE STILL *IN* THERE. WHAT YOU'RE DOING HERE--YOU STILL *CARE* ABOUT YOUR PAST.
BUT THE KILLING, THAT'S ***NOT YOU,*** EDDIE. YOU CAN ***STOP*** IT.
YOU'RE RIGHT...
...I ***AM*** STILL IN HERE.
BUT YOU'RE ***DEAD WRONG*** IF YOU THINK I'M NOT THE ONE WHO WANTS TO PUNISH THEM.
NOW...

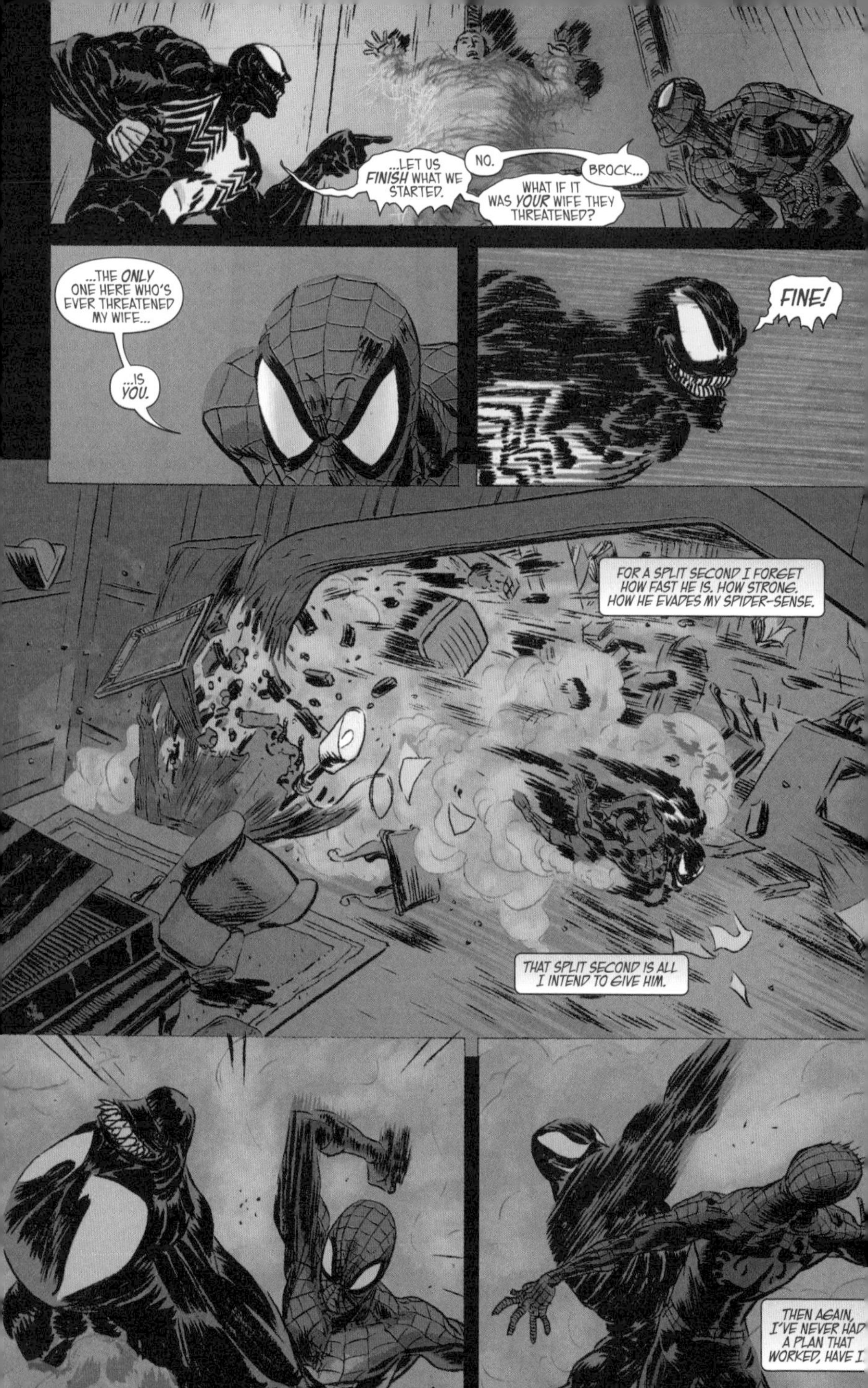
...LET US FINISH WHAT WE STARTED.
NO.
BROCK...
WHAT IF IT WAS YOUR WIFE THEY THREATENED?
...THE ONLY ONE HERE WHO'S EVER THREATENED MY WIFE...
...IS YOU.
FINE!
FOR A SPLIT SECOND I FORGET HOW FAST HE IS. HOW STRONG. HOW HE EVADES MY SPIDER-SENSE.
THAT SPLIT SECOND IS ALL I INTEND TO GIVE HIM.
THEN AGAIN, I'VE NEVER HAD A PLAN THAT WORKED, HAVE I.

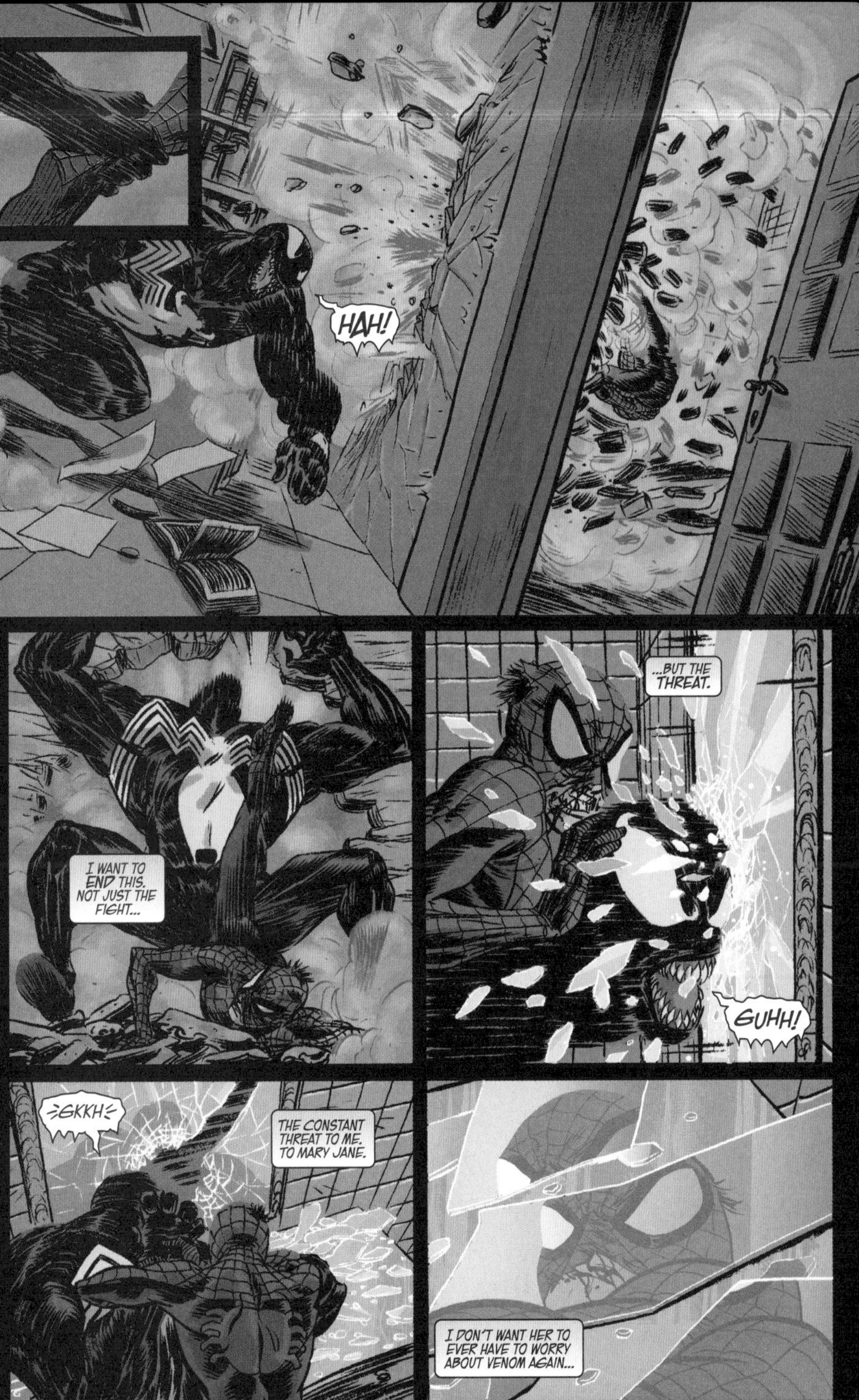
HAH!
I WANT TO END THIS. NOT JUST THE FIGHT...
...BUT THE THREAT.
GUHH!
GKKH
THE CONSTANT THREAT TO ME. TO MARY JANE.
I DON'T WANT HER TO EVER HAVE TO WORRY ABOUT VENOM AGAIN...

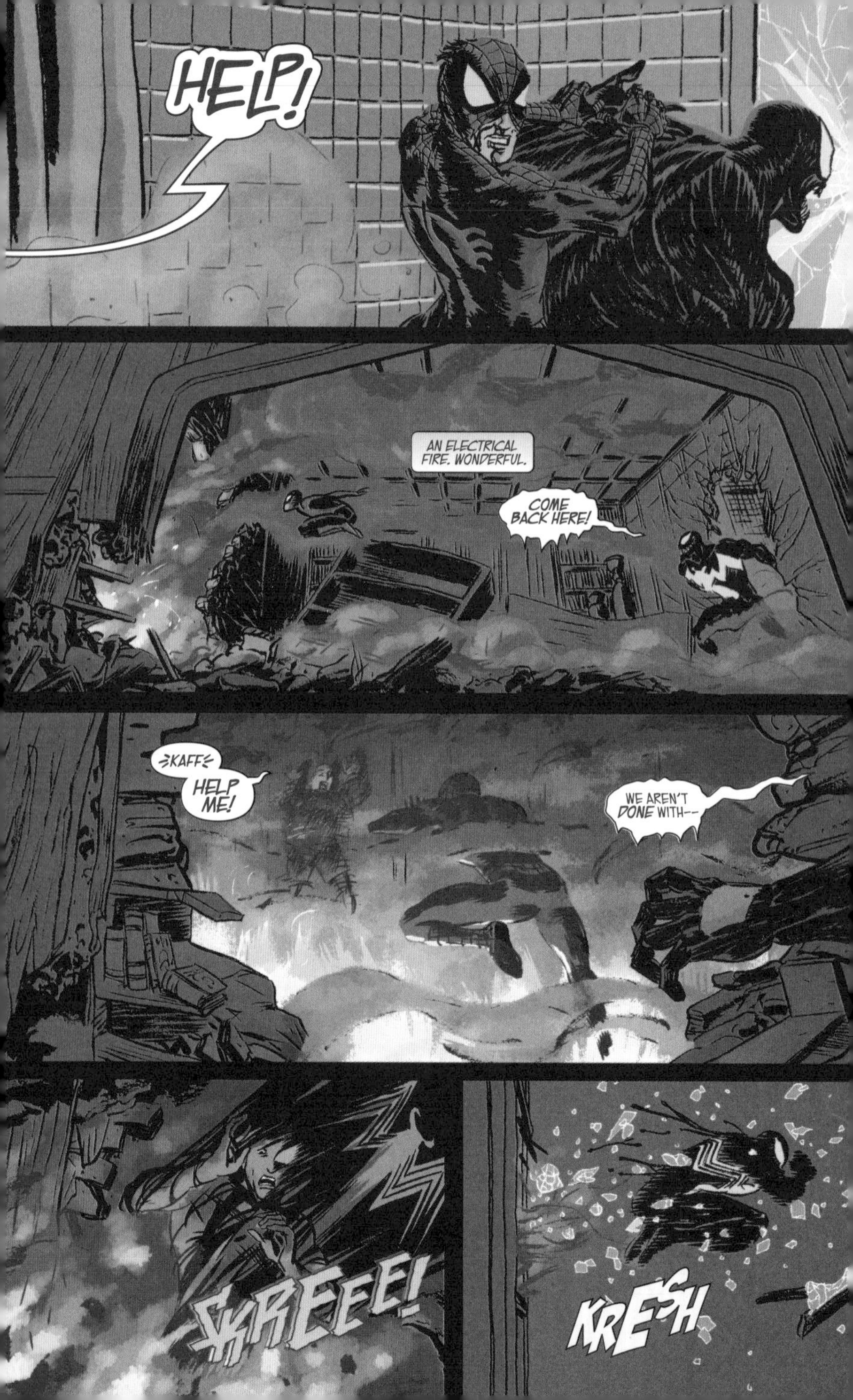
HELP!
AN ELECTRICAL FIRE. WONDERFUL.
COME BACK HERE!
KAFF
HELP ME!
WE AREN'T DONE WITH--
SKREEE!
KRESH

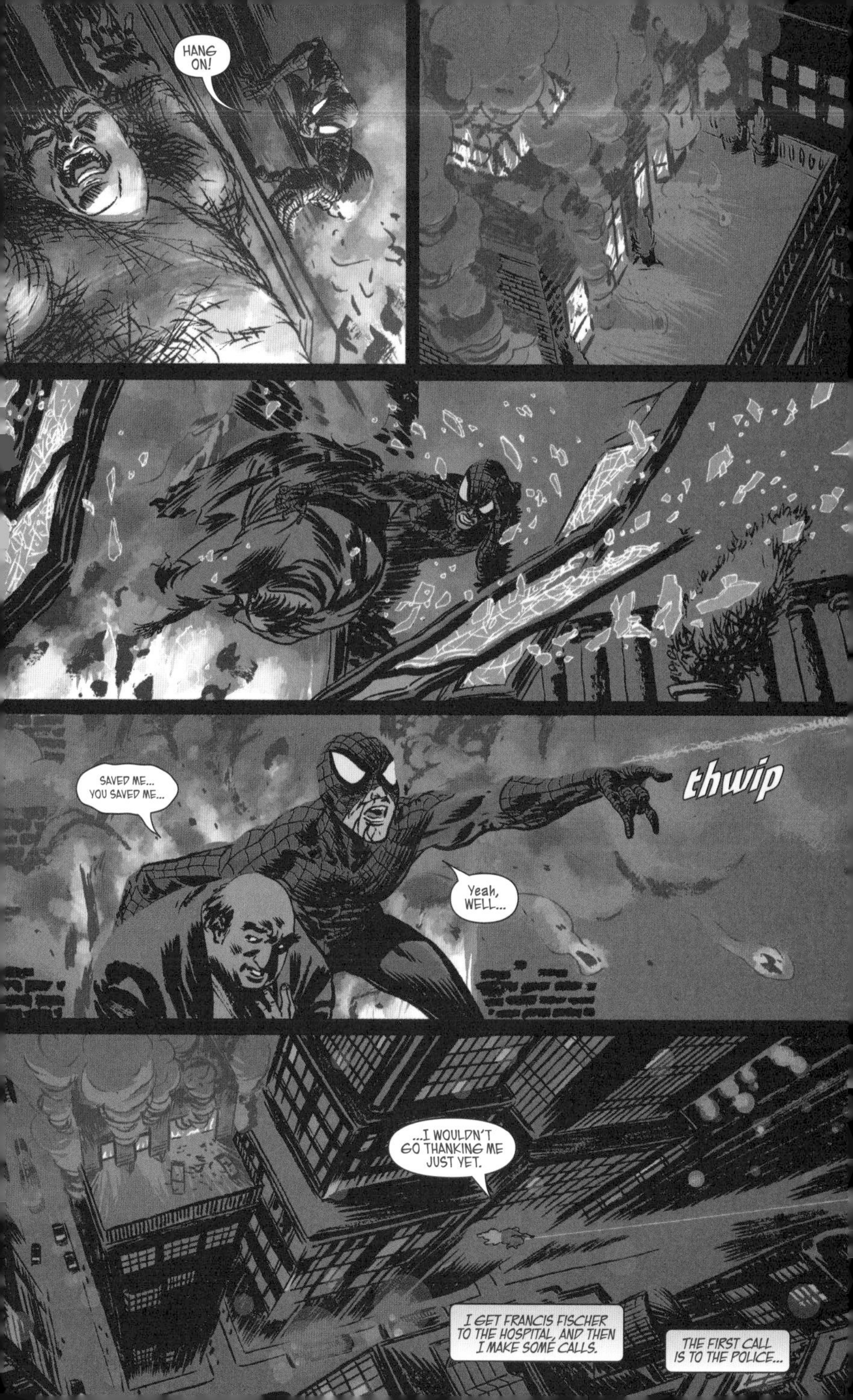
HANG ON!
SAVED ME... YOU SAVED ME...
thwip
Yeah, WELL...
...I WOULDN'T GO THANKING ME JUST YET.
I GET FRANCIS FISCHER TO THE HOSPITAL, AND THEN I MAKE SOME CALLS.
THE FIRST CALL IS TO THE POLICE...

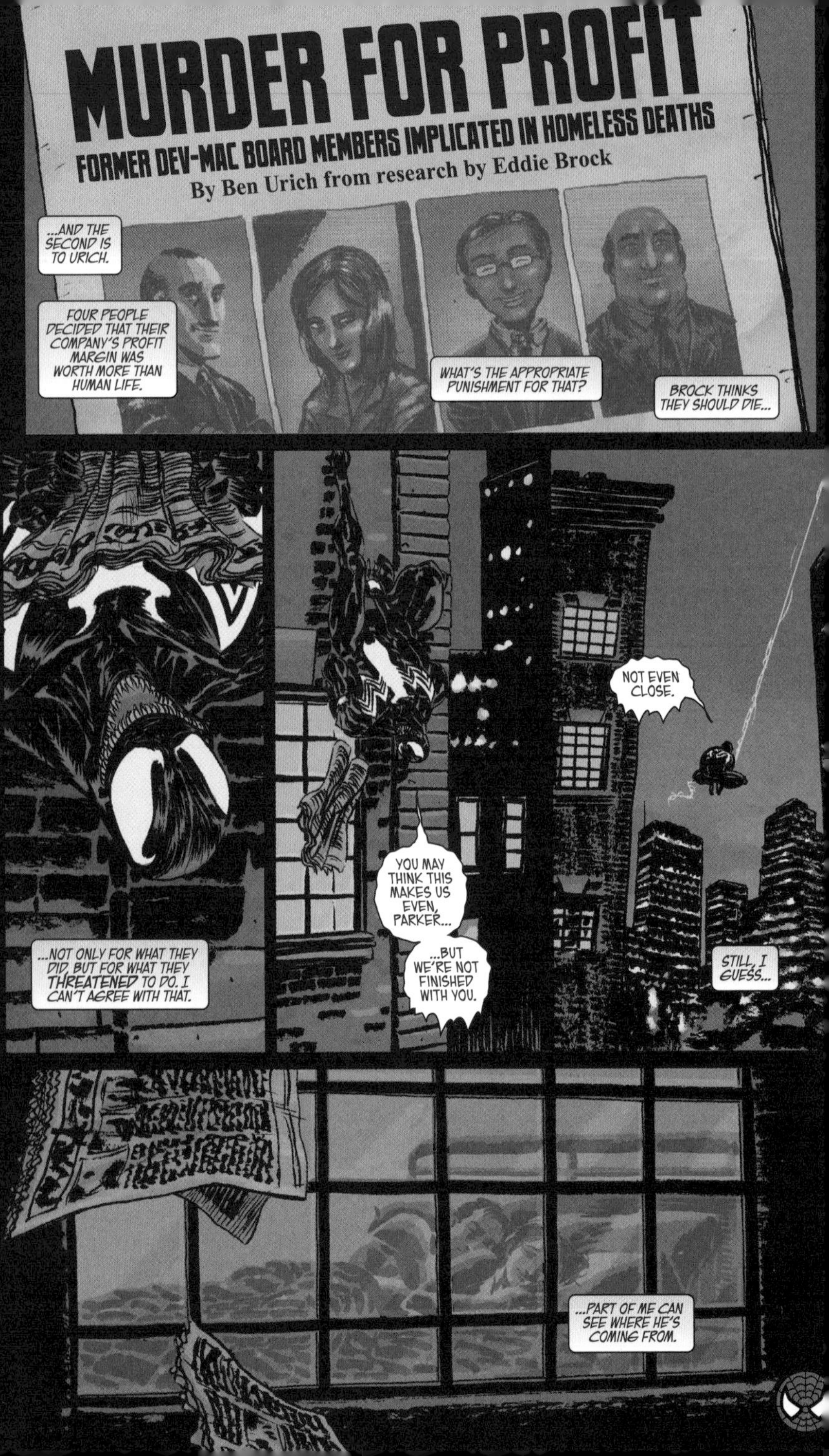
MURDER FOR PROFIT
FORMER DEV-MAC BOARD MEMBERS IMPLICATED IN HOMELESS DEATHS
By Ben Urich from research by Eddie Brock
...AND THE SECOND IS TO URICH.
FOUR PEOPLE DECIDED THAT THEIR COMPANY'S PROFIT MARGIN WAS WORTH MORE THAN HUMAN LIFE.
WHAT'S THE APPROPRIATE PUNISHMENT FOR THAT?
BROCK THINKS THEY SHOULD DIE...
...NOT ONLY FOR WHAT THEY DID, BUT FOR WHAT THEY THREATENED TO DO. I CAN'T AGREE WITH THAT.
YOU MAY THINK THIS MAKES US EVEN, PARKER...
...BUT WE'RE NOT FINISHED WITH YOU.
NOT EVEN CLOSE.
STILL, I GUESS...
...PART OF ME CAN SEE WHERE HE'S COMING FROM.

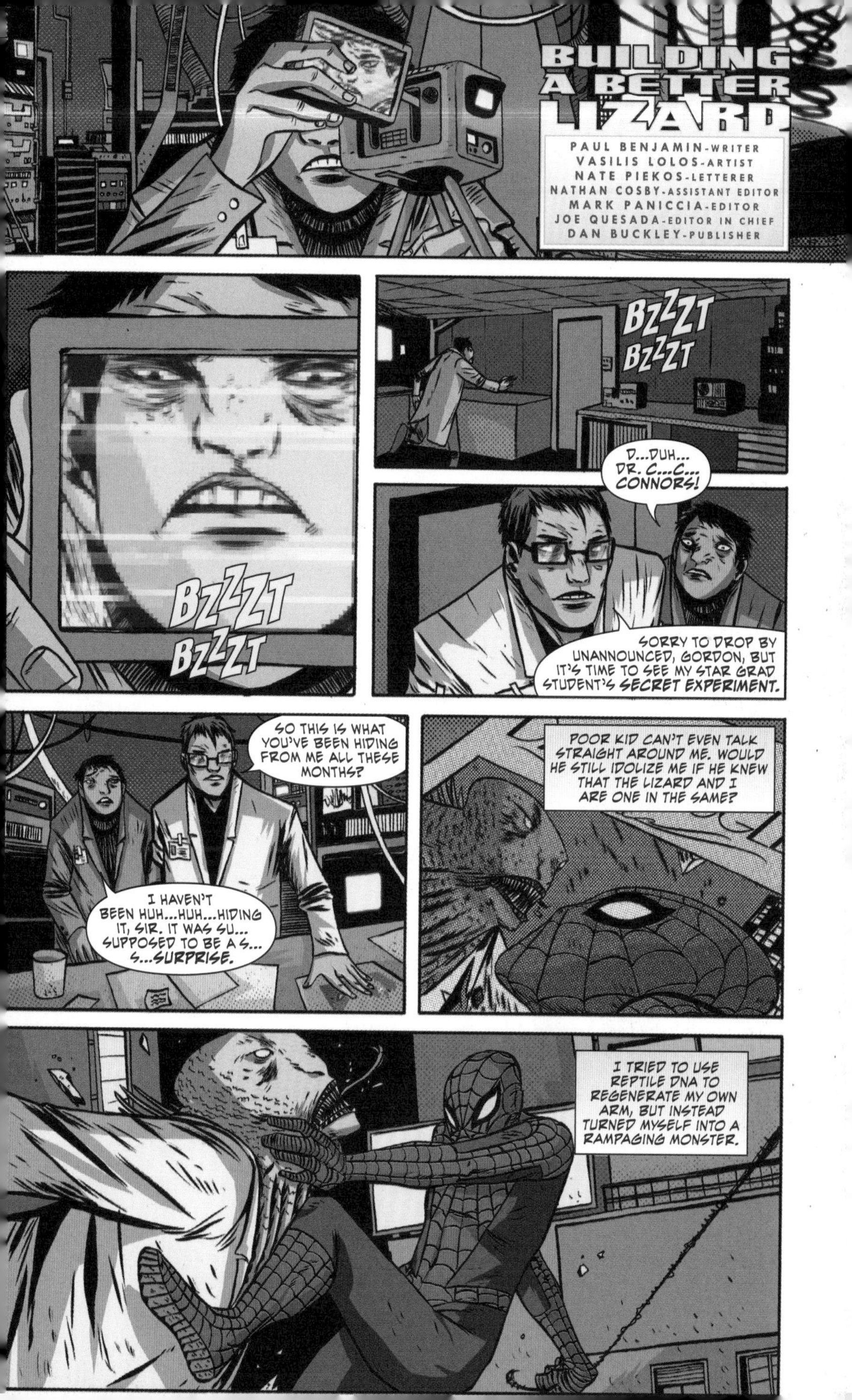
BUILDING A BETTER LIZARD
PAUL BENJAMIN-WRITER
VASILIS LOLOS-ARTIST
NATE PIEKOS-LETTERER
NATHAN COSBY-ASSISTANT EDITOR
MARK PANICCIA-EDITOR
JOE QUESADA-EDITOR IN CHIEF
DAN BUCKLEY-PUBLISHER
BZZZT BZZZT
BZZZT BZZZT
D...DUH... DR. C...C... CONNORS!
SORRY TO DROP BY UNANNOUNCED, GORDON, BUT IT'S TIME TO SEE MY STAR GRAD STUDENT'S SECRET EXPERIMENT.
SO THIS IS WHAT YOU'VE BEEN HIDING FROM ME ALL THESE MONTHS?
I HAVEN'T BEEN HUH...HUH...HIDING IT, SIR. IT WAS SU... SUPPOSED TO BE A S... S...SURPRISE.
POOR KID CAN'T EVEN TALK STRAIGHT AROUND ME. WOULD HE STILL IDOLIZE ME IF HE KNEW THAT THE LIZARD AND I ARE ONE IN THE SAME?
I TRIED TO USE REPTILE DNA TO REGENERATE MY OWN ARM, BUT INSTEAD TURNED MYSELF INTO A RAMPAGING MONSTER.

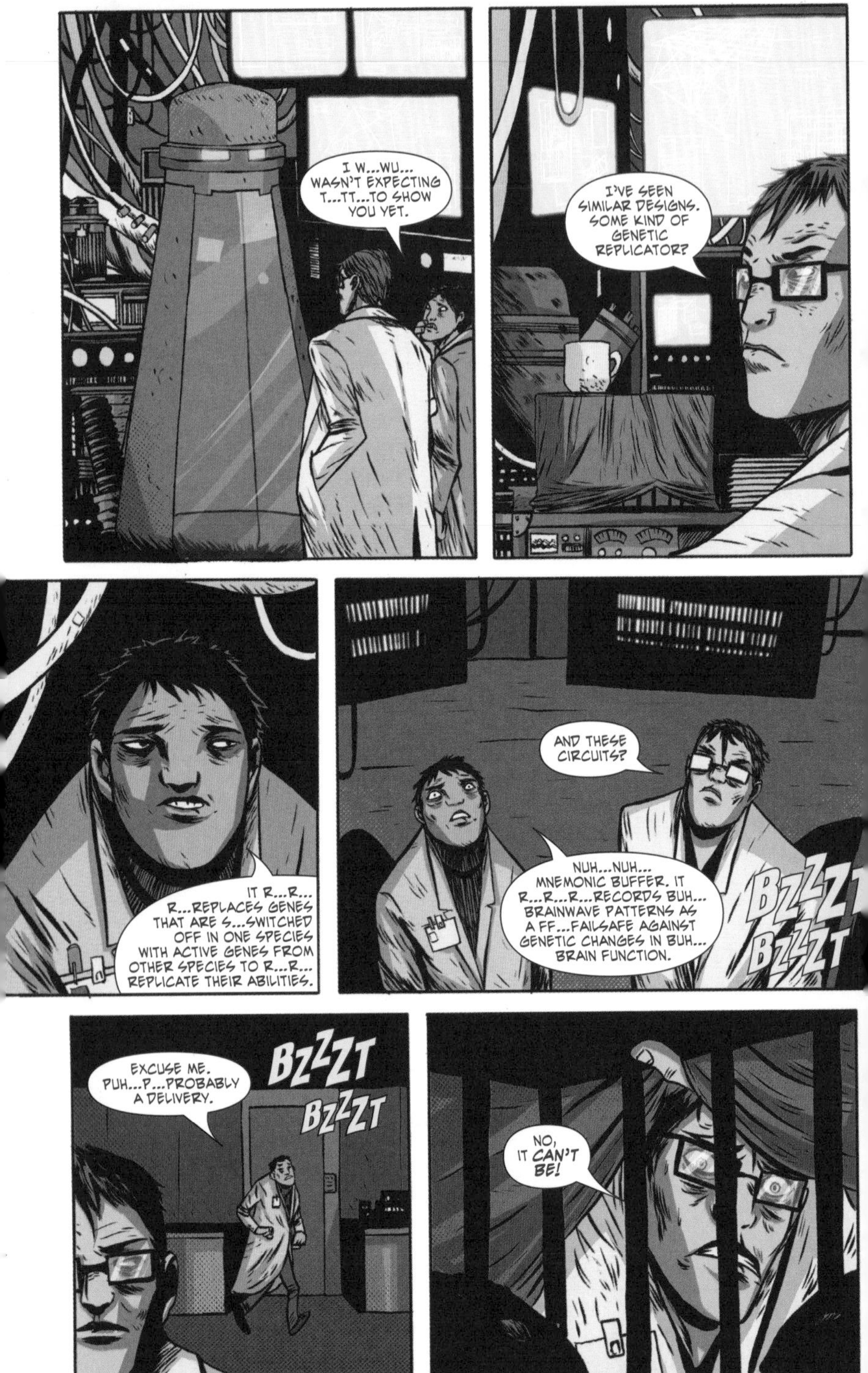
I W...WU... WASN'T EXPECTING T...TT...TO SHOW YOU YET.
I'VE SEEN SIMILAR DESIGNS. SOME KIND OF GENETIC REPLICATOR?
IT R...R... R...REPLACES GENES THAT ARE S...SWITCHED OFF IN ONE SPECIES WITH ACTIVE GENES FROM OTHER SPECIES TO R...R... REPLICATE THEIR ABILITIES.
AND THESE CIRCUITS?
NUH...NUH... MNEMONIC BUFFER. IT R...R...R...RECORDS BUH... BRAINWAVE PATTERNS AS A FF...FAILSAFE AGAINST GENETIC CHANGES IN BUH... BRAIN FUNCTION.
BZZZT
BZZZT
BZZZT
BZZZT
EXCUSE ME. PUH...P...PROBABLY A DELIVERY.
NO, IT CAN'T BE!

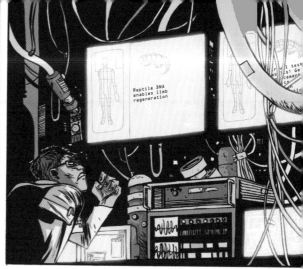

Reptile DNA
enables limb
regeneration

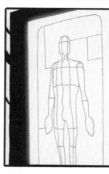

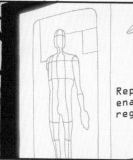

Reptile DNA
enables limb
regeneration

Virtual test
results: Gene
replacement
results
in human
regeneration

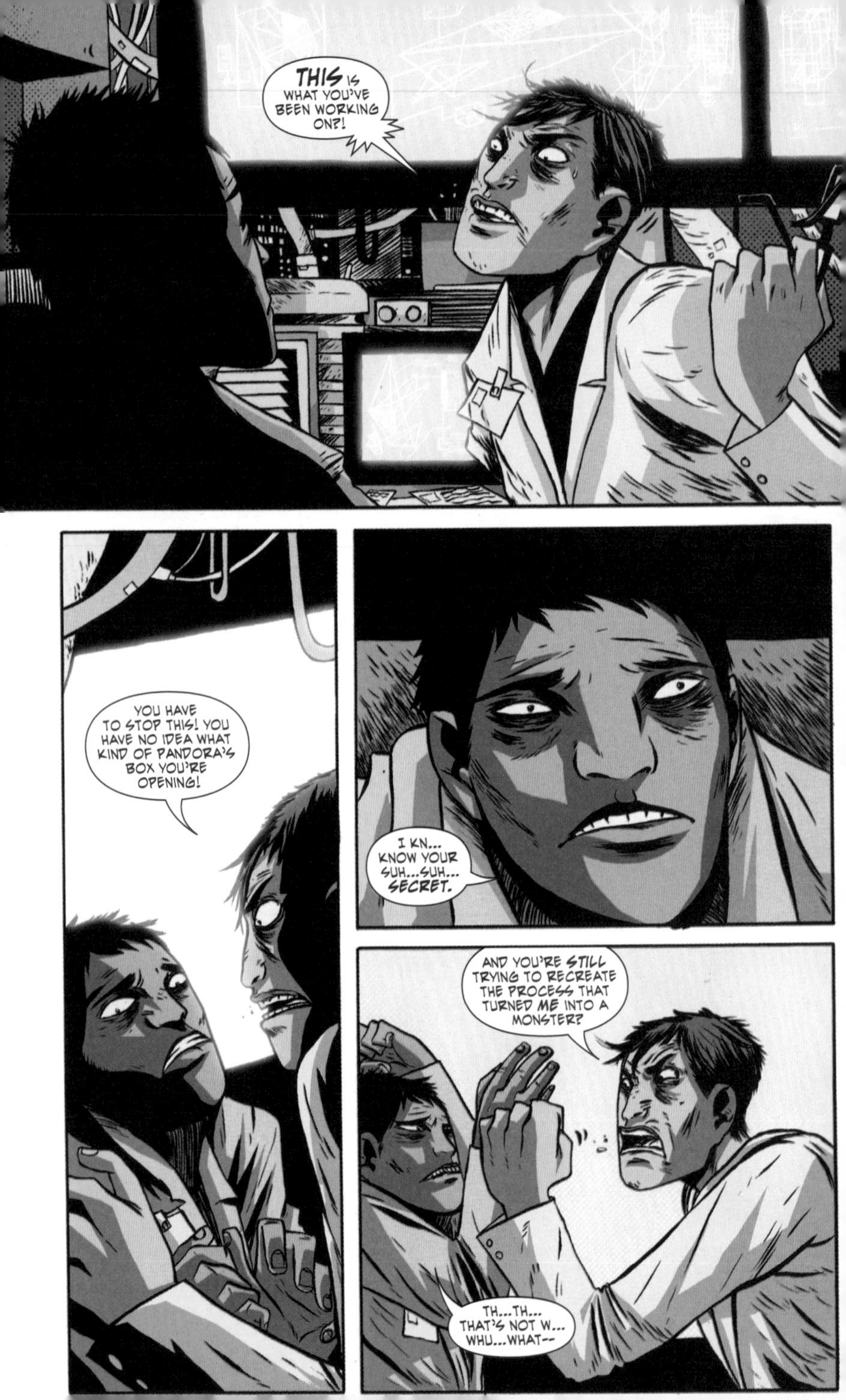
THIS IS WHAT YOU'VE BEEN WORKING ON?!
YOU HAVE TO STOP THIS! YOU HAVE NO IDEA WHAT KIND OF PANDORA'S BOX YOU'RE OPENING!
I KN... KNOW YOUR SUH...SUH... SECRET.
AND YOU'RE STILL TRYING TO RECREATE THE PROCESS THAT TURNED ME INTO A MONSTER?
TH...TH... THAT'S NOT W... WHU...WHAT--

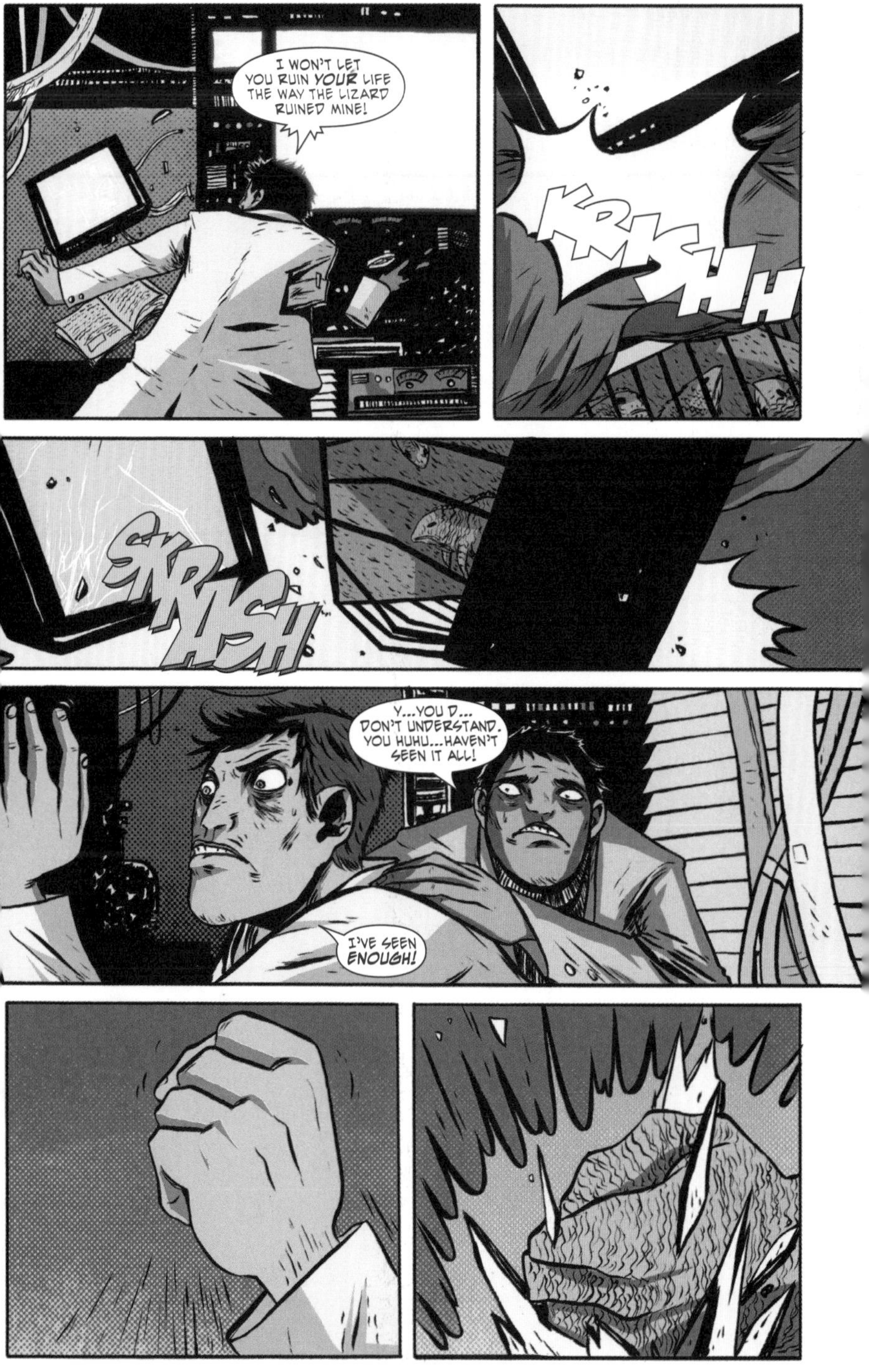
I WON'T LET YOU RUIN YOUR LIFE THE WAY THE LIZARD RUINED MINE!
KRISHH
SKRASH
Y...YOU D... DON'T UNDERSTAND. YOU HUHU...HAVEN'T SEEN IT ALL!
I'VE SEEN ENOUGH!

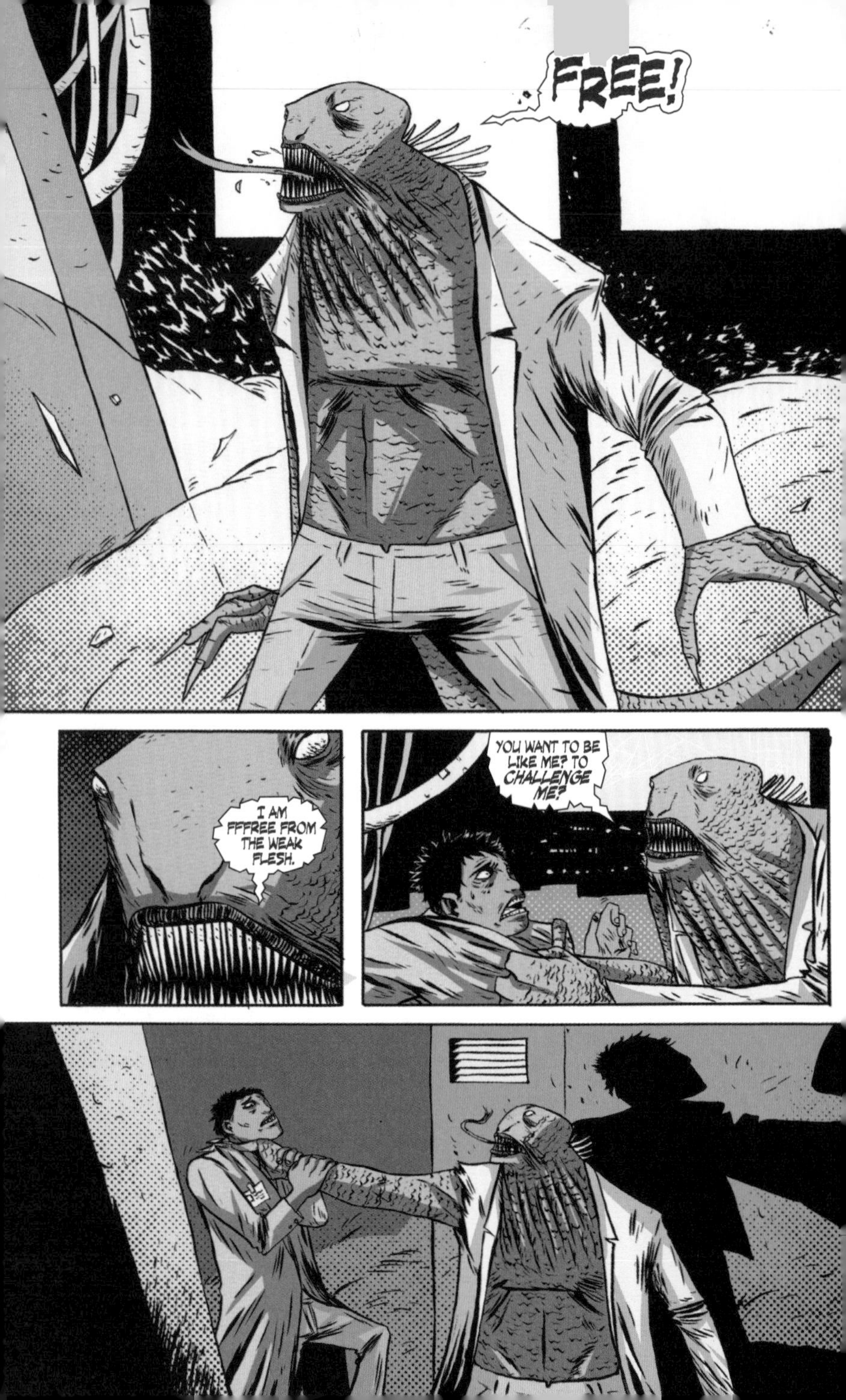
FREE!
I AM FFFREE FROM THE WEAK FLESH.
YOU WANT TO BE LIKE ME? TO CHALLENGE ME?

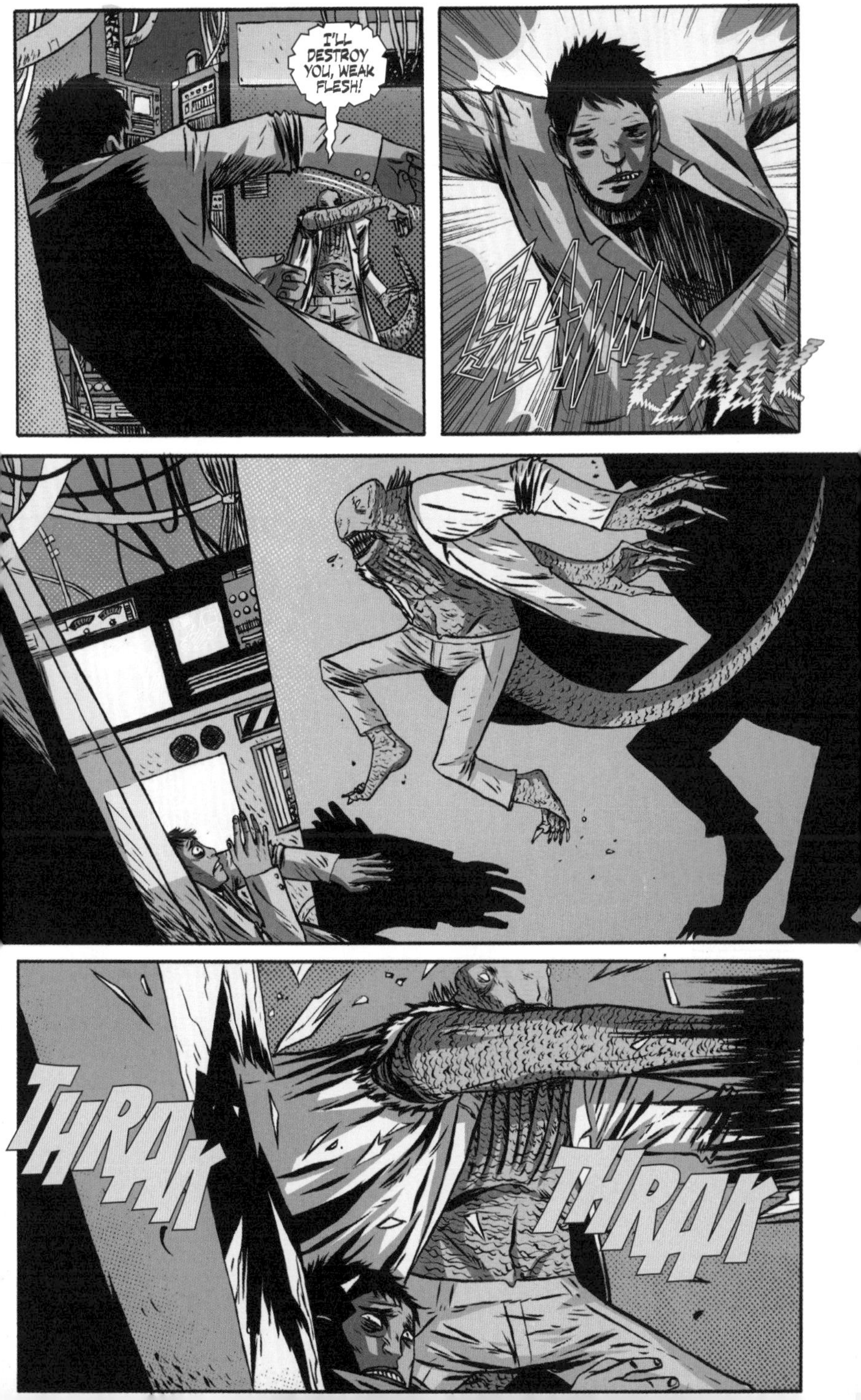
I'LL DESTROY YOU, WEAK FLESH!
THRAK
THRAK

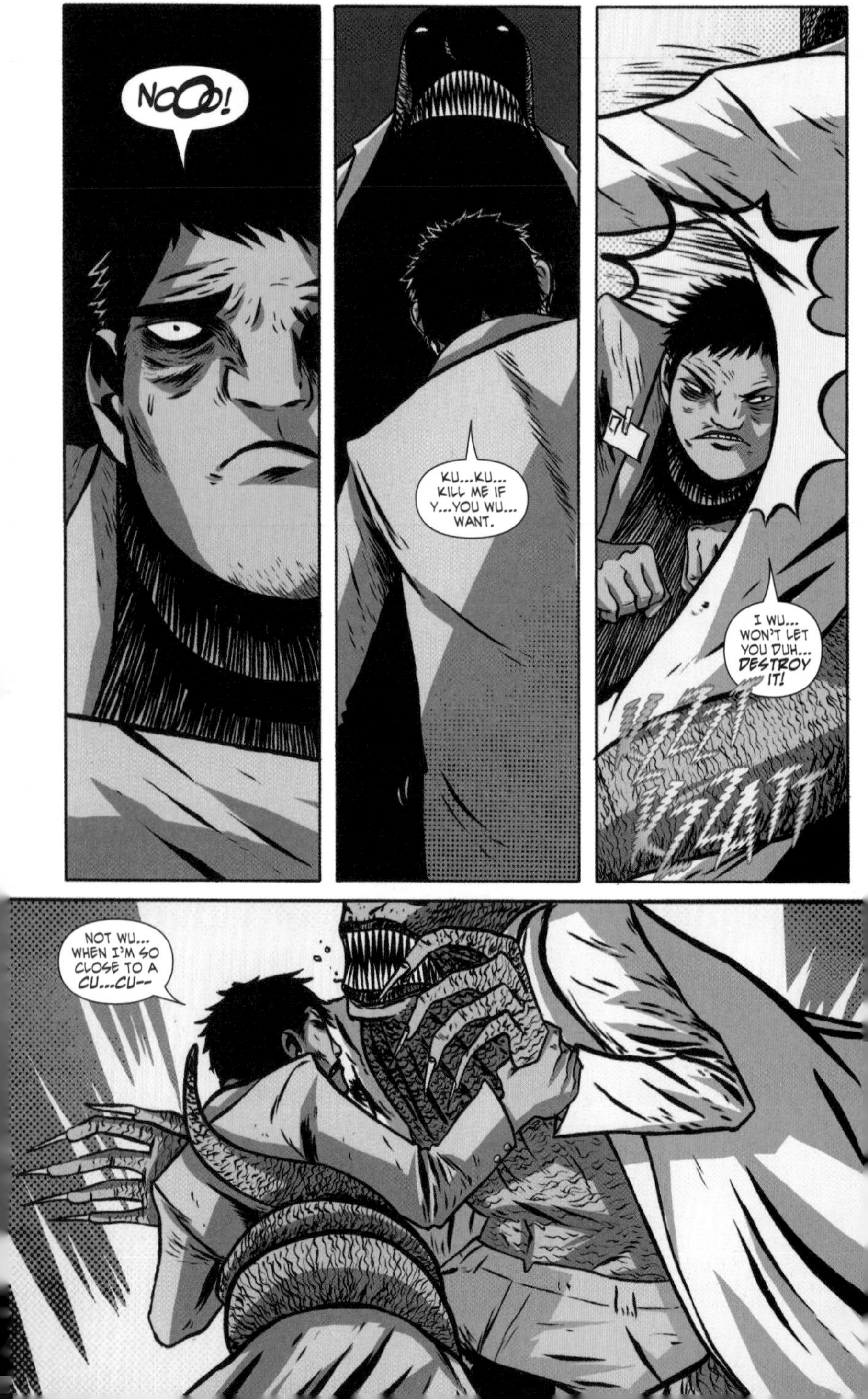
NOOO!
KU...KU... KILL ME IF Y...YOU WU... WANT.
I WU... WON'T LET YOU DUH... DESTROY IT!
NOT WU... WHEN I'M SO CLOSE TO A CU...CU--

--CURE FOR YOU.

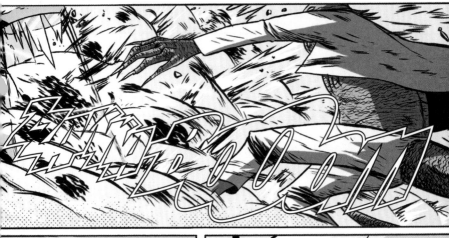

FMMMMMROOOM!!!

WHAT HAVE I DONE?

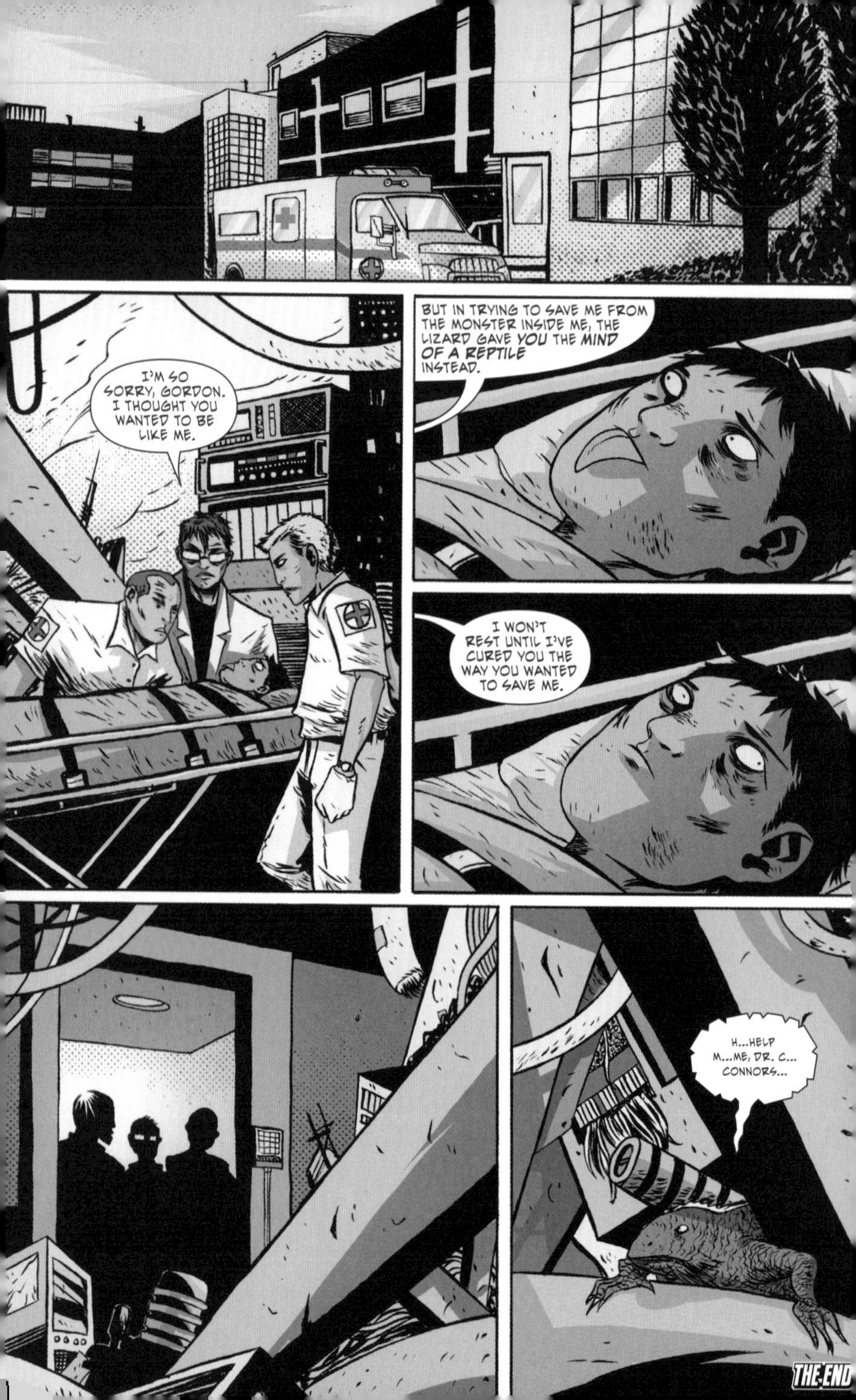
I'M SO SORRY, GORDON. I THOUGHT YOU WANTED TO BE LIKE ME.
BUT IN TRYING TO SAVE ME FROM THE MONSTER INSIDE ME, THE LIZARD GAVE YOU THE MIND OF A REPTILE INSTEAD.
I WON'T REST UNTIL I'VE CURED YOU THE WAY YOU WANTED TO SAVE ME.
H...HELP M...ME, DR. C... CONNORS...
THE END

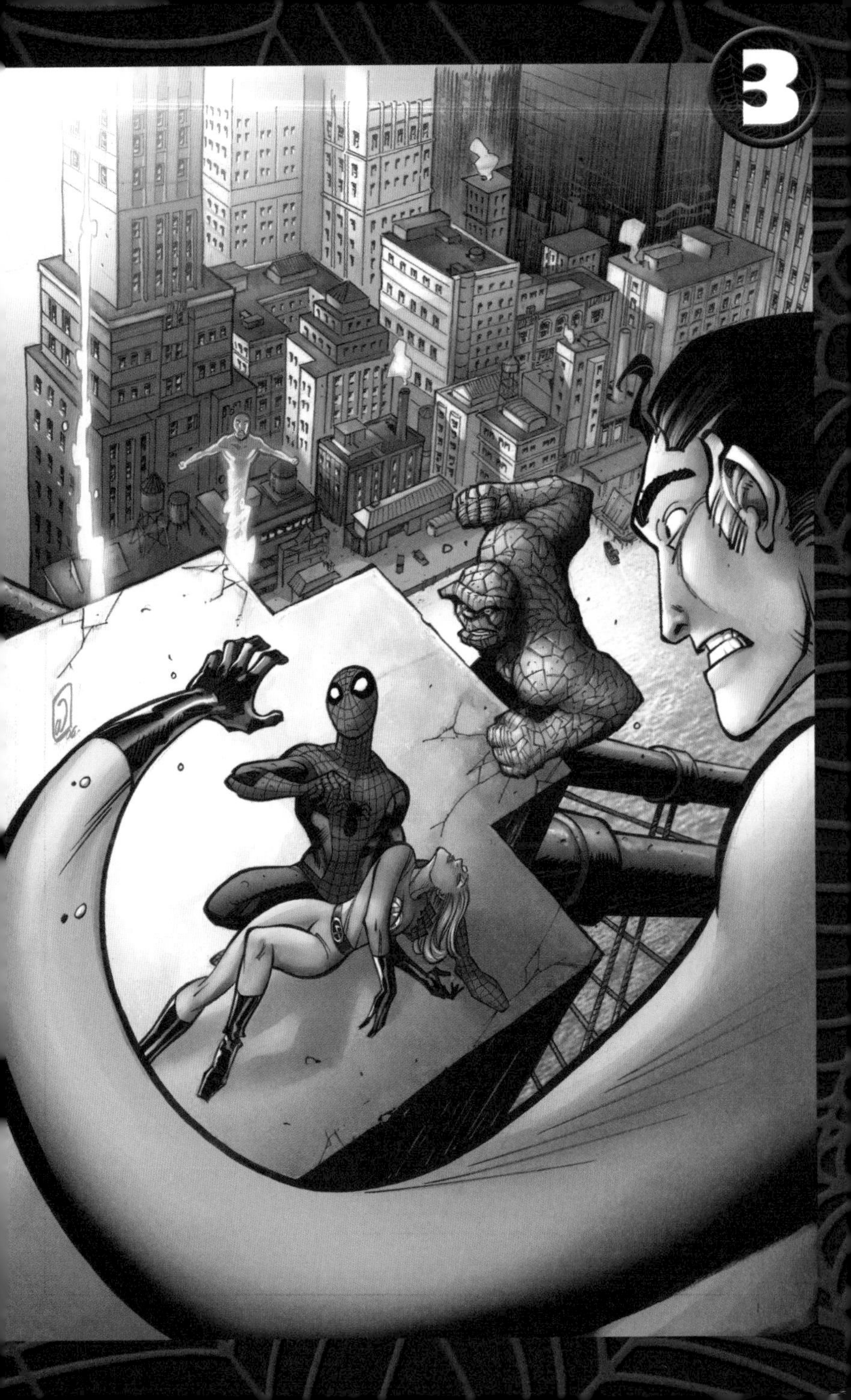
3

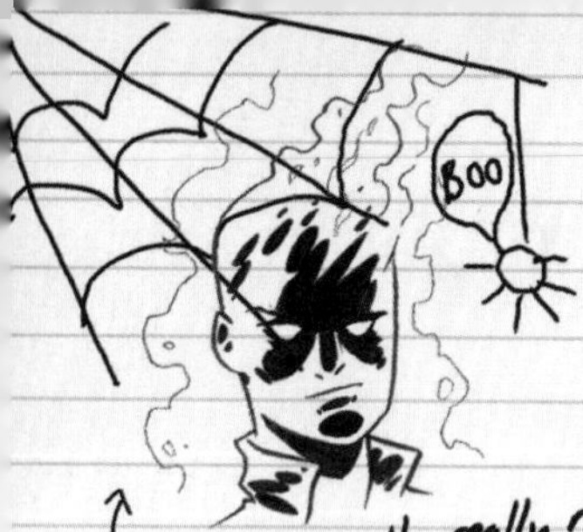
BOO

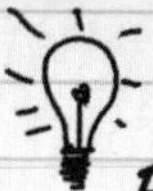

REED RICHARDS
=
MR. FANTASTIC (stretchy)

★ SUE STORM
=
INVISIBLE GIRL (suuuuper HOT)

BEN GRIMM
=
THING (rocky)

Johnny "I really really really REALLY hate him" Storm
or HUMAN TORCH
or MATCHSTICK
or FLAMEBRAIN
or DUMB ON FIRE GUY

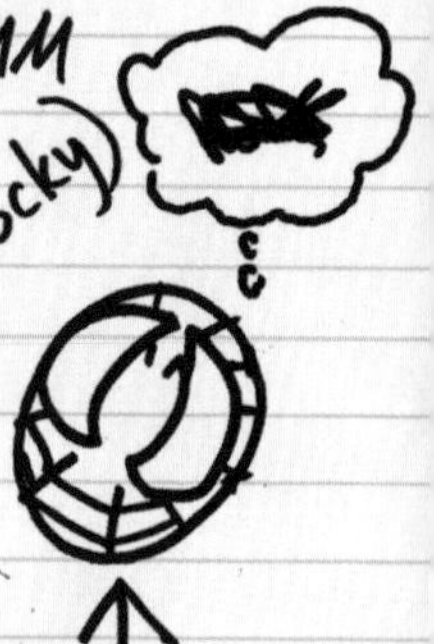

↑
ME

Why I hate Torch

1. doesn't have to keep identity secret
2. has car
3. when he shows up, people yell "YAY!" when I show up, people yell "GET AWAY FROM MY BABY!"
4. smells kinda like kerosene

(reasons 5-796 coming soon)

...

ELECTRICAL PROBLEMS!

Written by PAUL TOBIN
Art by PIERRE ALARY
Color by JEAN PAUL FERNANDEZ

Lettering by Blambot's NATE PIEKOS
Cover by ALARY & SOTOMAYOR
Production by BRAD JOHANSEN
Special Thanks to DAVID GABRIEL
Consulting by MARK PANICCIA
Edited by NATHAN COSBY
Editor in Chief JOE QUESADA
Publisher DAN BUCKLEY

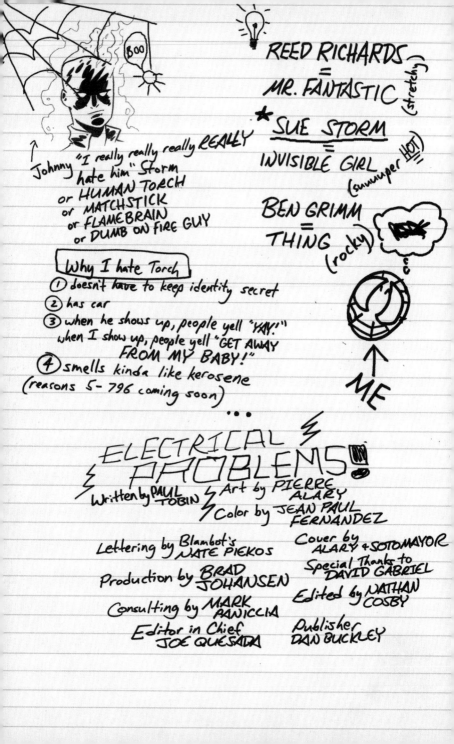

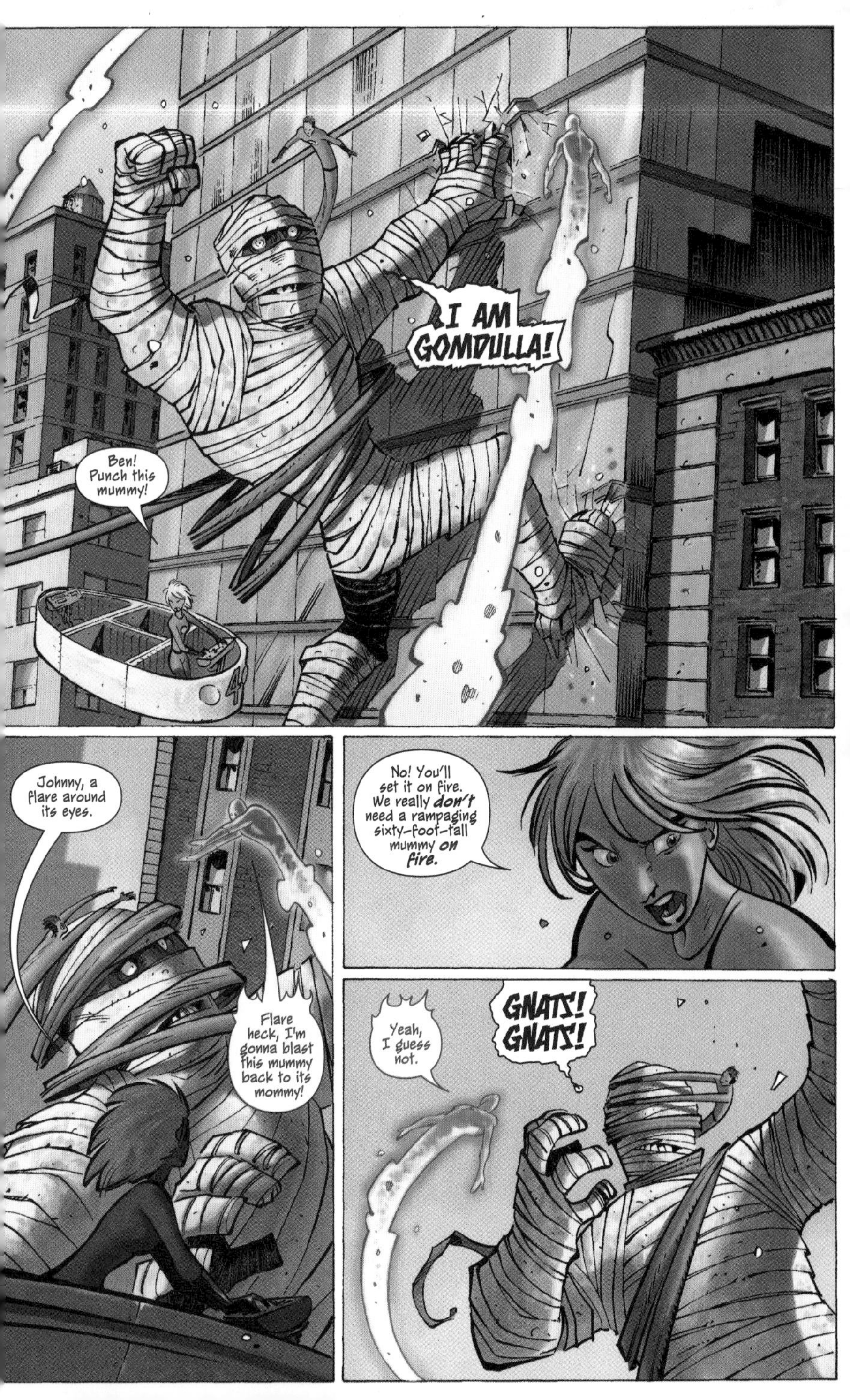
I AM GOMDULLA!
Ben! Punch this mummy!
Johnny, a flare around its eyes.
Flare heck, I'm gonna blast this mummy back to its mommy!
No! You'll set it on fire. We really don't need a rampaging sixty-foot-tall mummy on fire.
Yeah, I guess not.
GNATS! GNATS!

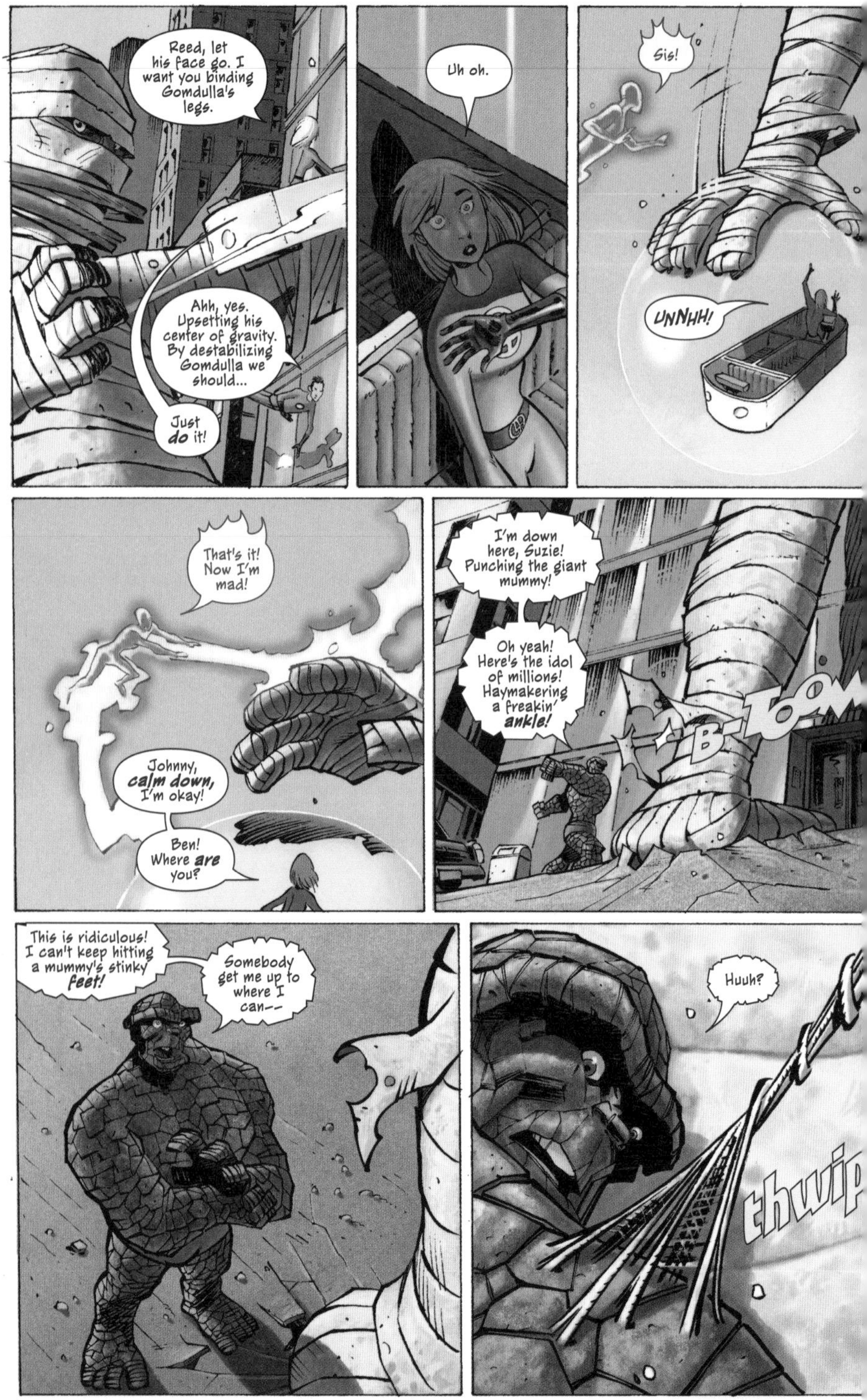

Reed, let his face go. I want you binding Gomdulla's legs.
Ahh, yes. Upsetting his center of gravity. By destabilizing Gomdulla we should...
Just do it!
Uh oh.
Sis!
UNNHH!
That's it! Now I'm mad!
Johnny, calm down, I'm okay!
Ben! Where are you?
I'm down here, Suzie! Punching the giant mummy!
Oh yeah! Here's the idol of millions! Haymakering a freakin' ankle!
B-TOO
This is ridiculous! I can't keep hitting a mummy's stinky feet!
Somebody get me up to where I can--
Huuh?
thwip

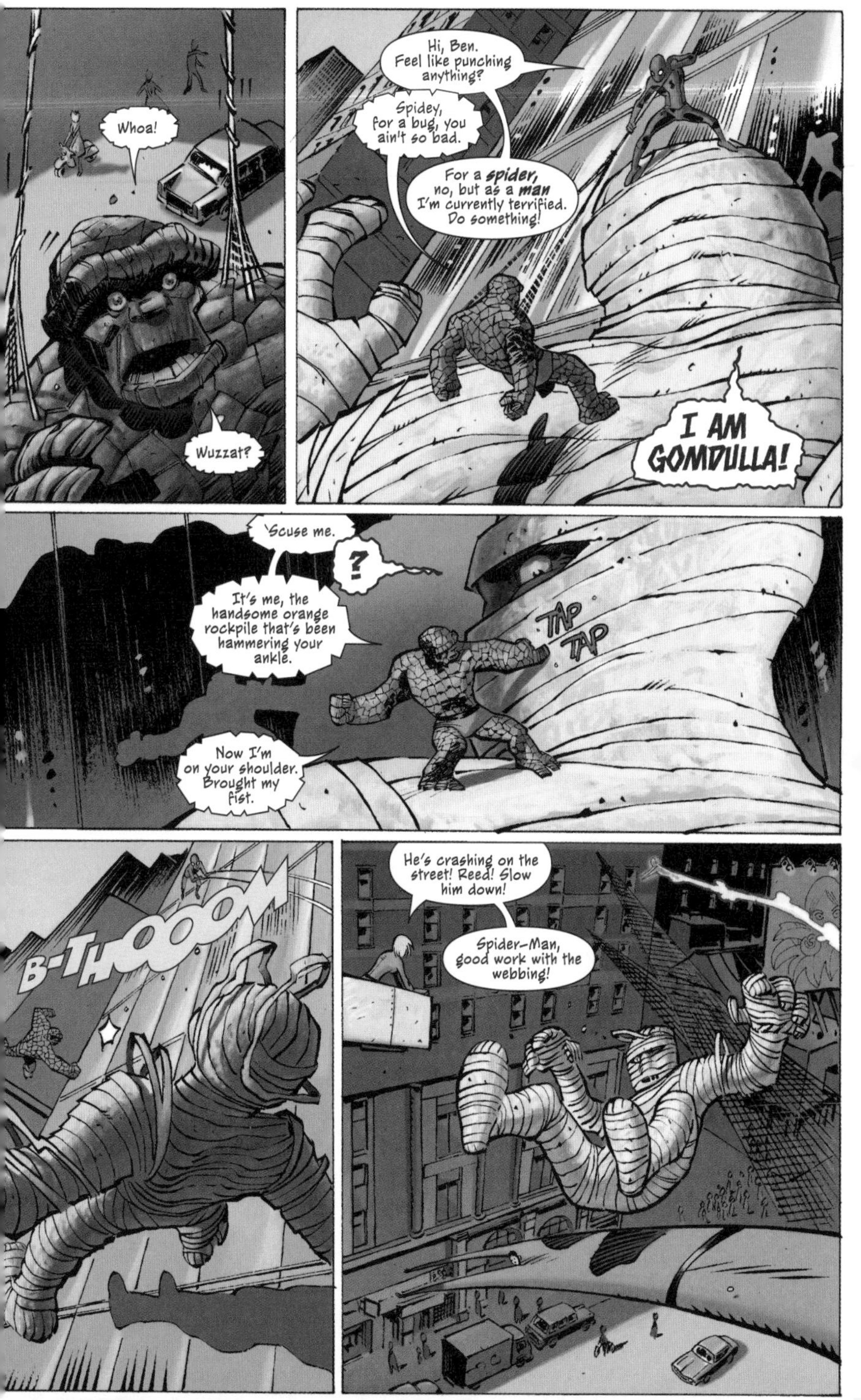

Whoa!
Wuzzat?
Hi, Ben. Feel like punching anything?
Spidey, for a bug, you ain't so bad.
For a spider, no, but as a man I'm currently terrified. Do something!
I AM GOMDULLA!
'Scuse me.
?
It's me, the handsome orange rockpile that's been hammering your ankle.
TAP TAP
Now I'm on your shoulder. Brought my fist.
B-THOOOOM
He's crashing on the street! Reed! Slow him down!
Spider-Man, good work with the webbing!

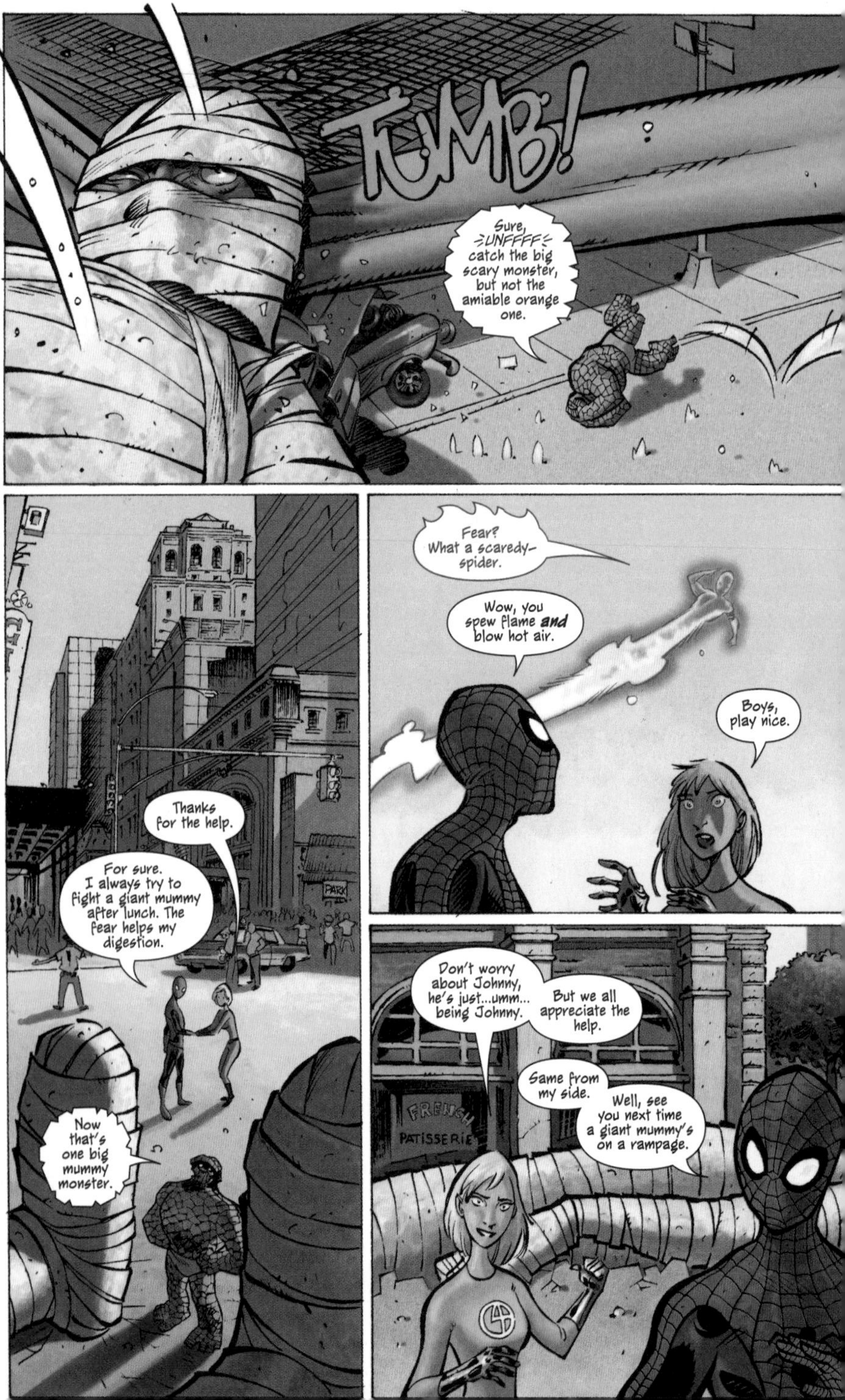

TUMB!
Sure, UNFFFF catch the big scary monster, but not the amiable orange one.
Thanks for the help.
For sure. I always try to fight a giant mummy after lunch. The fear helps my digestion.
PARK
Now that's one big mummy monster.
Fear? What a scaredy-spider.
Wow, you spew flame and blow hot air.
Boys, play nice.
Don't worry about Johnny, he's just...umm... being Johnny.
But we all appreciate the help.
Same from my side.
Well, see you next time a giant mummy's on a rampage.
FRENCH
PATISSERIE

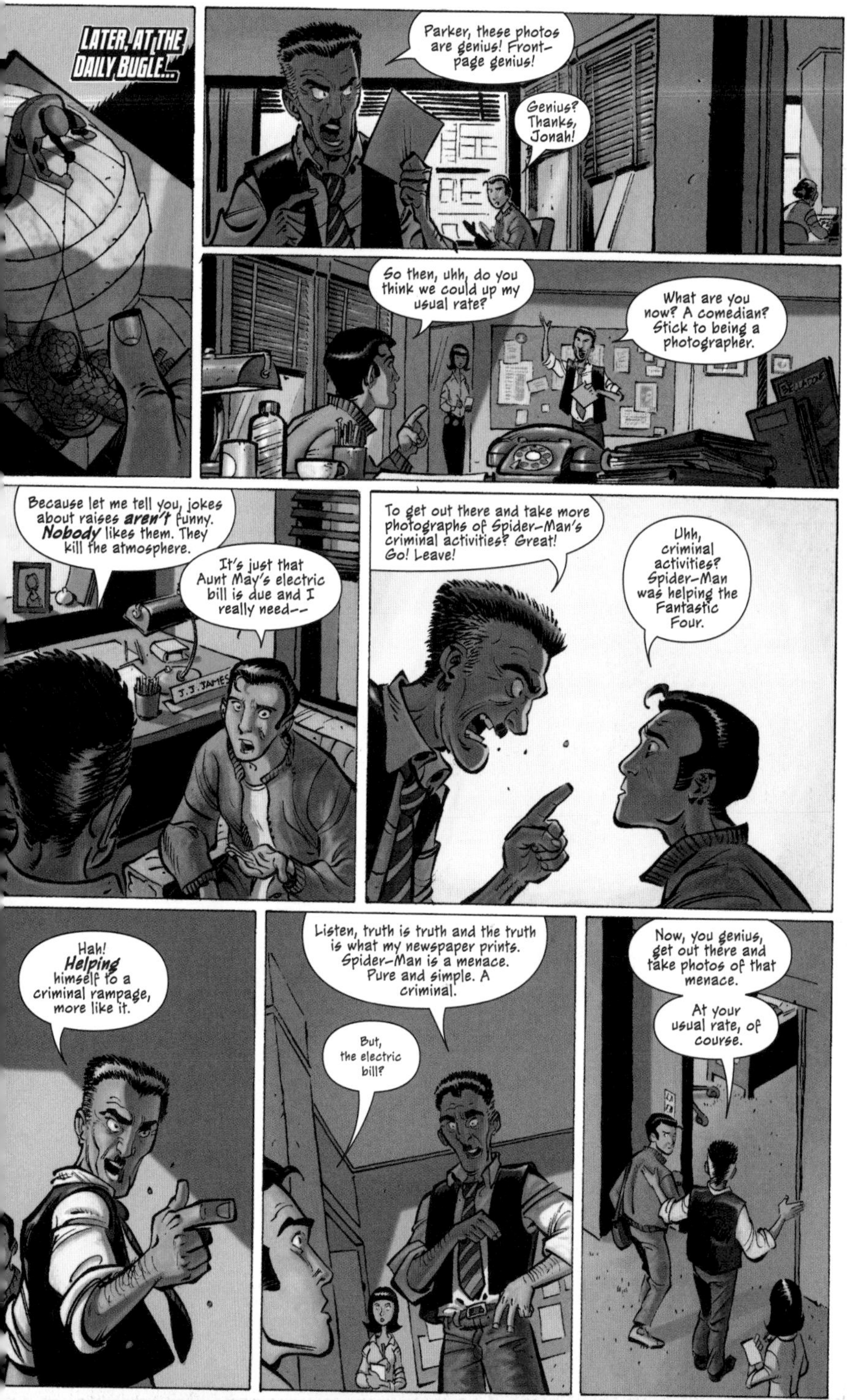
LATER, AT THE DAILY BUGLE...
Parker, these photos are genius! Front-page genius!
Genius? Thanks, Jonah!
So then, uhh, do you think we could up my usual rate?
What are you now? A comedian? Stick to being a photographer.
Because let me tell you, jokes about raises ***aren't*** funny. ***Nobody*** likes them. They kill the atmosphere.
It's just that Aunt May's electric bill is due and I really need--
J.J. JAMES
To get out there and take more photographs of Spider-Man's criminal activities? Great! Go! Leave!
Uhh, criminal activities? Spider-Man was helping the Fantastic Four.
Hah! ***Helping*** himself to a criminal rampage, more like it.
Listen, truth is truth and the truth is what my newspaper prints. Spider-Man is a menace. Pure and simple. A criminal.
But, the electric bill?
Now, you genius, get out there and take photos of that menace.
At your usual rate, of course.

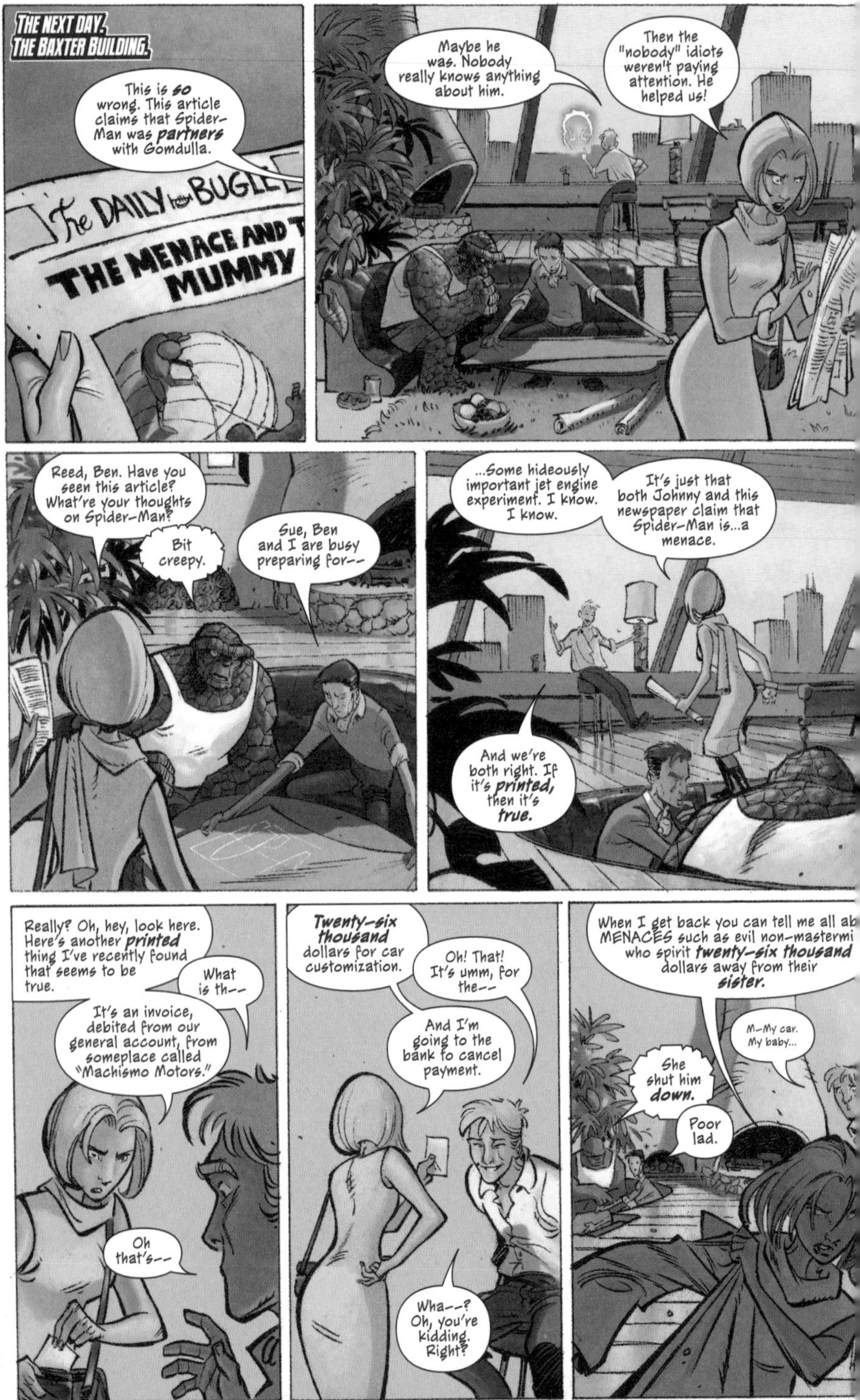
THE NEXT DAY. THE BAXTER BUILDING.
This is *so* wrong. This article claims that Spider-Man was *partners* with Gomdulla.
The DAILY BUGLE
THE MENACE AND T MUMMY
Maybe he was. Nobody really knows anything about him.
Then the "nobody" idiots weren't paying attention. He helped us!
Reed, Ben. Have you seen this article? What're your thoughts on Spider-Man?
Bit creepy.
Sue, Ben and I are busy preparing for--
...Some hideously important jet engine experiment. I know. I know.
It's just that both Johnny and this newspaper claim that Spider-Man is...a menace.
And we're both right. If it's *printed,* then it's *true.*
Really? Oh, hey, look here. Here's another *printed* thing I've recently found that seems to be true.
What is th--
It's an invoice, debited from our general account, from someplace called "Machismo Motors."
Oh that's--
Twenty-six thousand dollars for car customization.
Oh! That! It's umm, for the--
And I'm going to the bank to cancel payment.
Wha--? Oh, you're kidding. Right?
When I get back you can tell me all ab MENACES such as evil non-mastermi who spirit *twenty-six thousand* dollars away from their *sister.*
M-My car. My baby...
She shut him *down.*
Poor lad.

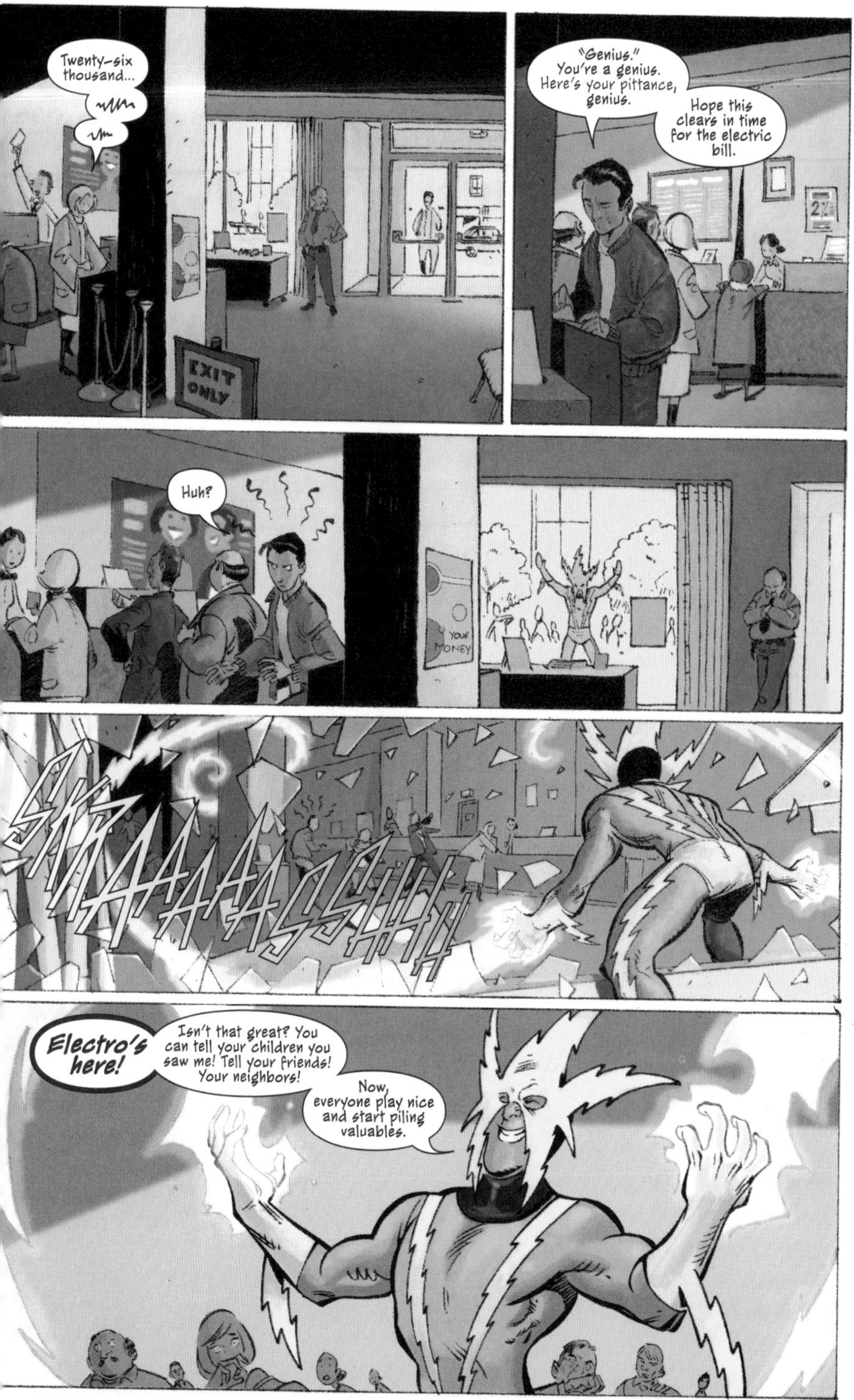

Twenty-six thousand...
EXIT ONLY
"Genius." You're a genius. Here's your pittance, genius.
Hope this clears in time for the electric bill.
Huh?
YOUR MONEY
SKRAAAAASSHHH
Electro's here!
Isn't that great? You can tell your children you saw me! Tell your friends! Your neighbors!
Now, everyone play nice and start piling valuables.

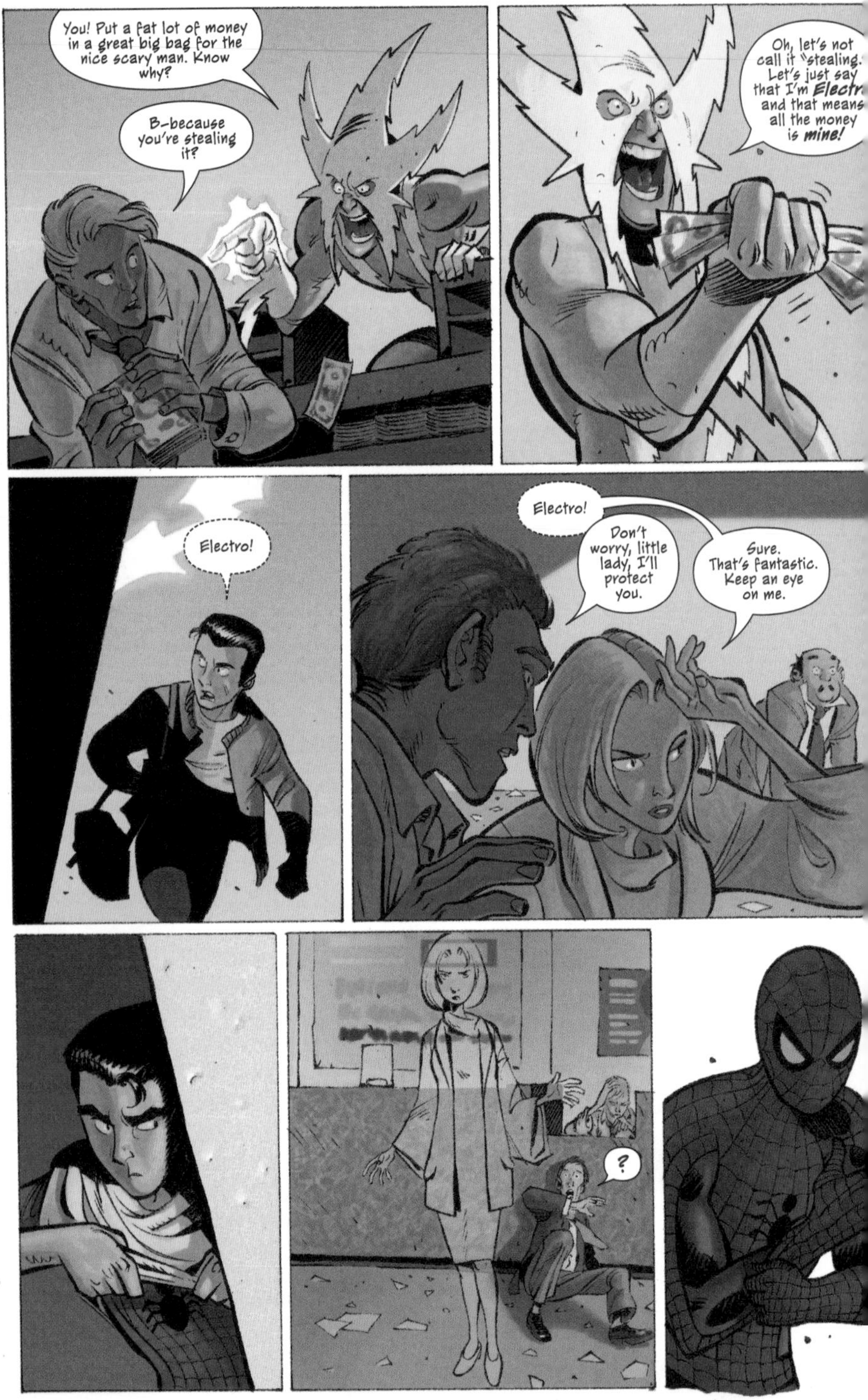
You! Put a fat lot of money in a great big bag for the nice scary man. Know why?
B-because you're stealing it?
Oh, let's not call it "stealing." Let's just say that I'm Electr and that means all the money is mine!
Electro!
Electro!
Don't worry, little lady, I'll protect you.
Sure. That's fantastic. Keep an eye on me.
?

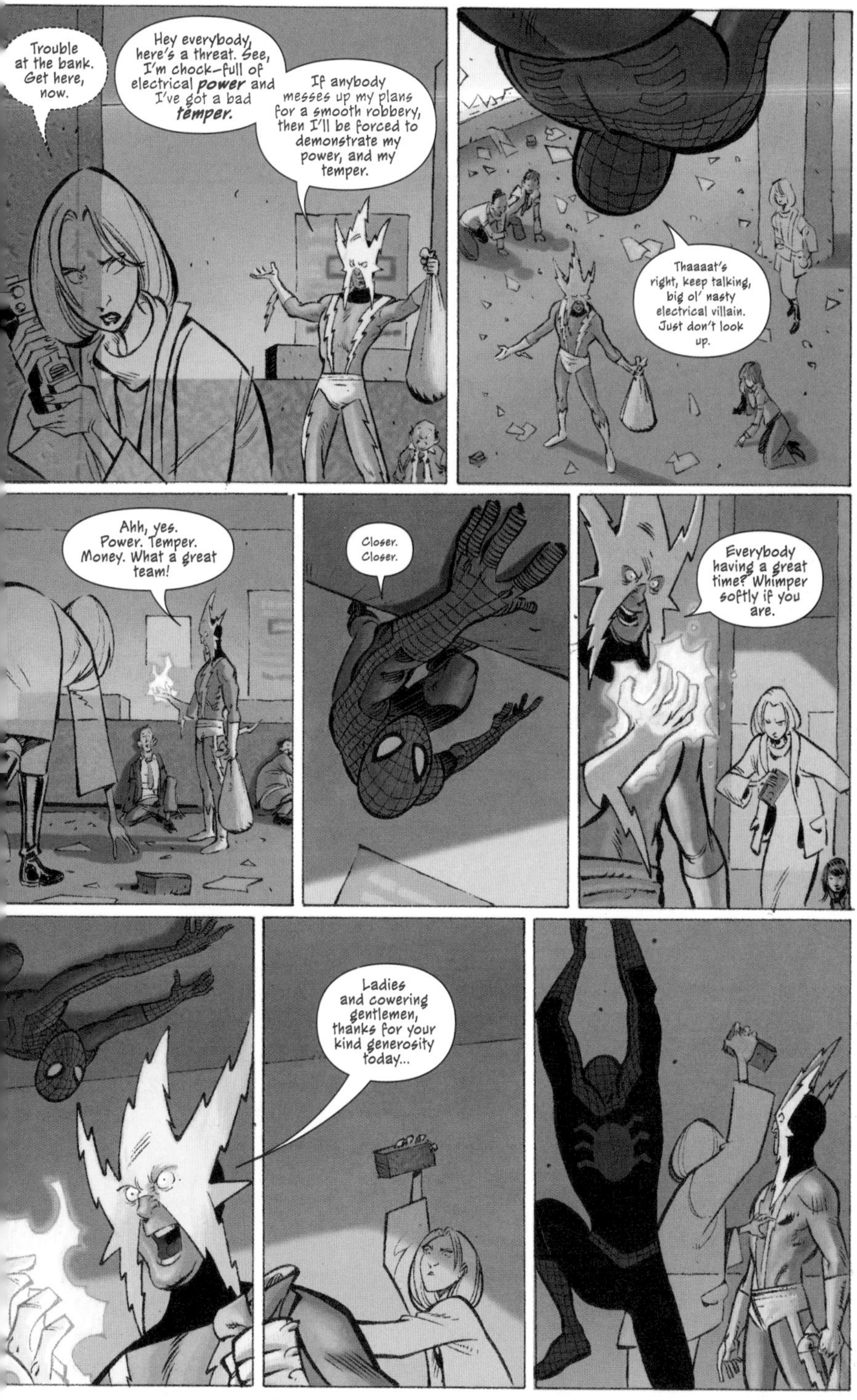
Trouble at the bank. Get here, now.
Hey everybody, here's a threat. See, I'm chock-full of electrical **power** and I've got a bad ***temper.***
If anybody messes up my plans for a smooth robbery, then I'll be forced to demonstrate my power, and my temper.
Thaaaat's right, keep talking, big ol' nasty electrical villain. Just don't look up.
Ahh, yes. Power. Temper. Money. What a great team!
Closer. Closer.
Everybody having a great time? Whimper softly if you are.
Ladies and cowering gentlemen, thanks for your kind generosity today...

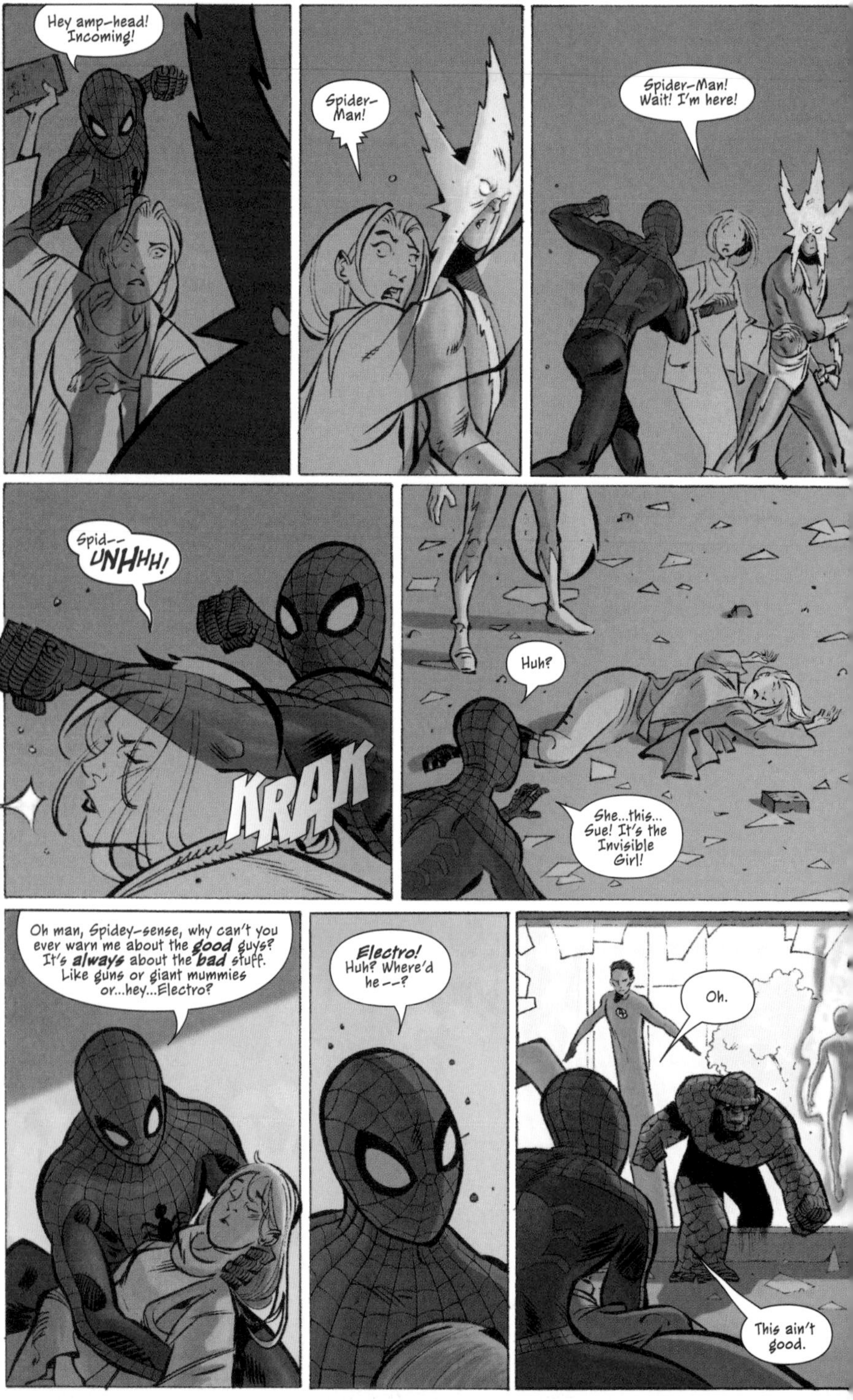
Hey amp-head! Incoming!
Spider-Man!
Spider-Man! Wait! I'm here!
Spid-- UNHHH!
KRAK
Huh?
She...this... Sue! It's the Invisible Girl!
Oh man, Spidey-sense, why can't you ever warn me about the **good** guys? It's **always** about the **bad** stuff. Like guns or giant mummies or...hey...Electro?
Electro! Huh? Where'd he --?
Oh.
This ain't good.

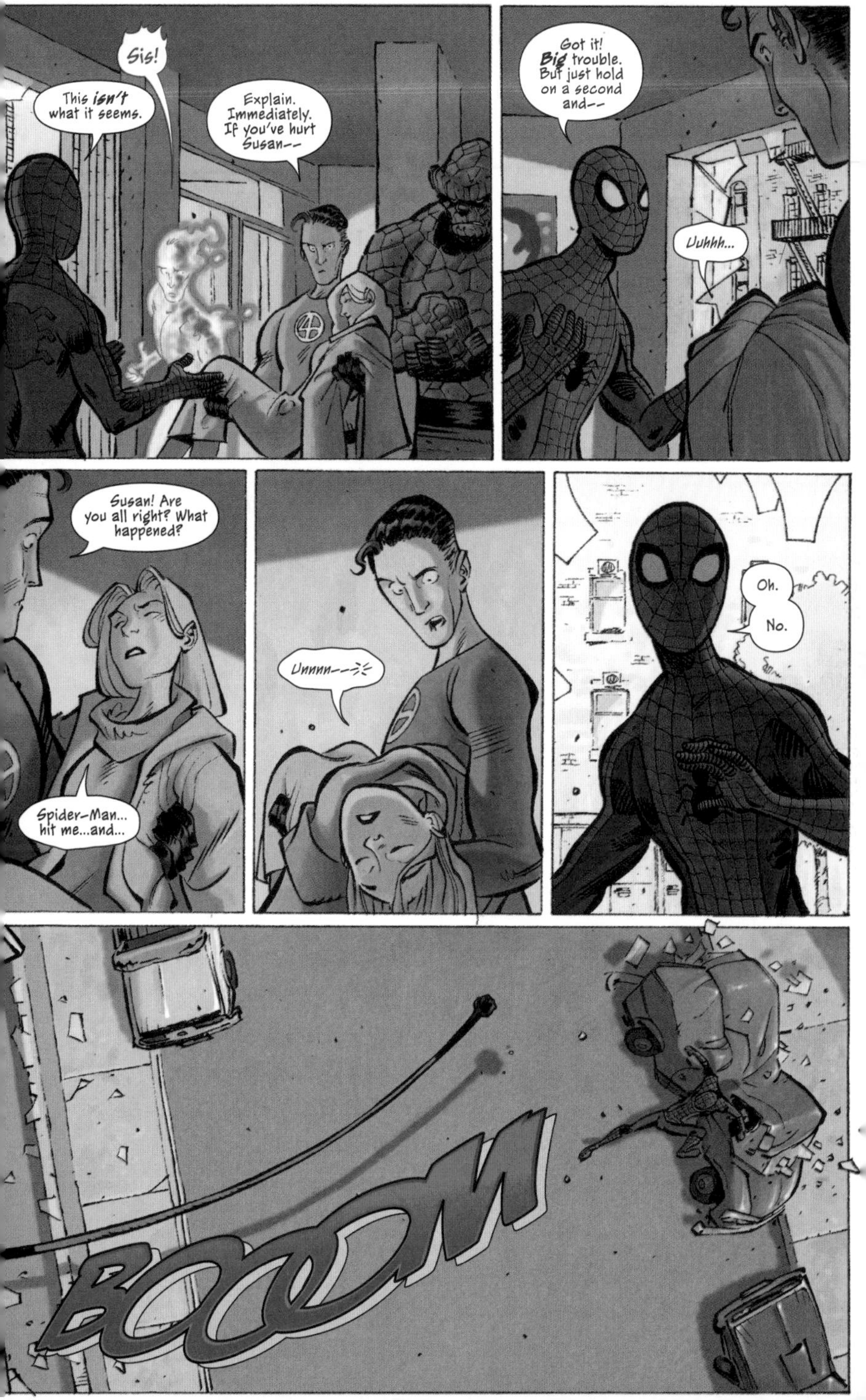
This isn't what it seems.
Sis!
Explain. Immediately. If you've hurt Susan--
Got it! Big trouble. But just hold on a second and--
Uuhhh...
Susan! Are you all right? What happened?
Spider-Man... hit me...and...
Unnnn--
Oh.
No.
BOOOM

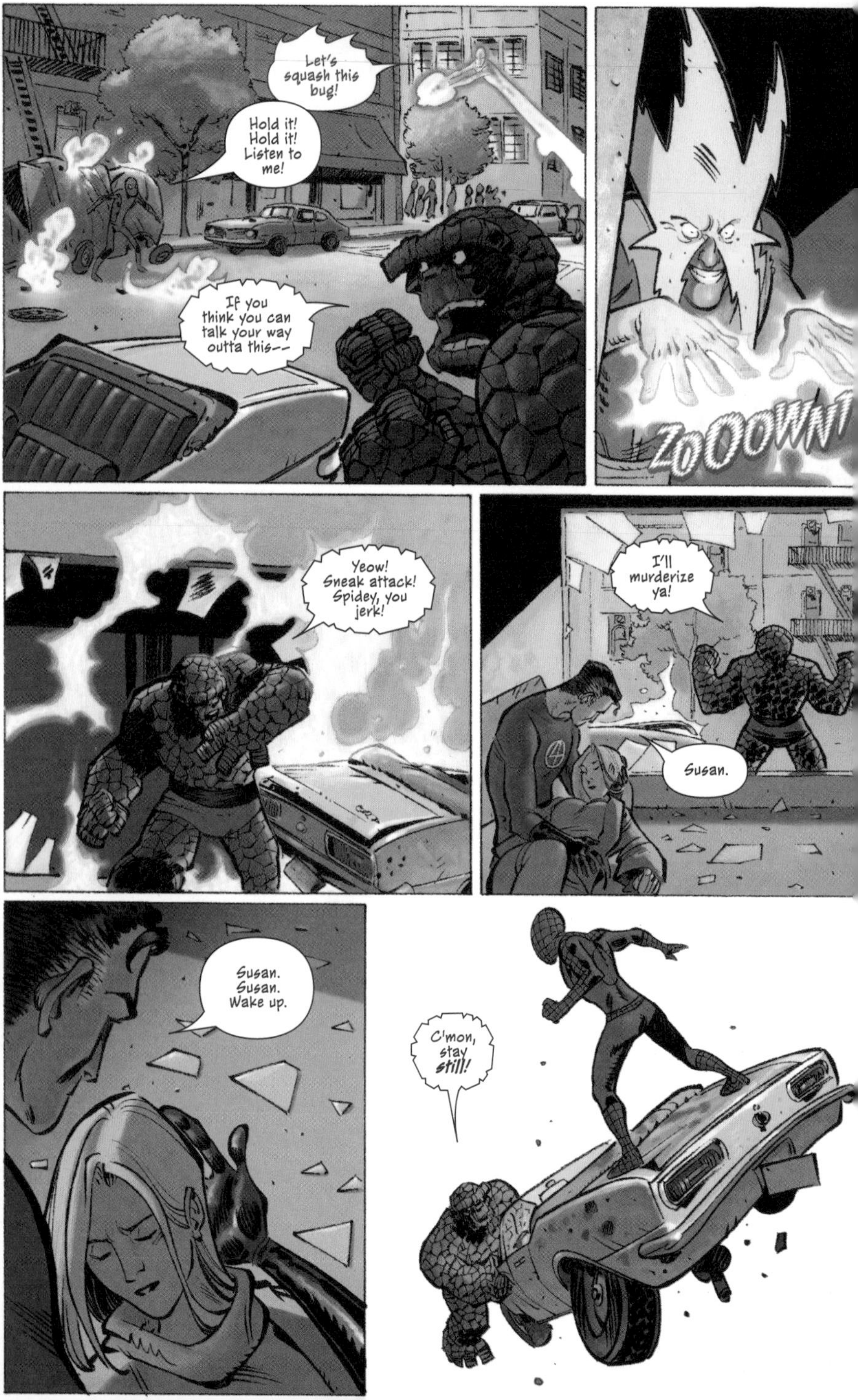
Let's squash this bug!
Hold it! Hold it! Listen to me!
If you think you can talk your way outta this--
ZOOOWN!
Yeow! Sneak attack! Spidey, you jerk!
I'll murderize ya!
Susan.
Susan. Susan. Wake up.
C'mon, stay still!

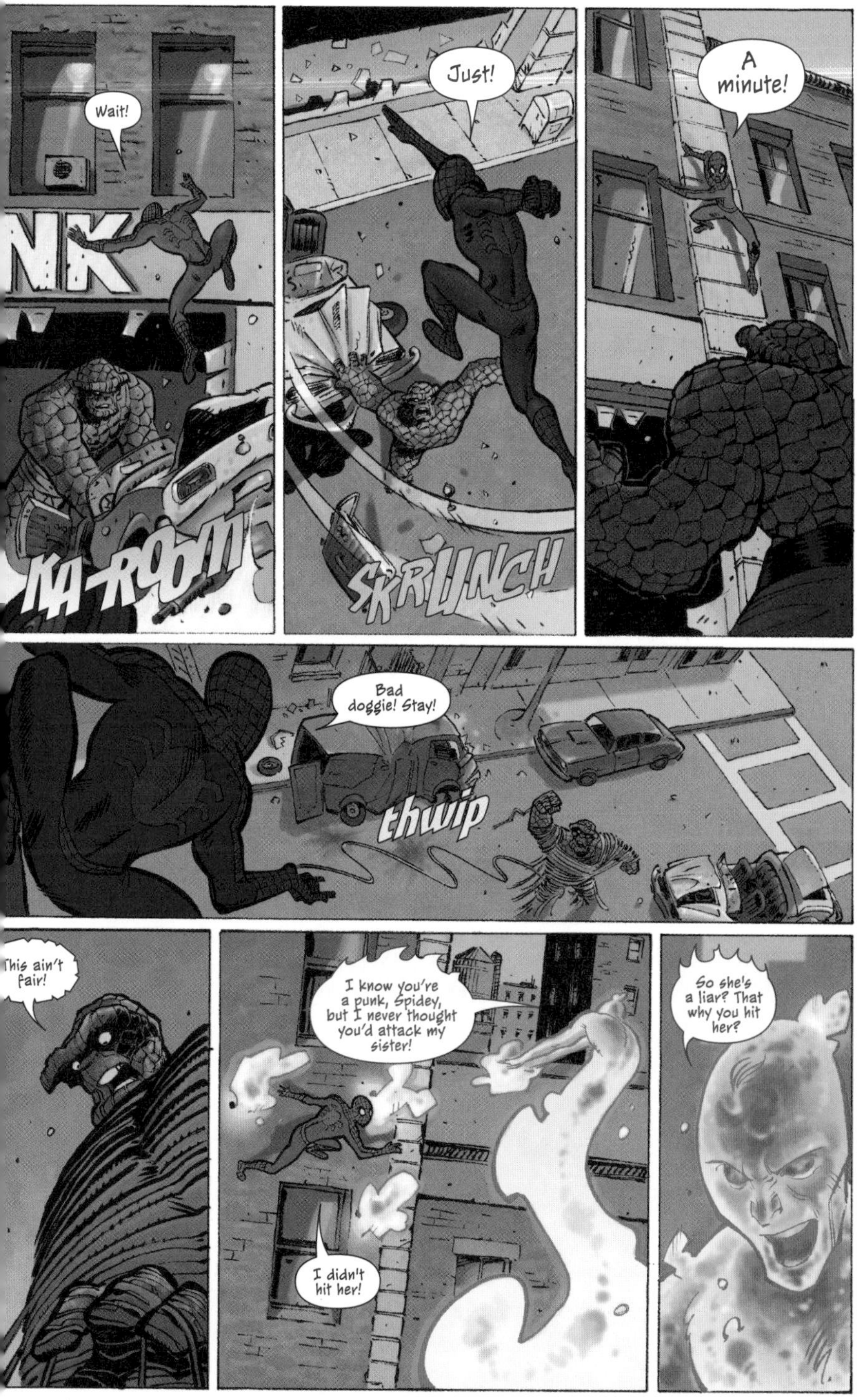
Wait!
KA-ROOM
Just!
SKRUNCH
A minute!
Bad doggie! Stay!
thwip
This ain't fair!
I know you're a punk, Spidey, but I never thought you'd attack my sister!
I didn't hit her!
So she's a liar? That why you hit her?

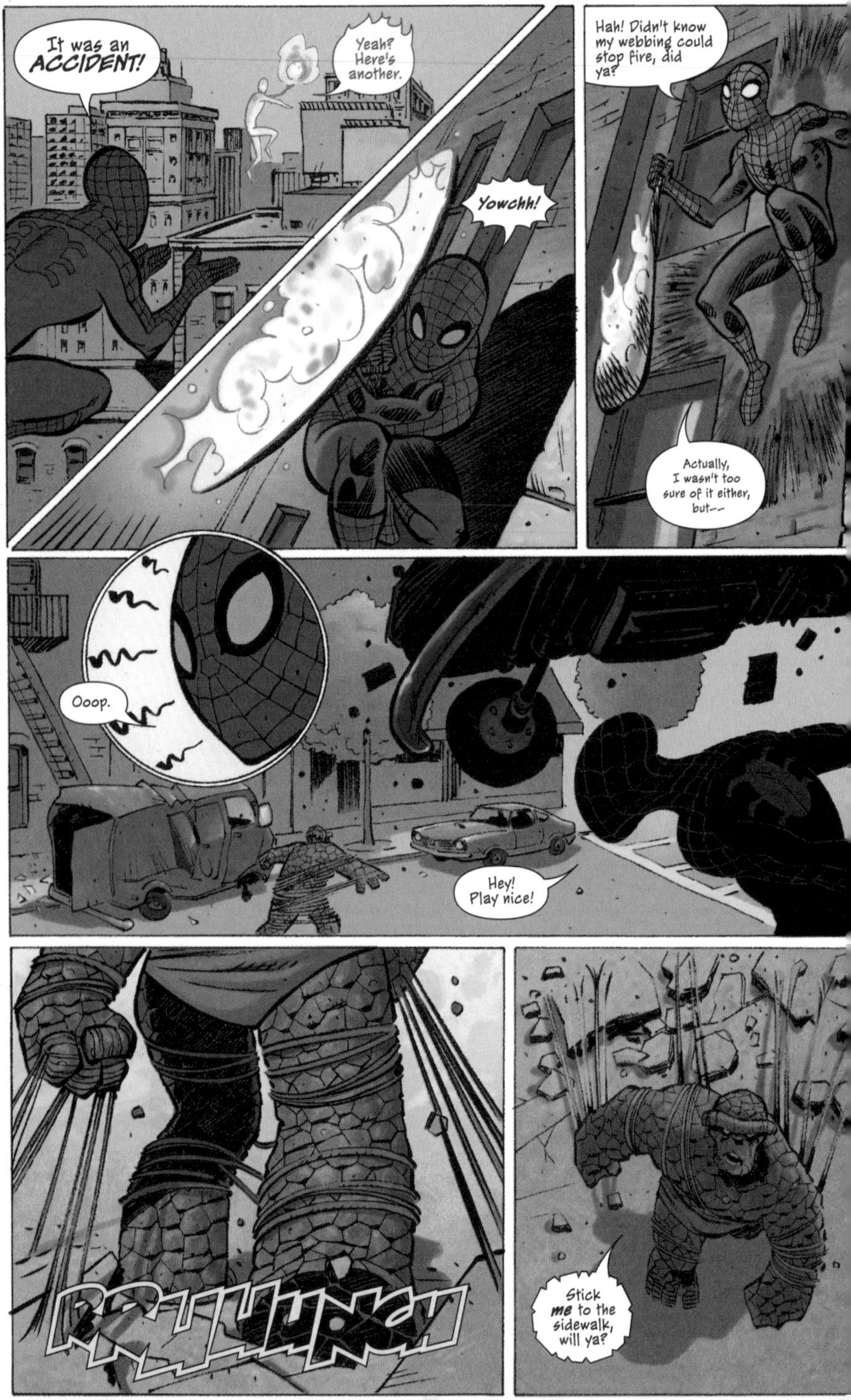

It was an ACCIDENT!
Yeah? Here's another.
Yowchh!
Hah! Didn't know my webbing could stop fire, did ya?
Actually, I wasn't too sure of it either, but--
Ooop.
Hey! Play nice!
Stick me to the sidewalk, will ya?

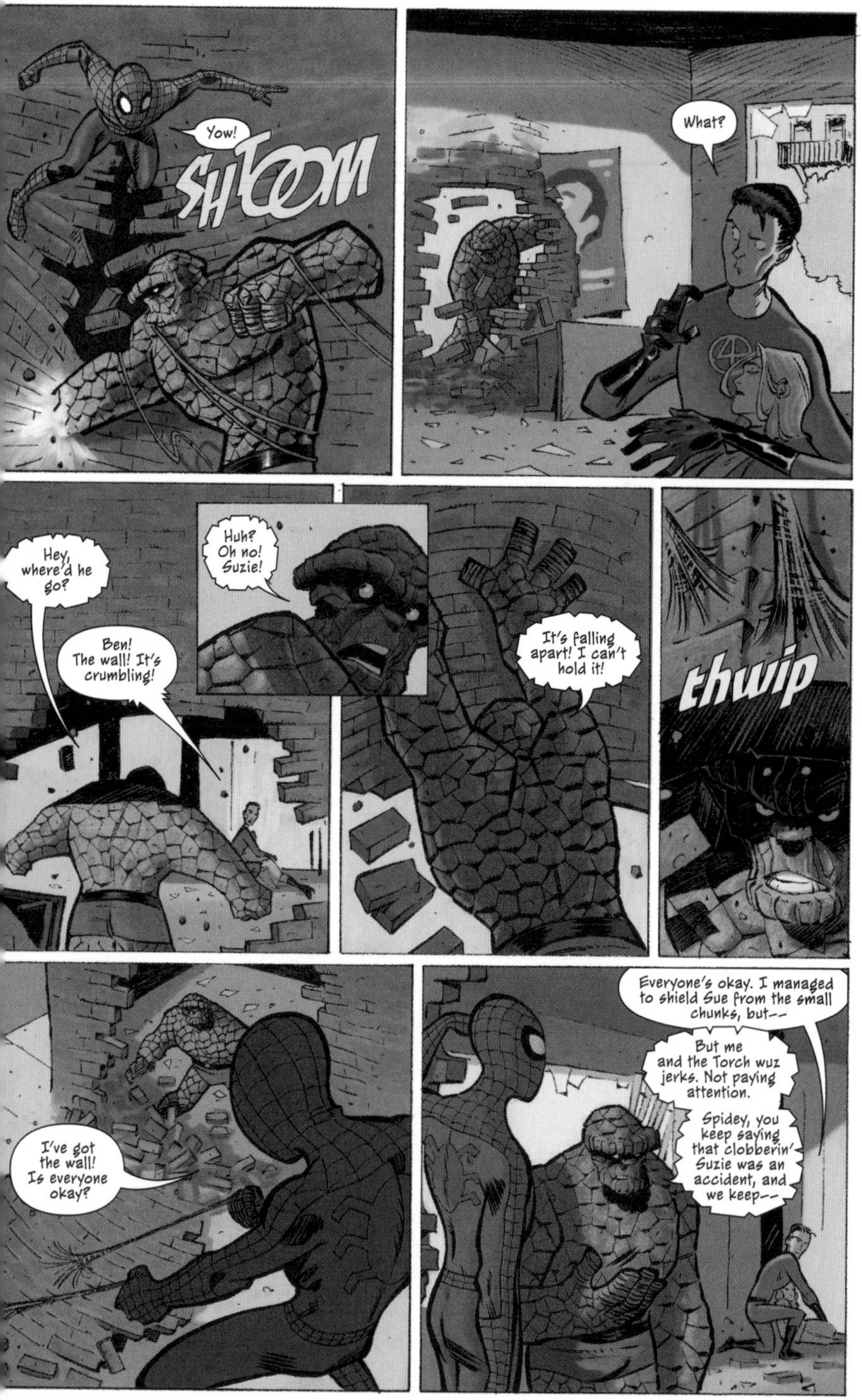

Yow!
SHTOOM
What?
Hey, where'd he go?
Ben! The wall! It's crumbling!
Huh? Oh no! Suzie!
It's falling apart! I can't hold it!
thwip
I've got the wall! Is everyone okay?
Everyone's okay. I managed to shield Sue from the small chunks, but--
But me and the Torch wuz jerks. Not paying attention.
Spidey, you keep saying that clobberin' Suzie was an accident, and we keep--

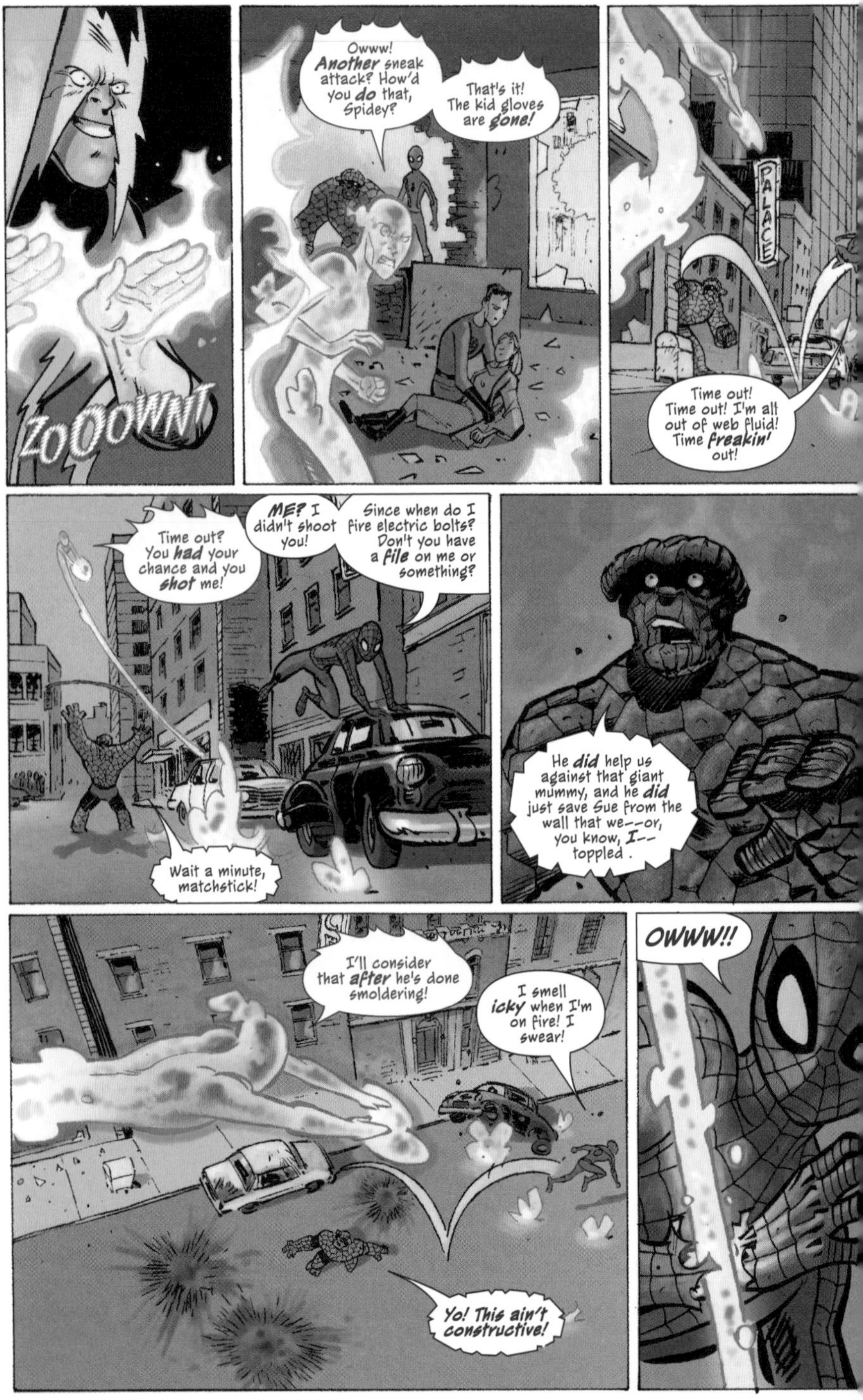
ZOOOWNT
Owww! Another sneak attack? How'd you do that, Spidey?
That's it! The kid gloves are gone!
PALACE
Time out! Time out! I'm all out of web fluid! Time freakin' out!
Time out? You had your chance and you shot me!
ME? I didn't shoot you!
Since when do I fire electric bolts? Don't you have a file on me or something?
Wait a minute, matchstick!
He did help us against that giant mummy, and he did just save Sue from the wall that we--or, you know, I-- toppled.
I'll consider that after he's done smoldering!
I smell icky when I'm on fire! I swear!
Yo! This ain't constructive!
OWWW!!

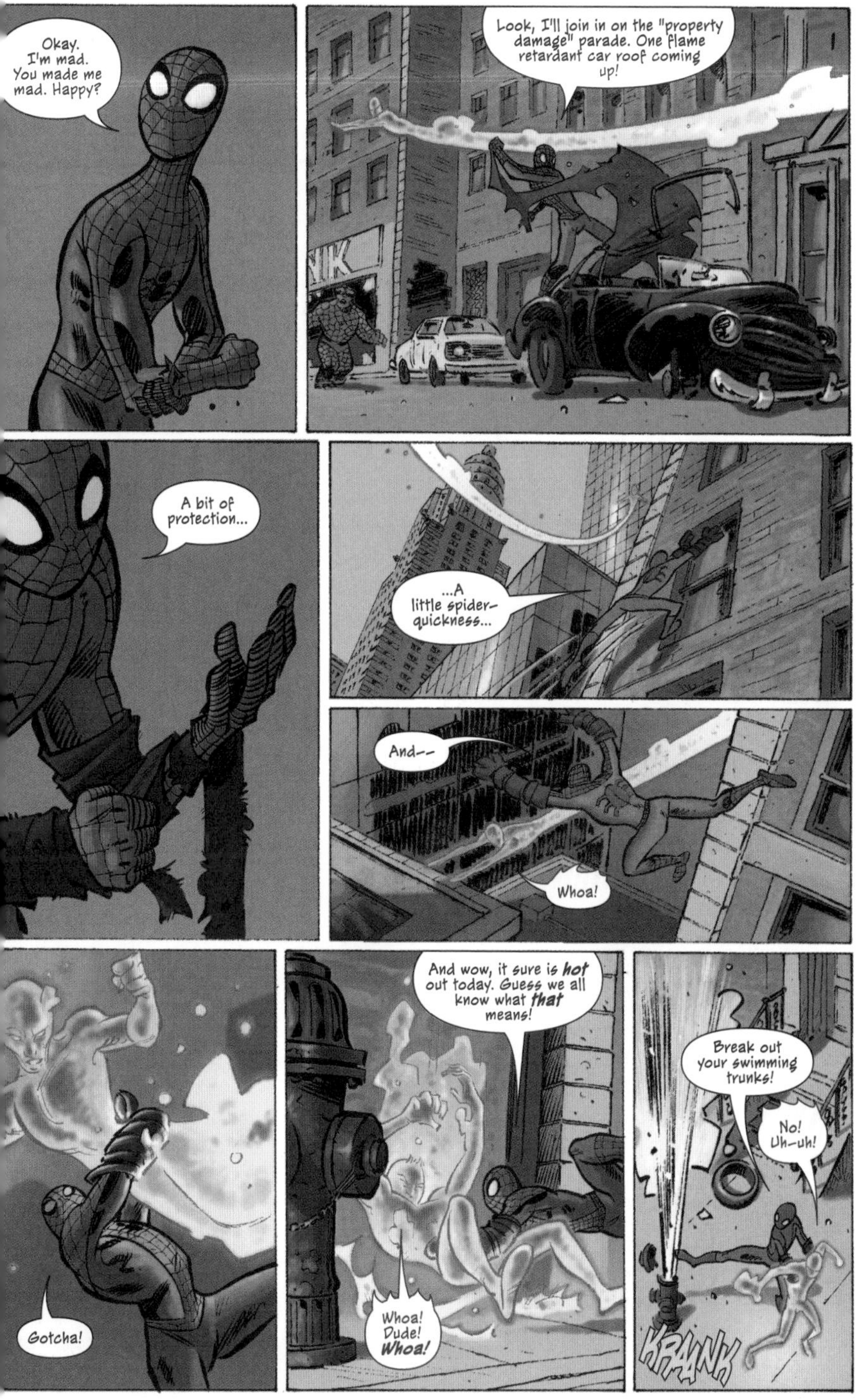

Okay. I'm mad. You made me mad. Happy?
Look, I'll join in on the "property damage" parade. One flame retardant car roof coming up!
A bit of protection...
...A little spider-quickness...
And--
Whoa!
Gotcha!
And wow, it sure is **hot** out today. Guess we all know what **that** means!
Whoa! Dude! **Whoa!**
Break out your swimming trunks!
No! Uh-uh!
KRANK

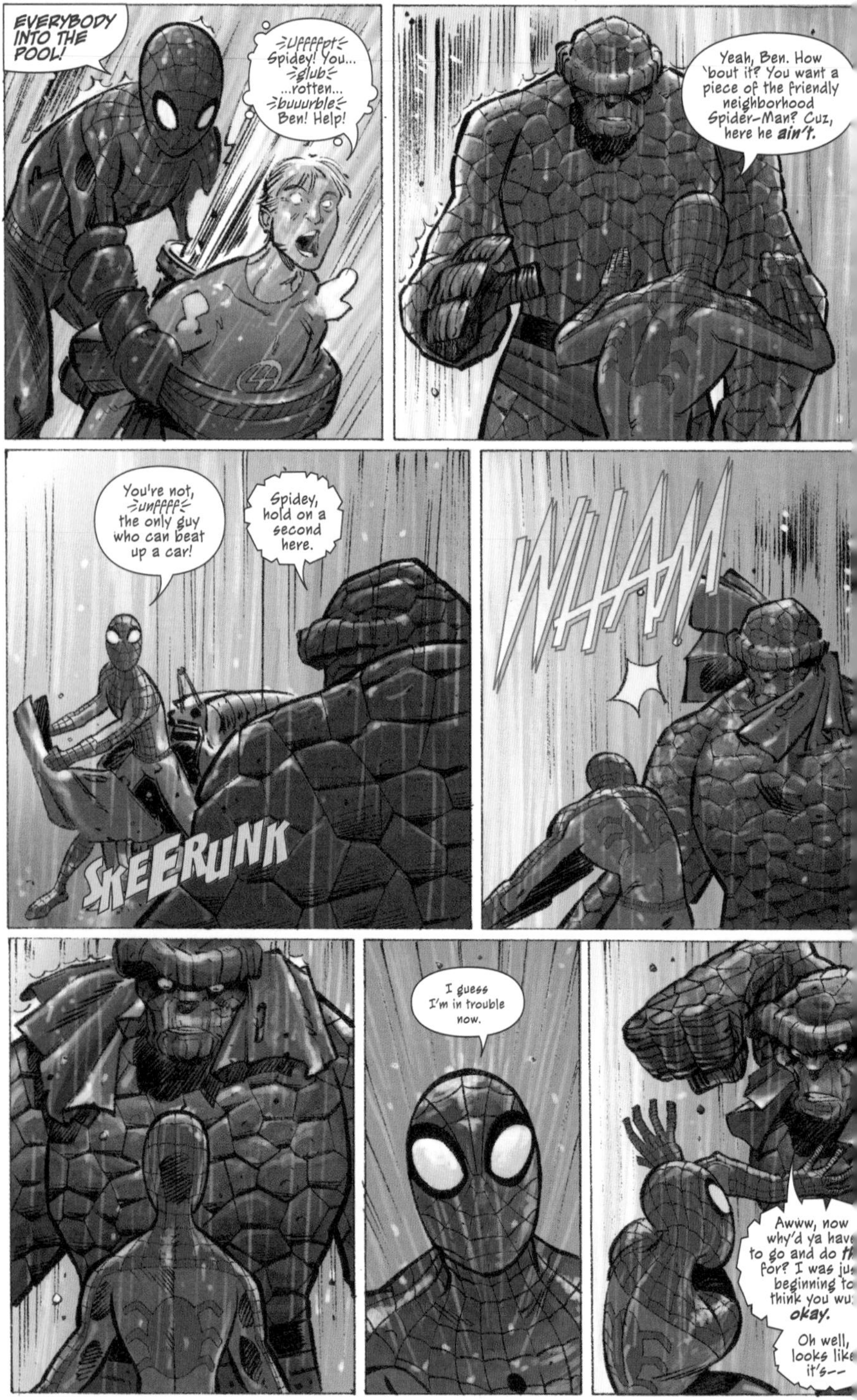

EVERYBODY INTO THE POOL!
Uffffpt Spidey! You... glub ...rotten... buuurble Ben! Help!
Yeah, Ben. How 'bout it? You want a piece of the friendly neighborhood Spider-Man? Cuz, here he ain't.
You're not, unffff the only guy who can beat up a car!
Spidey, hold on a second here.
SKEERUNK
WHAM
I guess I'm in trouble now.
Awww, now why'd ya have to go and do th for? I was jus beginning to think you wu okay.
Oh well, looks like it's--

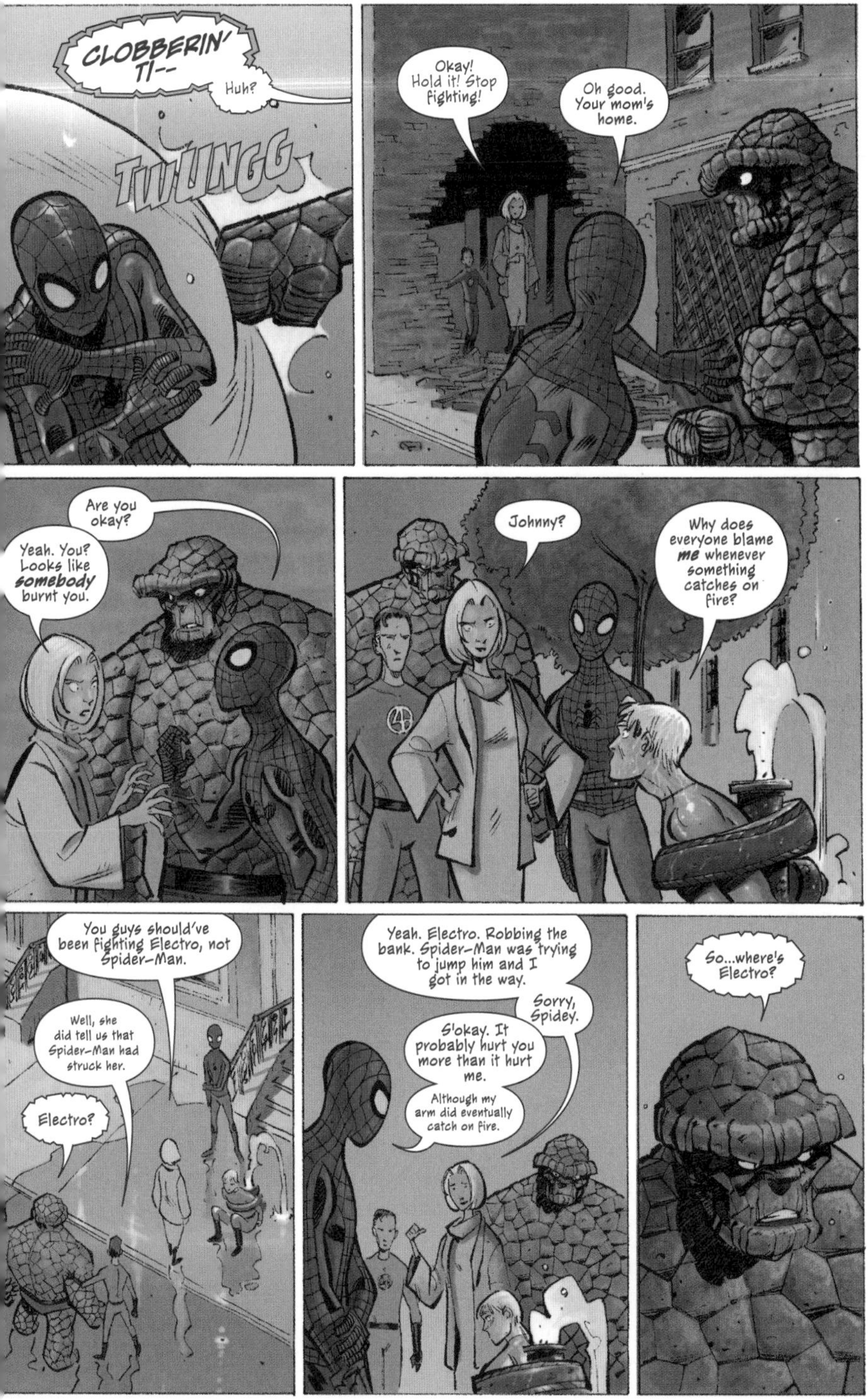
CLOBBERIN' TI--
Huh?
TWUNGG
Okay! Hold it! Stop fighting!
Oh good. Your mom's home.
Are you okay?
Yeah. You? Looks like **somebody** burnt you.
Johnny?
Why does everyone blame **me** whenever something catches on fire?
You guys should've been fighting Electro, not Spider-Man.
Well, she did tell us that Spider-Man had struck her.
Electro?
Yeah. Electro. Robbing the bank. Spider-Man was trying to jump him and I got in the way.
Sorry, Spidey.
S'okay. It probably hurt you more than it hurt me.
Although my arm did eventually catch on fire.
So...where's Electro?

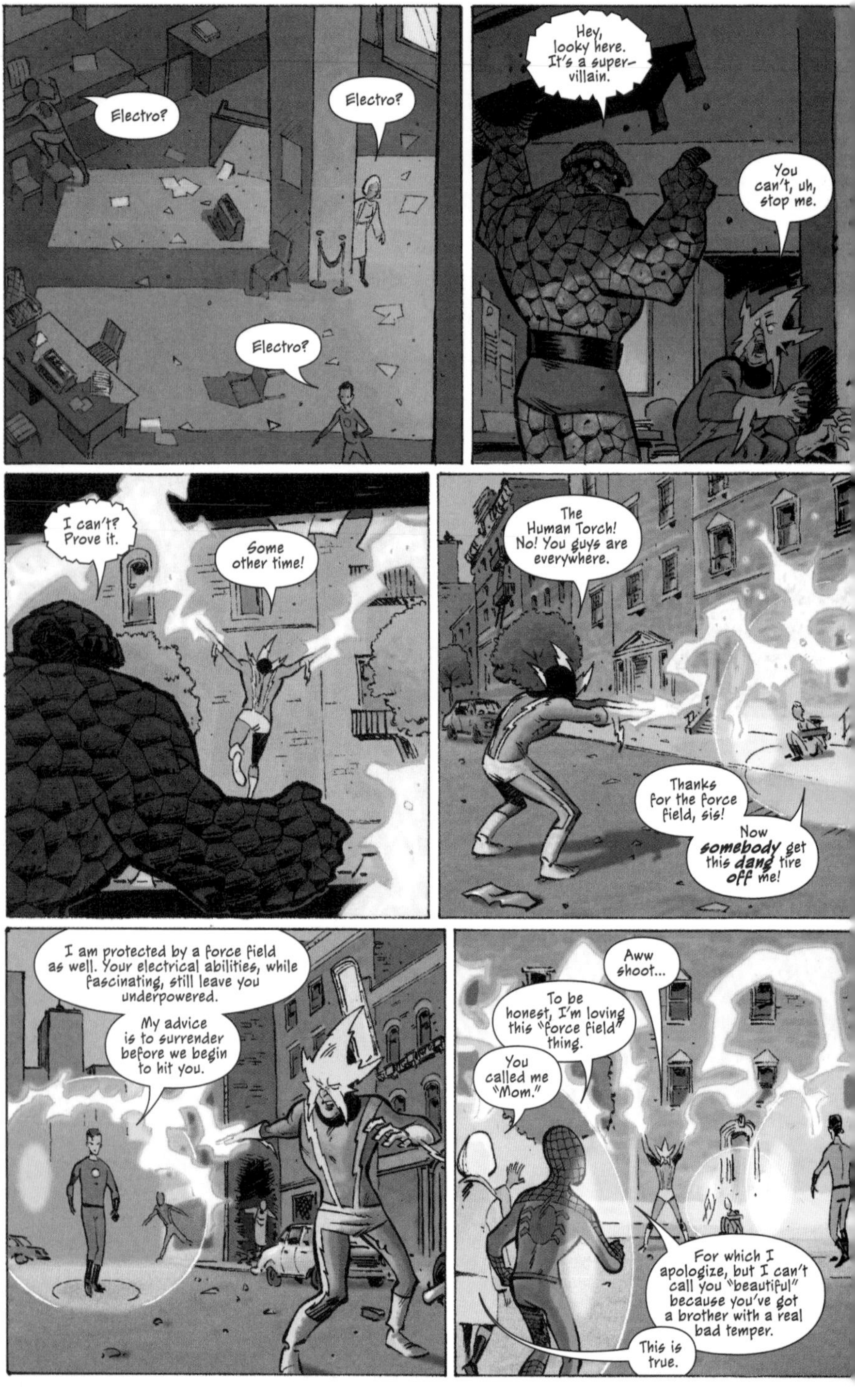
Electro?
Electro?
Electro?
Hey, looky here. It's a super-villain.
You can't, uh, stop me.
I can't? Prove it.
Some other time!
The Human Torch! No! You guys are everywhere.
Thanks for the force field, sis!
Now somebody get this dang tire off me!
I am protected by a force field as well. Your electrical abilities, while fascinating, still leave you underpowered.
My advice is to surrender before we begin to hit you.
Aww shoot...
To be honest, I'm loving this "force field" thing.
You called me "Mom."
For which I apologize, but I can't call you "beautiful" because you've got a brother with a real bad temper.
This is true.

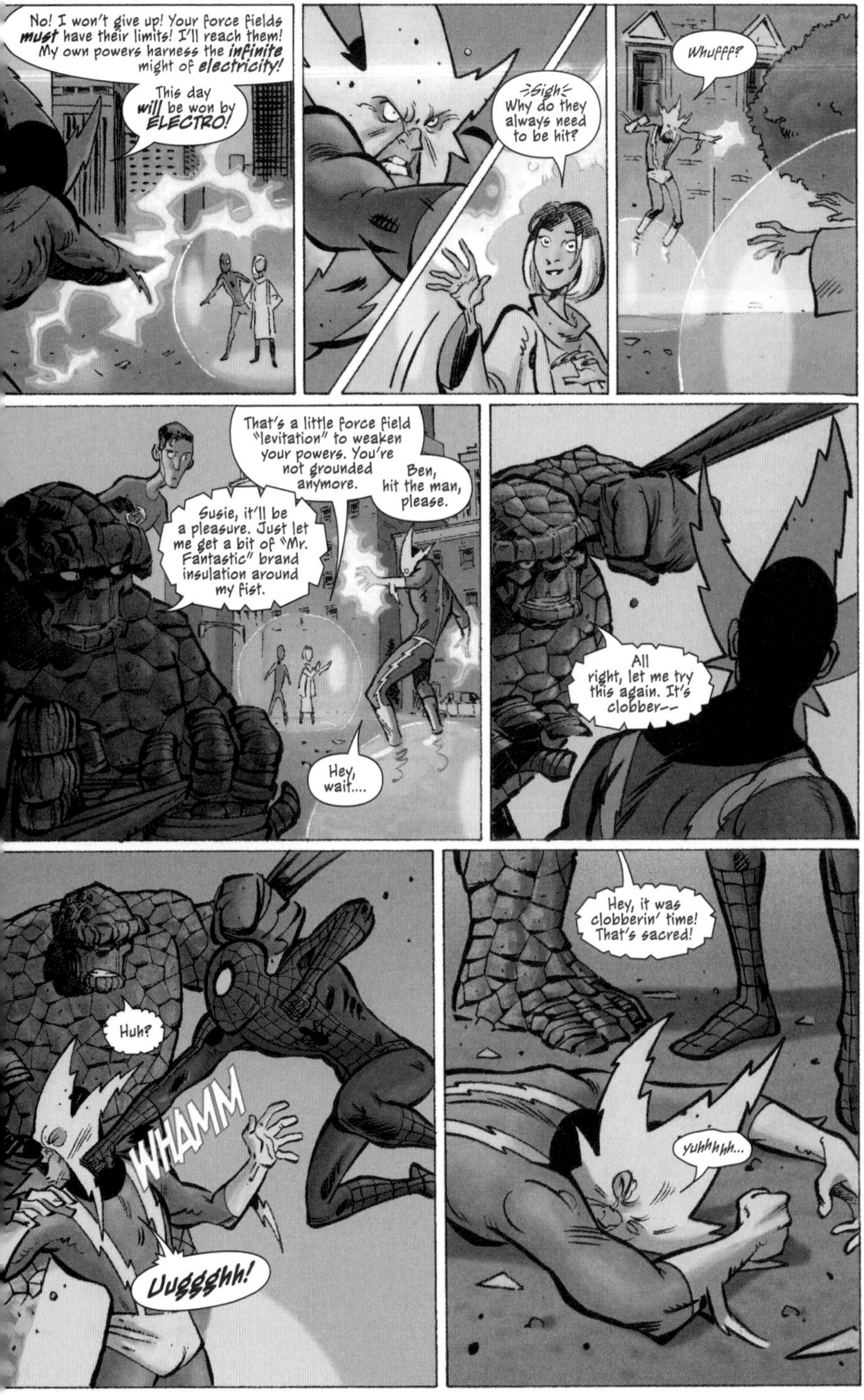
No! I won't give up! Your force fields must have their limits! I'll reach them! My own powers harness the infinite might of electricity!
This day will be won by ELECTRO!
Sigh
Why do they always need to be hit?
Whufff?
That's a little force field "levitation" to weaken your powers. You're not grounded anymore.
Ben, hit the man, please.
Susie, it'll be a pleasure. Just let me get a bit of "Mr. Fantastic" brand insulation around my fist.
Hey, wait....
All right, let me try this again. It's clobber--
Huh?
WHAMM
Uuggghh!
Hey, it was clobberin' time! That's sacred!
yuhhhhh...

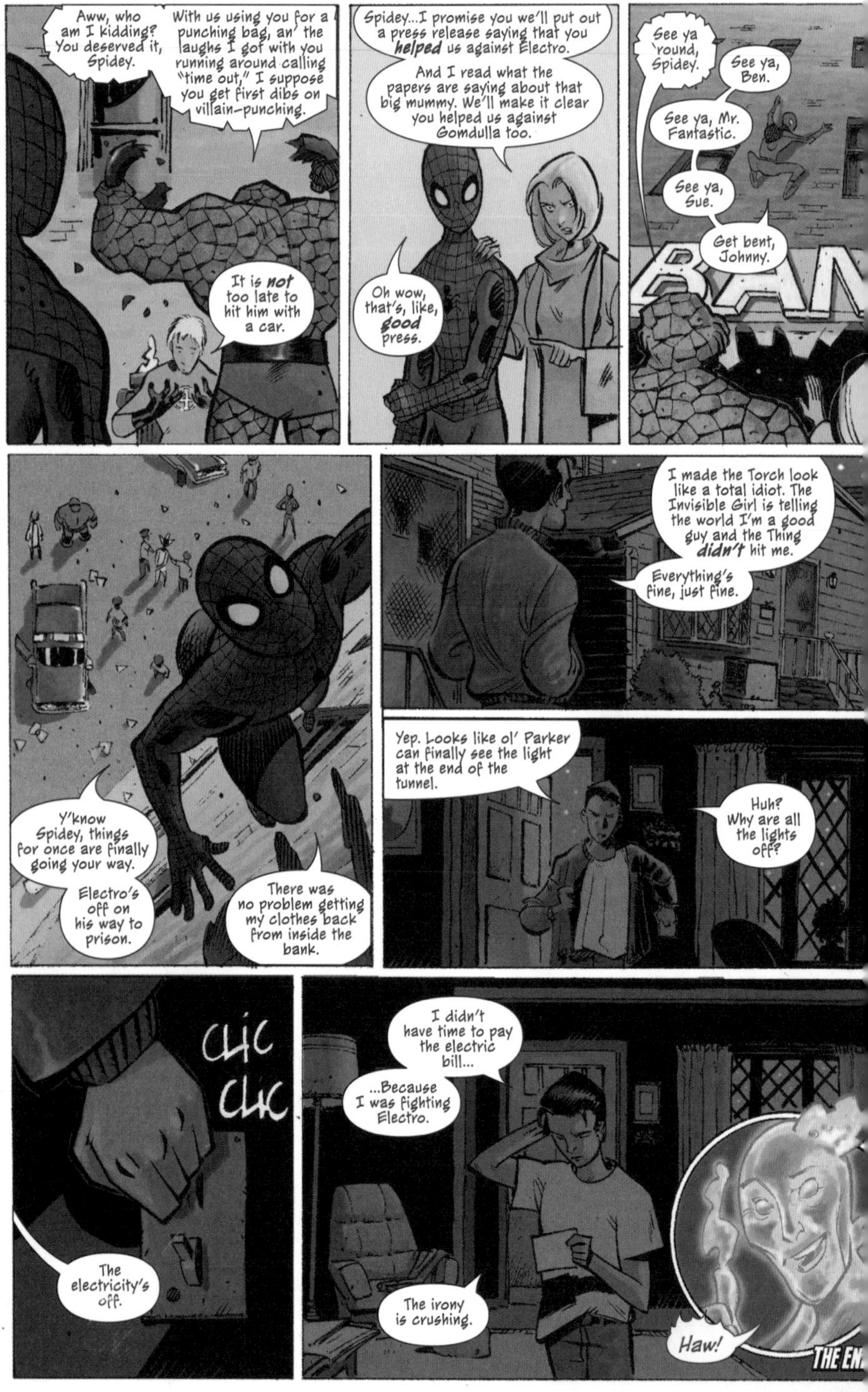

Aww, who am I kidding? You deserved it, Spidey.
With us using you for a punching bag, an' the laughs I got with you running around calling "time out," I suppose you get first dibs on villain-punching.
It is *not* too late to hit him with a car.
Spidey...I promise you we'll put out a press release saying that you *helped* us against Electro.
And I read what the papers are saying about that big mummy. We'll make it clear you helped us against Gomdulla too.
Oh wow, that's, like, *good* press.
See ya 'round, Spidey.
See ya, Ben.
See ya, Mr. Fantastic.
See ya, Sue.
Get bent, Johnny.
Y'know Spidey, things for once are finally going your way.
Electro's off on his way to prison.
There was no problem getting my clothes back from inside the bank.
I made the Torch look like a total idiot. The Invisible Girl is telling the world I'm a good guy and the Thing *didn't* hit me.
Everything's fine, just fine.
Yep. Looks like ol' Parker can finally see the light at the end of the tunnel.
Huh? Why are all the lights off?
CLIC
CLIC
The electricity's off.
I didn't have time to pay the electric bill...
...Because I was fighting Electro.
The irony is crushing.
Haw!

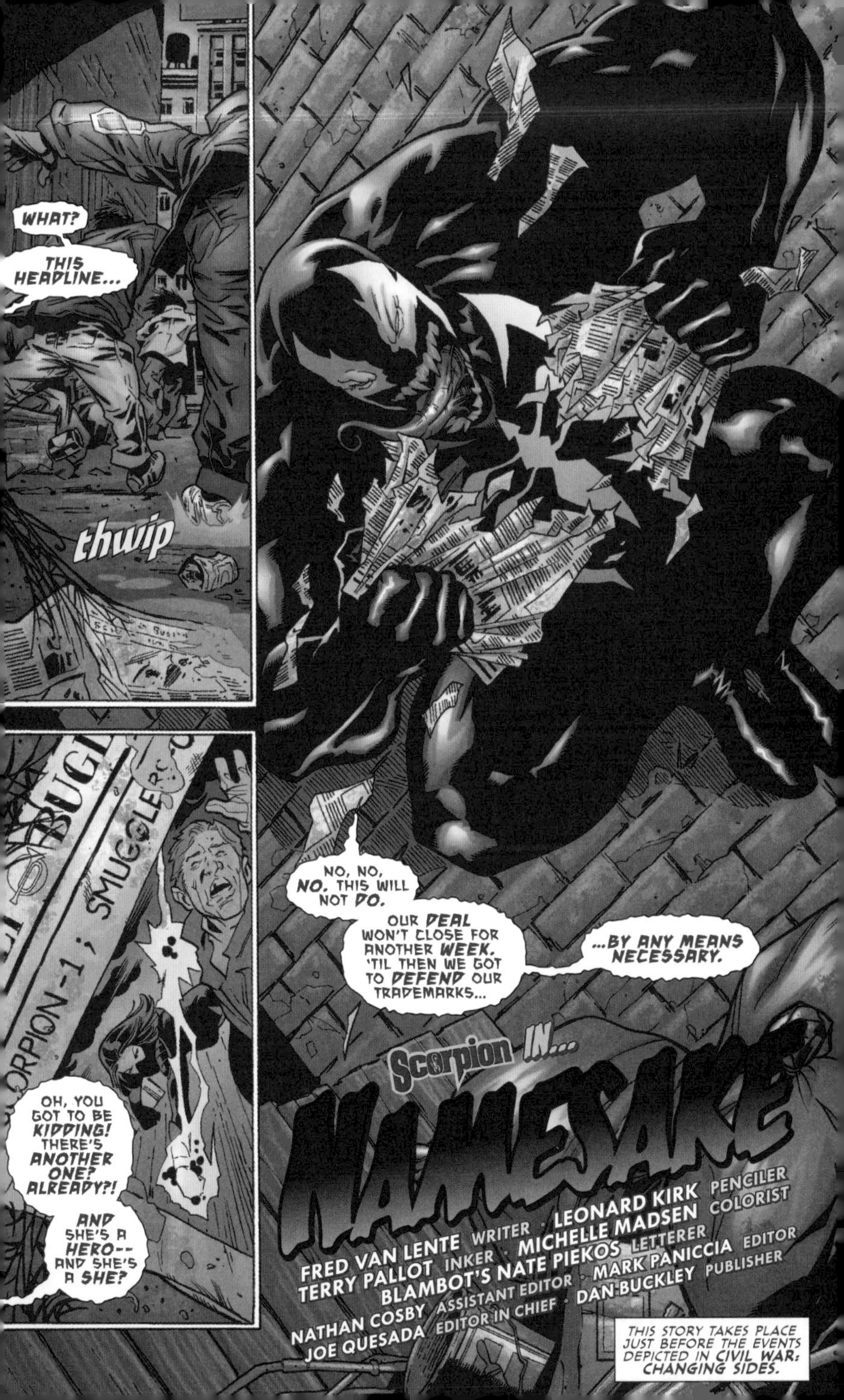
WHAT?
THIS HEADLINE...
thwip
NO, NO, NO. THIS WILL NOT DO.
OUR DEAL WON'T CLOSE FOR ANOTHER WEEK. 'TIL THEN WE GOT TO DEFEND OUR TRADEMARKS...
...BY ANY MEANS NECESSARY.
BUGL
SCORPION-1; SMUGGLER C
OH, YOU GOT TO BE KIDDING! THERE'S ANOTHER ONE? ALREADY?!
AND SHE'S A HERO-- AND SHE'S A SHE?
Scorpion IN...
NAMESAKE
FRED VAN LENTE WRITER · LEONARD KIRK PENCILER
TERRY PALLOT INKER · MICHELLE MADSEN COLORIST
BLAMBOT'S NATE PIEKOS LETTERER
NATHAN COSBY ASSISTANT EDITOR · MARK PANICCIA EDITOR
JOE QUESADA EDITOR IN CHIEF · DAN BUCKLEY PUBLISHER
THIS STORY TAKES PLACE JUST BEFORE THE EVENTS DEPICTED IN CIVIL WAR: CHANGING SIDES.

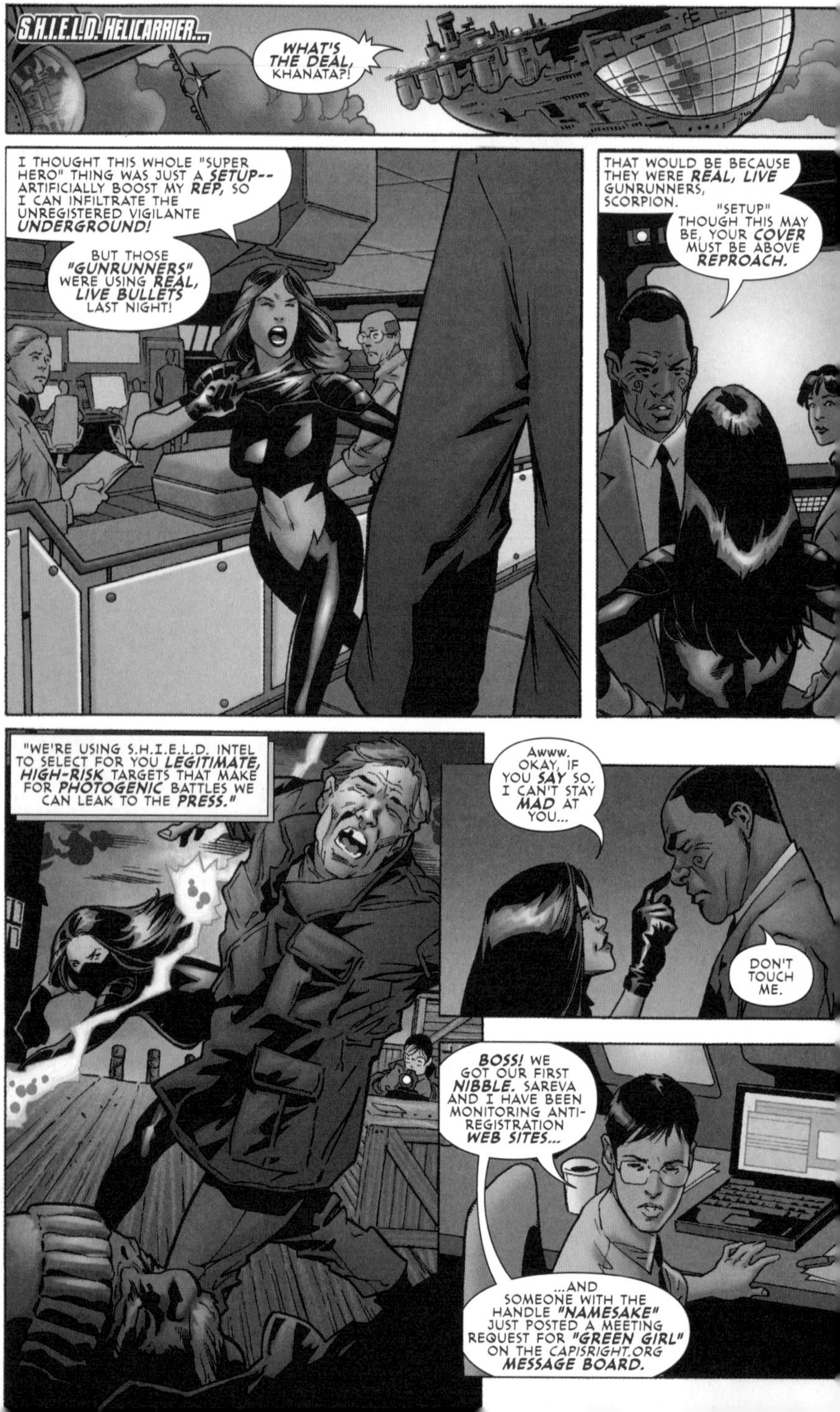
S.H.I.E.L.D. HELICARRIER...
WHAT'S THE DEAL, KHANATA?!
I THOUGHT THIS WHOLE "SUPER HERO" THING WAS JUST A SETUP-- ARTIFICIALLY BOOST MY REP, SO I CAN INFILTRATE THE UNREGISTERED VIGILANTE UNDERGROUND!
BUT THOSE "GUNRUNNERS" WERE USING REAL, LIVE BULLETS LAST NIGHT!
THAT WOULD BE BECAUSE THEY WERE REAL, LIVE GUNRUNNERS, SCORPION.
"SETUP" THOUGH THIS MAY BE, YOUR COVER MUST BE ABOVE REPROACH.
"WE'RE USING S.H.I.E.L.D. INTEL TO SELECT FOR YOU LEGITIMATE, HIGH-RISK TARGETS THAT MAKE FOR PHOTOGENIC BATTLES WE CAN LEAK TO THE PRESS."
Awww. OKAY, IF YOU SAY SO. I CAN'T STAY MAD AT YOU...
DON'T TOUCH ME.
BOSS! WE GOT OUR FIRST NIBBLE. SAREVA AND I HAVE BEEN MONITORING ANTI-REGISTRATION WEB SITES...
...AND SOMEONE WITH THE HANDLE "NAMESAKE" JUST POSTED A MEETING REQUEST FOR "GREEN GIRL" ON THE CAPISRIGHT.ORG MESSAGE BOARD.

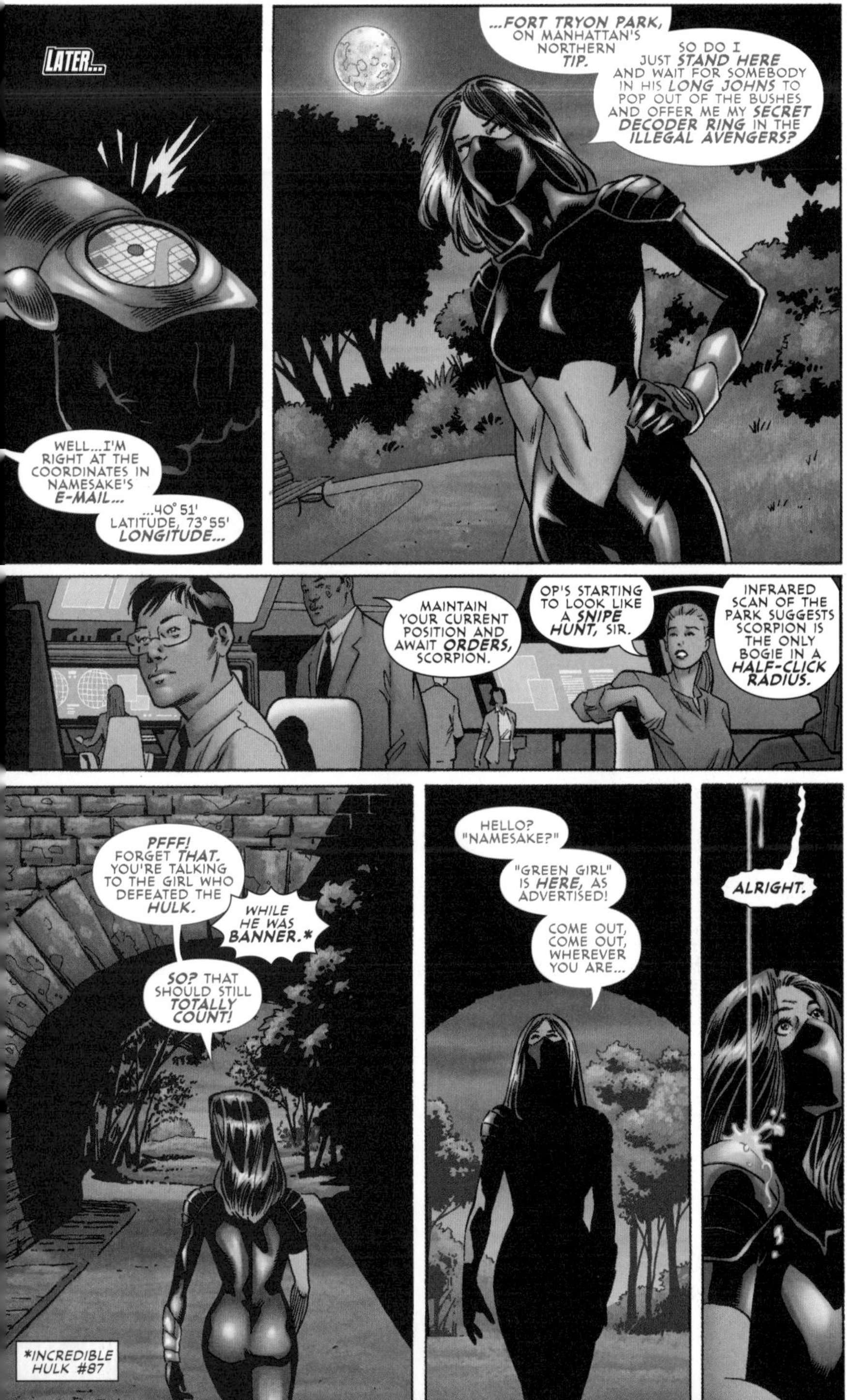
LATER...
WELL...I'M RIGHT AT THE COORDINATES IN NAMESAKE'S E-MAIL...
...40° 51' LATITUDE, 73°55' LONGITUDE...
...FORT TRYON PARK, ON MANHATTAN'S NORTHERN TIP.
SO DO I JUST STAND HERE AND WAIT FOR SOMEBODY IN HIS LONG JOHNS TO POP OUT OF THE BUSHES AND OFFER ME MY SECRET DECODER RING IN THE ILLEGAL AVENGERS?
MAINTAIN YOUR CURRENT POSITION AND AWAIT ORDERS, SCORPION.
OP'S STARTING TO LOOK LIKE A SNIPE HUNT, SIR.
INFRARED SCAN OF THE PARK SUGGESTS SCORPION IS THE ONLY BOGIE IN A HALF-CLICK RADIUS.
PFFF! FORGET THAT. YOU'RE TALKING TO THE GIRL WHO DEFEATED THE HULK.
WHILE HE WAS BANNER.*
SO? THAT SHOULD STILL TOTALLY COUNT!
*INCREDIBLE HULK #87
HELLO? "NAMESAKE?"
"GREEN GIRL" IS HERE, AS ADVERTISED!
COME OUT, COME OUT, WHEREVER YOU ARE...
ALRIGHT.

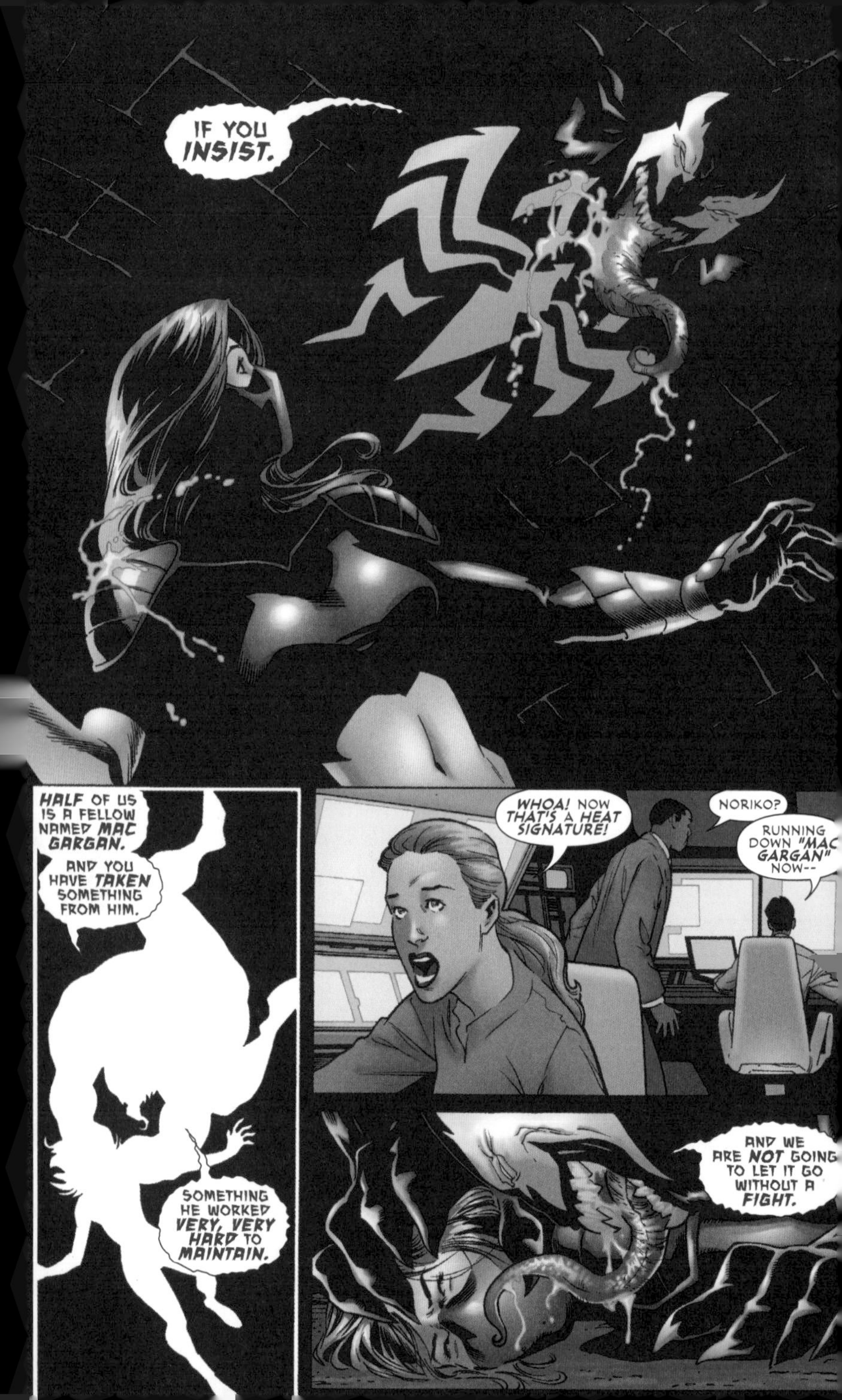
IF YOU INSIST.
HALF OF US IS A FELLOW NAMED MAC GARGAN.
AND YOU HAVE TAKEN SOMETHING FROM HIM.
WHOA! NOW THAT'S A HEAT SIGNATURE!
NORIKO?
RUNNING DOWN "MAC GARGAN" NOW--
SOMETHING HE WORKED VERY, VERY HARD TO MAINTAIN.
AND WE ARE NOT GOING TO LET IT GO WITHOUT A FIGHT.

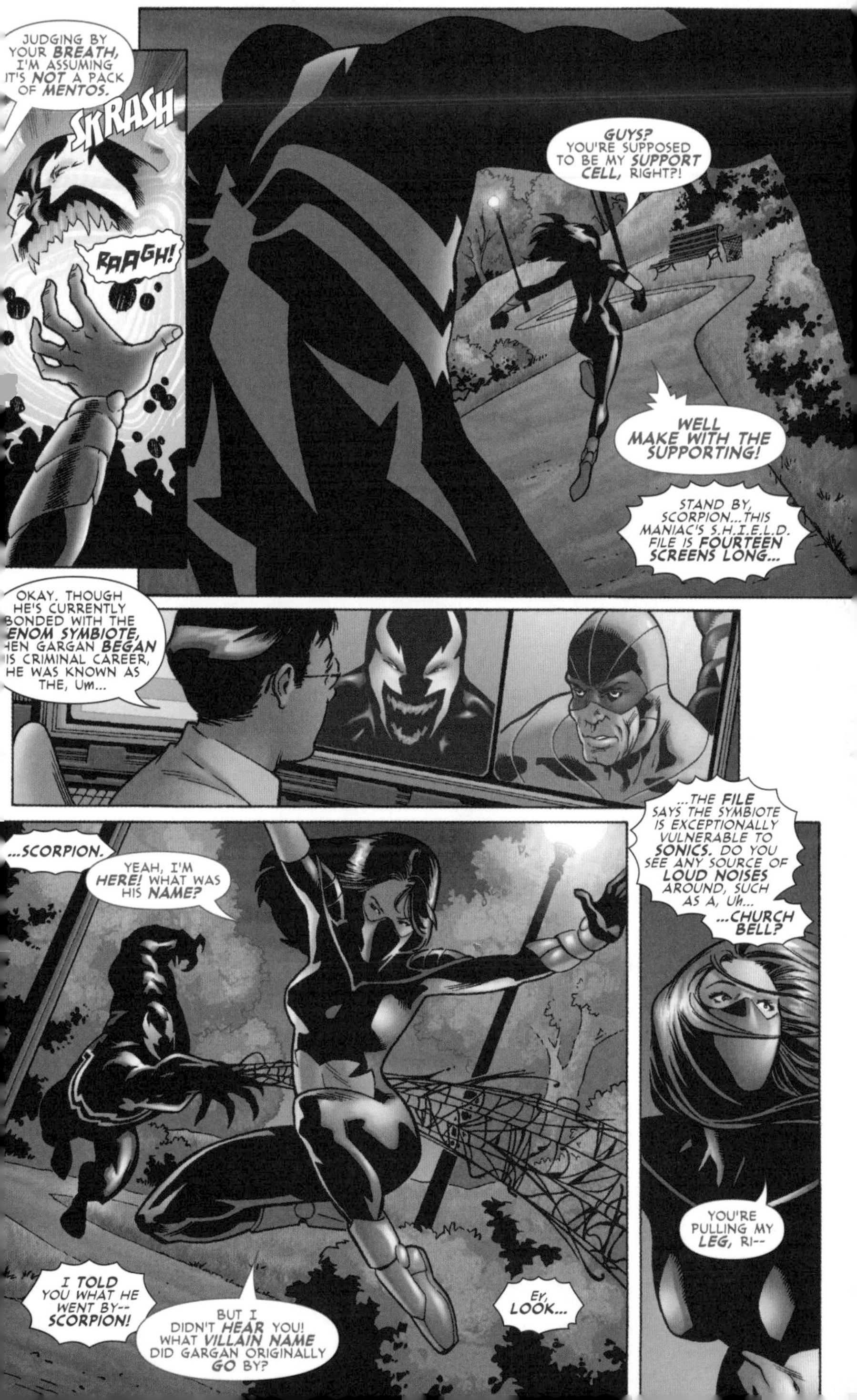

JUDGING BY YOUR BREATH, I'M ASSUMING IT'S NOT A PACK OF MENTOS.
SKRASH
RAAGH!
GUYS? YOU'RE SUPPOSED TO BE MY SUPPORT CELL, RIGHT?!
WELL MAKE WITH THE SUPPORTING!
STAND BY, SCORPION...THIS MANIAC'S S.H.I.E.L.D. FILE IS FOURTEEN SCREENS LONG...
OKAY. THOUGH HE'S CURRENTLY BONDED WITH THE ENOM SYMBIOTE, HEN GARGAN BEGAN IS CRIMINAL CAREER, HE WAS KNOWN AS THE, UM...
...SCORPION.
YEAH, I'M HERE! WHAT WAS HIS NAME?
...THE FILE SAYS THE SYMBIOTE IS EXCEPTIONALLY VULNERABLE TO SONICS. DO YOU SEE ANY SOURCE OF LOUD NOISES AROUND, SUCH AS A, UH...
...CHURCH BELL?
YOU'RE PULLING MY LEG, RI--
I TOLD YOU WHAT HE WENT BY-- SCORPION!
BUT I DIDN'T HEAR YOU! WHAT VILLAIN NAME DID GARGAN ORIGINALLY GO BY?
ER, LOOK...

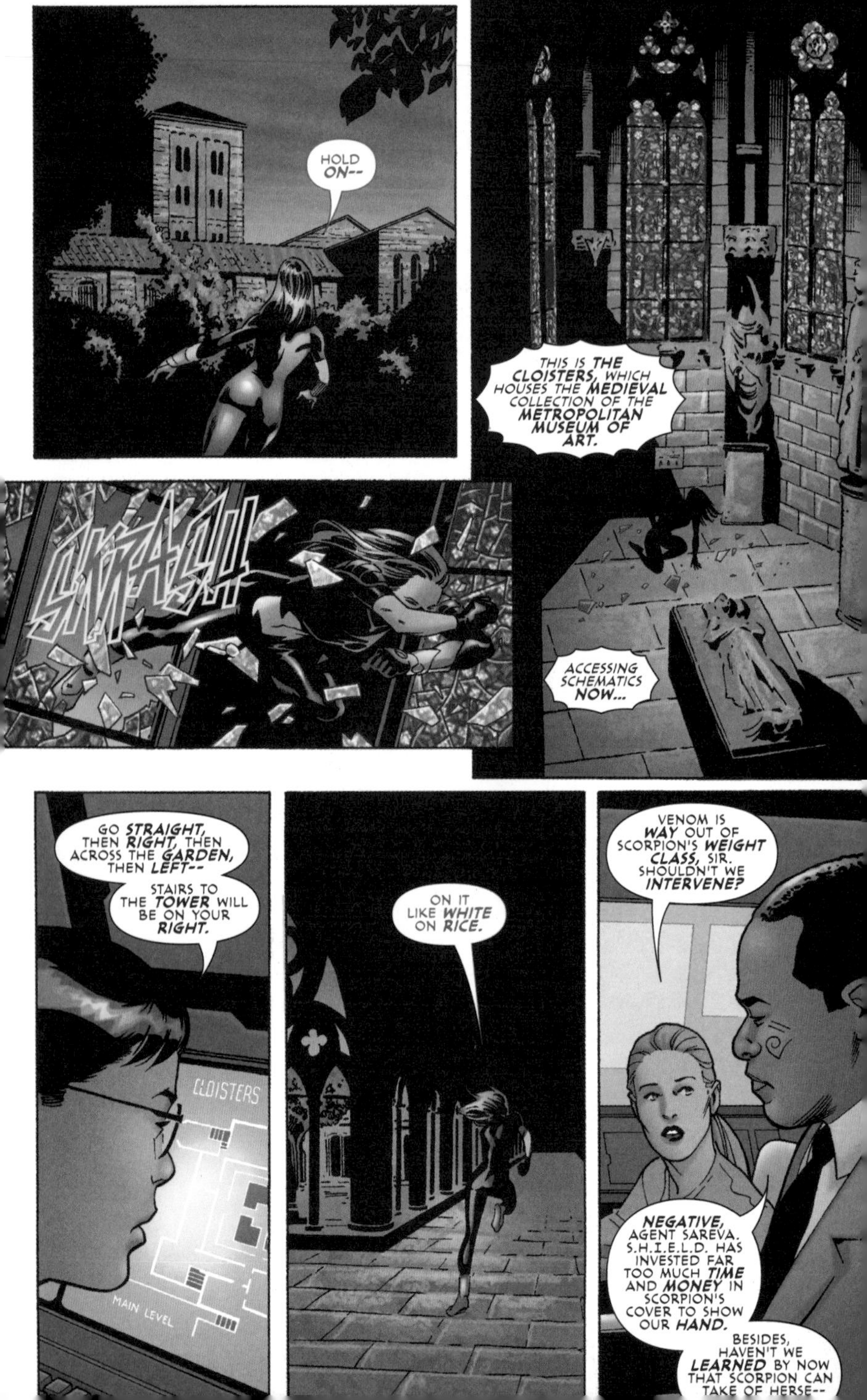
HOLD ON--
THIS IS THE CLOISTERS, WHICH HOUSES THE MEDIEVAL COLLECTION OF THE METROPOLITAN MUSEUM OF ART.
SKRASH!
ACCESSING SCHEMATICS NOW...
GO STRAIGHT, THEN RIGHT, THEN ACROSS THE GARDEN, THEN LEFT--
STAIRS TO THE TOWER WILL BE ON YOUR RIGHT.
CLOISTERS
MAIN LEVEL
ON IT LIKE WHITE ON RICE.
VENOM IS WAY OUT OF SCORPION'S WEIGHT CLASS, SIR. SHOULDN'T WE INTERVENE?
NEGATIVE, AGENT SAREVA. S.H.I.E.L.D. HAS INVESTED FAR TOO MUCH TIME AND MONEY IN SCORPION'S COVER TO SHOW OUR HAND.
BESIDES, HAVEN'T WE LEARNED BY NOW THAT SCORPION CAN TAKE OF HERSE--

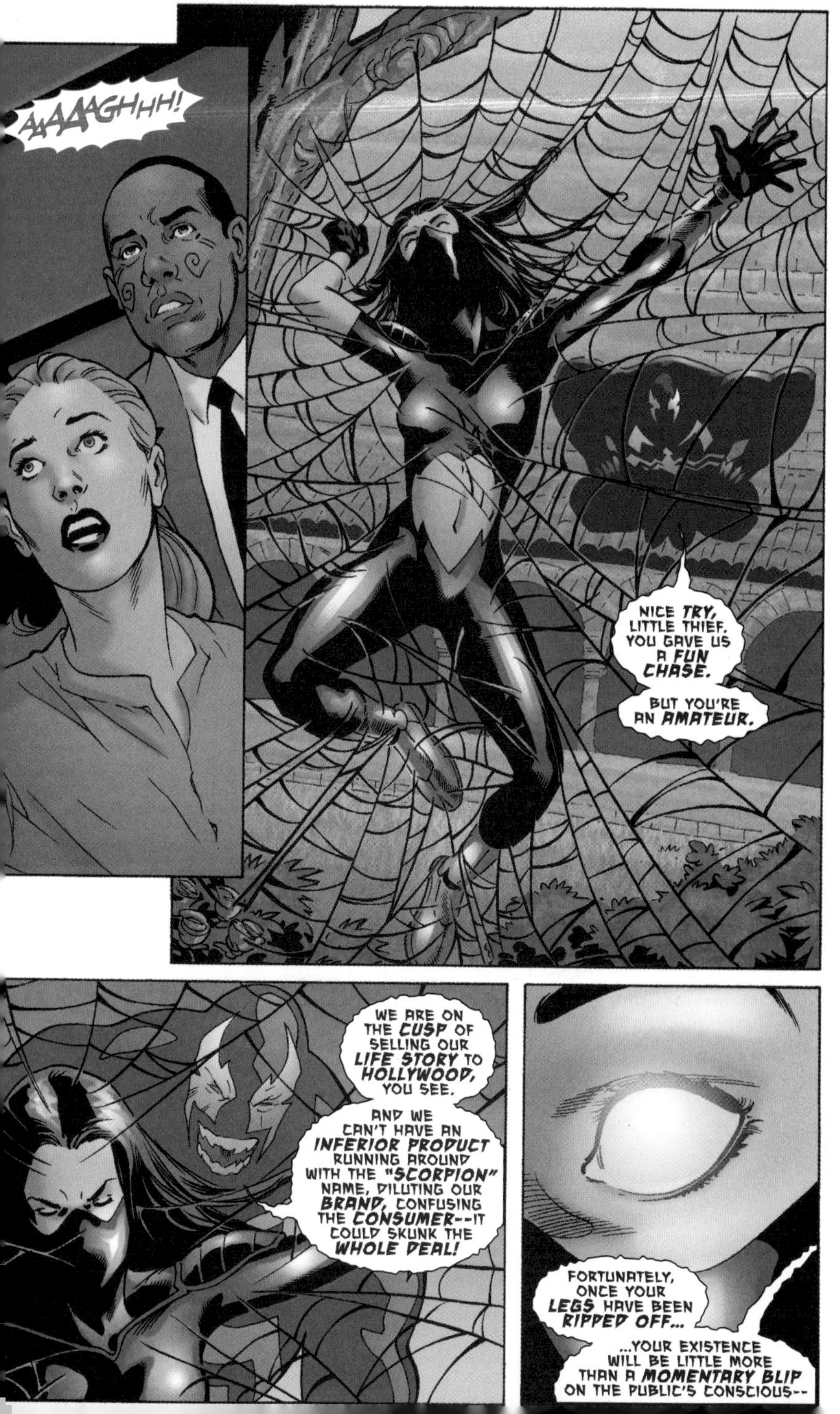
AAAAAGHHH!
NICE TRY, LITTLE THIEF. YOU GAVE US A FUN CHASE.
BUT YOU'RE AN AMATEUR.
WE ARE ON THE CUSP OF SELLING OUR LIFE STORY TO HOLLYWOOD, YOU SEE.
AND WE CAN'T HAVE AN INFERIOR PRODUCT RUNNING AROUND WITH THE "SCORPION" NAME, DILUTING OUR BRAND, CONFUSING THE CONSUMER--IT COULD SKUNK THE WHOLE DEAL!
FORTUNATELY, ONCE YOUR LEGS HAVE BEEN RIPPED OFF...
...YOUR EXISTENCE WILL BE LITTLE MORE THAN A MOMENTARY BLIP ON THE PUBLIC'S CONSCIOUS--

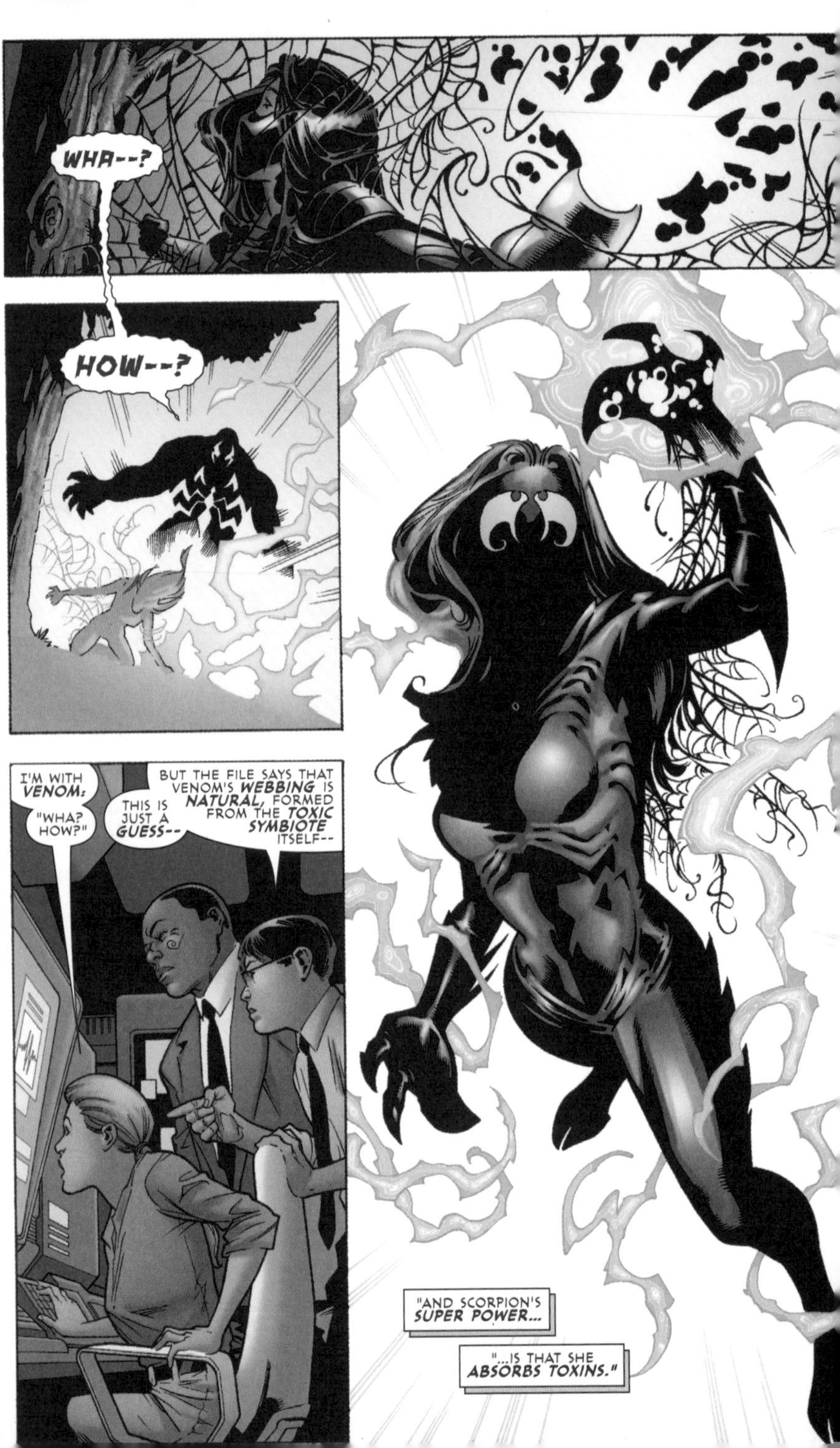
WHA--?
HOW--?
I'M WITH VENOM: "WHA? HOW?"
THIS IS JUST A GUESS--
BUT THE FILE SAYS THAT VENOM'S WEBBING IS NATURAL, FORMED FROM THE TOXIC SYMBIOTE ITSELF--
"AND SCORPION'S SUPER POWER...
"...IS THAT SHE ABSORBS TOXINS."

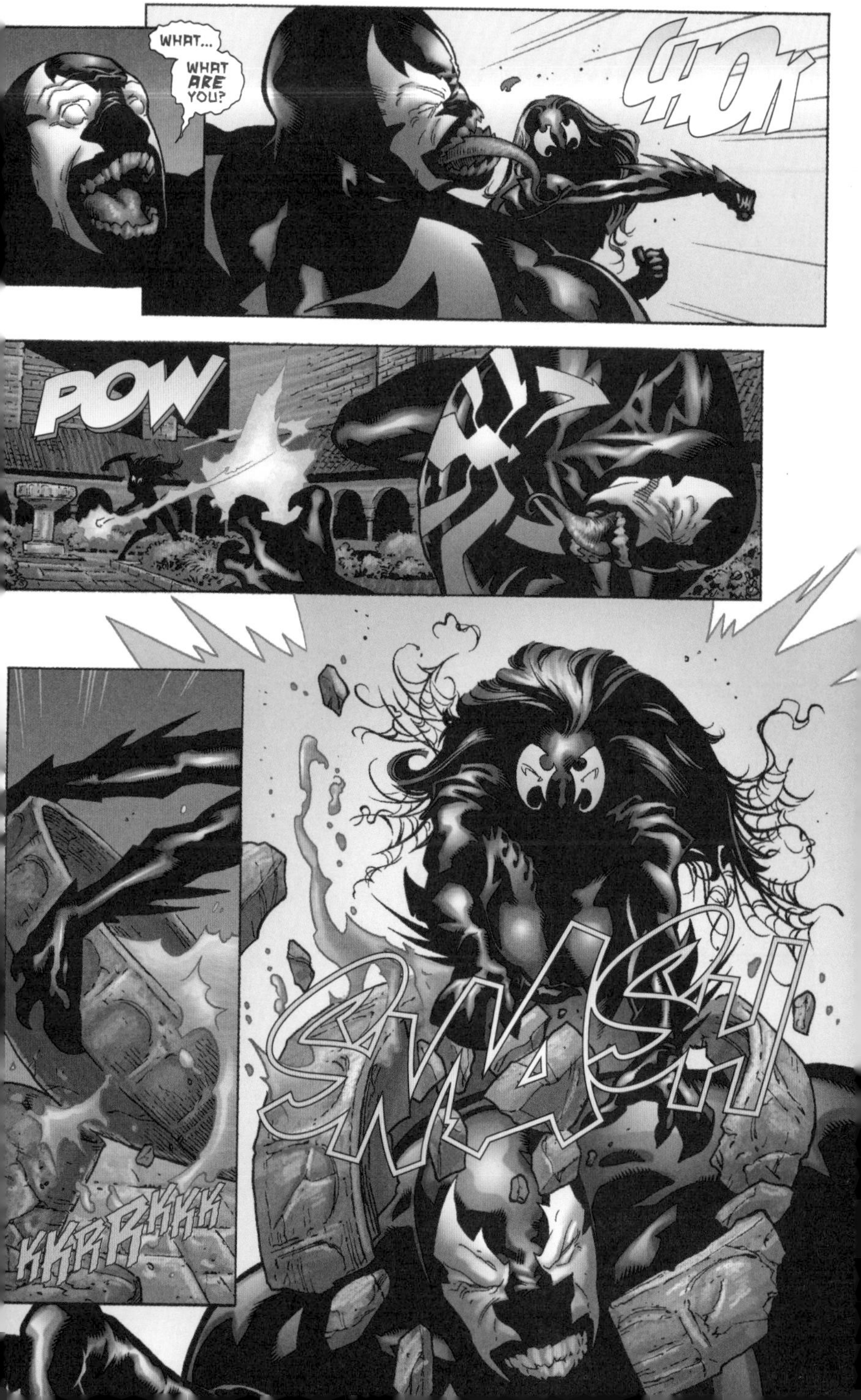
WHAT... WHAT ARE YOU?
CHOK
POW
SMASH
KKRRKKK

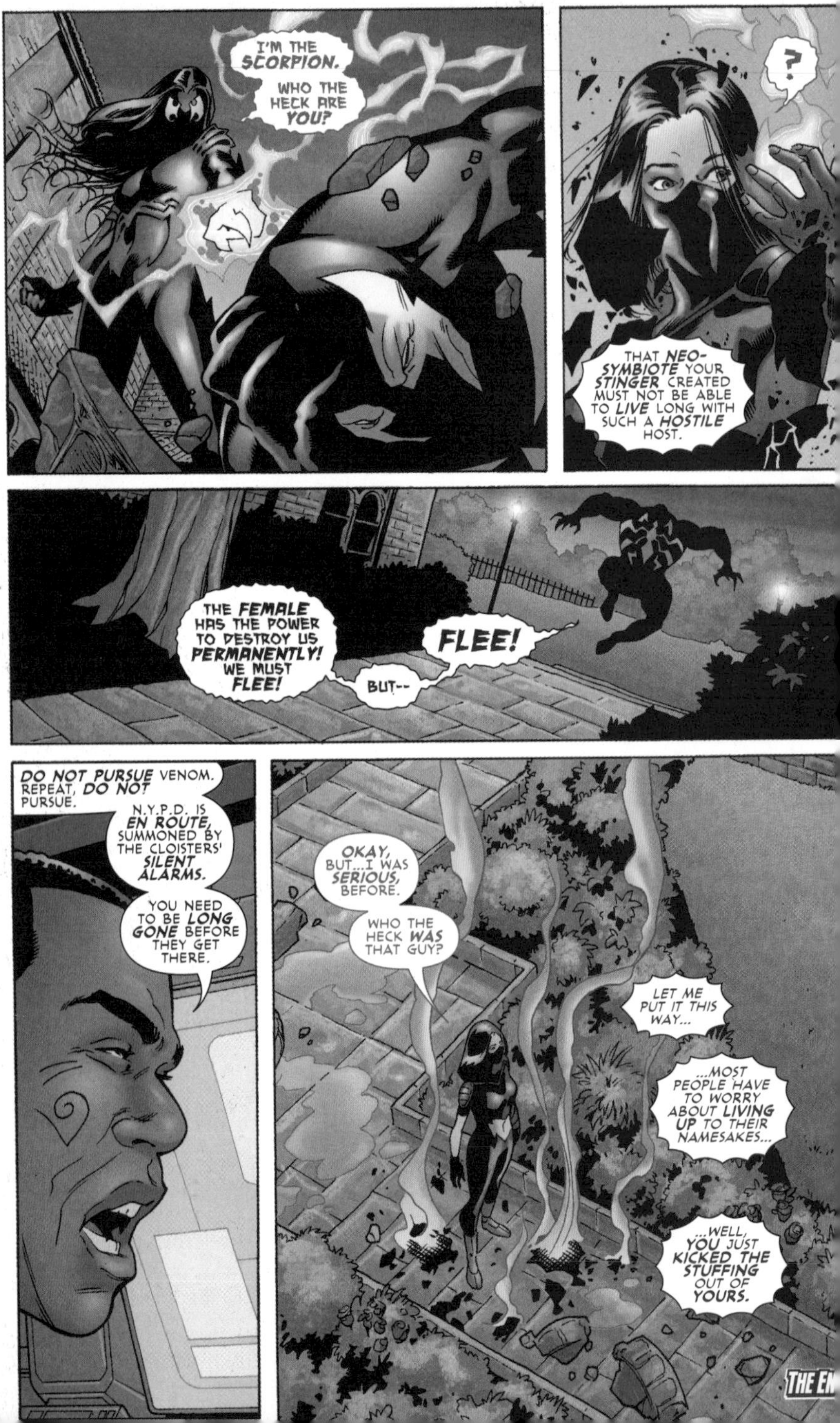

I'M THE SCORPION.
WHO THE HECK ARE YOU?
?
THAT NEO-SYMBIOTE YOUR STINGER CREATED MUST NOT BE ABLE TO LIVE LONG WITH SUCH A HOSTILE HOST.
THE FEMALE HAS THE POWER TO DESTROY US PERMANENTLY! WE MUST FLEE!
BUT--
FLEE!
DO NOT PURSUE VENOM. REPEAT, DO NOT PURSUE.
N.Y.P.D. IS EN ROUTE, SUMMONED BY THE CLOISTERS' SILENT ALARMS.
YOU NEED TO BE LONG GONE BEFORE THEY GET THERE.
OKAY, BUT...I WAS SERIOUS, BEFORE.
WHO THE HECK WAS THAT GUY?
LET ME PUT IT THIS WAY...
...MOST PEOPLE HAVE TO WORRY ABOUT LIVING UP TO THEIR NAMESAKES...
...WELL, YOU JUST KICKED THE STUFFING OUT OF YOURS.